DECLARATION

★ *of* ★

INDEPENDENCE

How Independent Compliance Officers and Directors Can Hold Management More Accountable

PART 1
Personal Lessons Learned

Eric T. Young

First Printing, 2021
Declaration of Independence: How Independent Compliance Officers and Directors Can Hold Management More Accountable, by Eric T. Young

ISBN 978-1-7374028-0-0 - paperback
ISBN 978-1-7374028-1-7 - ebook

Edited by Armin Brott
Proofreading by Dina Mangarella
Book design by Elena Reznikova

Ordering Information/Quantity Sales: Special discounts are available on quantity purchases by corporations, associations, business schools, U.S. trade bookstores, wholesalers, and others. For details, contact the publisher at the address below.

Ethical Pebble Publishing
2775 North Street
Fairfield, CT 06824
www.ethicalpebble.com

To my beautiful wife.

Table of Contents

Prologue and Introduction *1*

1.1 My Parents, Chess, and Sports as the Great Equalizer 8

1.2 Culture Meets Strategy Over Breakfast 15

1.3 If You Can't Stand the Heat, *Don't* Get Out of the Kitchen 22

1.4 Managing Change Means Managing Culture and Strategy 26

1.5 The Importance of Written Policy Controls *31*

1.6 On Special Assignment 37

1.7 Should I Stay, or Should I Go? 43

1.8 Two Cornerstones — Getting Married and the US Sentencing
Guidelines 48

1.9 Taking the Leap of Faith for Growth 54

1.10 The Voicemail—and the Important Relationship
Between Compliance and Marketing 62

1.11 Compliance, Baseball, and Corporate Strategy 66

1.12 Mind the Gap: Lessons Learned About Compliance
Risk Assessments from Subways and Trains *71*

1.13 The Rubik's Cube of Compliance Risk Assessments 76

1.14 Achieving Regulatory Exam Readiness — Without the Drama *80*

1.15 Do the Math to Better Evaluate Residual Risks *85*

1.16 The Trader and the Compliance Officer's Kneecap —
Underestimating Risks *91*

1.17 CRADs and TIGRs *98*

1.18 Corporate Culture and the Role of Compliance & Ethics *106*

1.19 Building—but Then Sadly Dismantling— an Effective
Compliance & Ethics Program *120*

1.20 Compliance: Fish out of Water or Amphibious Evolution? *130*

1.21 The Bermuda Triangle: Credibility and Culture
Within Compliance *140*

1.22 Bricks, Horseshoes, Storytelling, and the Importance
of Meaningful Reporting *150*

1.23 "That Was Then, This is Now, and This is Where
We're Heading" *159*

Prologue and Introduction

Chief auditor meeting with the chief compliance officer

Source: Sam Wordley/Shutterstock.com, edits by author

You could hear the rain pounding heavily against my home office windows. Our quarterly compliance update meeting with Internal Audit wasn't going well, compounded by the fact that we were still working remotely via Zoom. The exasperated chief auditor on my screen asked me point blank if I could "declare that our compliance & ethics function was finally independent from the businesses, and was therefore effective and sustainable."

"No, not yet; not even close," I replied. There was an incredibly awkward pause.

"Why not? What do you mean?" she asked.

Lightning lit the sky and the overhead lights in my office flickered. "Well," I said with a sigh, thunder nearly drowning out my voice. "I have three major concerns. One: The businesses pay our salaries, which means we're not independent from them. They also control our budget, whom

1

Source: Cory Seamer/Shutterstock.com

and how many we hire and fire, and staff salaries and bonuses. Our Group CFO prevents us from investing in essential compliance technology that would allow us to monitor, escalate, and ultimately address our compliance & ethics risks in a robust, risk-based, predictive, and analytical manner."

The chief auditor opened her mouth, about to interrupt me, but I continued. "Two: We have no direct access to—or dialogue with—our board of directors because our general counsel and chief risk officer prefer to filter my information by speaking with the board themselves. As a result, we can't alert them in a timely manner as to the company's key reputational, regulatory, or ethical risks. And three," I said, raising my hand to indicate that I wasn't done, "the chief executive officer and executive management have no incentive to listen to us because they aren't accountable or even liable for their misconduct. Clearly, we have to completely change the overall compliance program."

Another thunderous boom. Our video conference went completely quiet and my screen pixilated and froze for an instant. Finally, the chief auditor broke the silence: "Wow, you've got your work cut out for you. How on earth are you going to do that?"

* * *

After that stormy meeting was over and my discussion with the chief auditor was just a memory, I had a splitting headache and felt forever shackled by our C-suite executives. As my mind wandered, I was reminded of Plato's Allegory of the Cave.[1] In the Allegory, a group of people are living

---

1   From Plato's *Republic*, written about 375 BC

in an underground cave that has only one entrance and exit. Most of them are chained facing a wall and are unable to move either their bodies or their heads. They've spent their entire lives like this and it's all they know.

Behind these prisoners is a roaring fire, in front of which, the remaining residents of the cave project shadows on the wall that the prisoners sit in front of. Those shadows are their only "reality." By some near miracle, one of the prisoners escapes the cave. Outside, the bright sun hurts her eyes, and it takes her some time to get used to seeing the world as it truly is. Eventually, she returns to the cave, intending to tell the other prisoners the truth and to help them escape.

So why am I telling you this 2,500-year-old story? Because it's a perfect metaphor for many of the issues I'll be talking about throughout this book. All we need to do is swap some of Plato's characters with those you'll find in most companies.

- The chained-up prisoners (A on the illustration below) are the company's board of directors and employees, including compliance & ethics officers.

- The shadow-masters (B on the illustration) are the same company's chief executive officer (CEOs), chief financial officer (CFOs), and general counsel.

Source: delcarmat/Shutterstock.com (edits by author)

Revisiting the Allegory, but with the new cast, we can see the cave itself is your company; and the CEO, CFO, and general counsel are showing the board, employees, and compliance & ethics officers a highly edited, short-term-profit-maximized version of "reality." But since it's the only reality that the prisoners know, they blindly follow the shadow-masters. Unfortunately, when things go wrong, the prisoners (board, employees[2] and compliance)—*not* the shadow-masters who created the problems—are the ones who are held responsible, accountable, and personally liable.

Consider this book, *Declaration of Independence*, the key that unlocks your chains. In it, you'll learn two important things:

- The truth about how unaccountable C-suite shadow-masters can deceive—and endanger—the board, compliance, and the company as a whole.

- How you can return to the cave and use your newfound knowledge to enlighten and unshackle your fellow "prisoners."

In Plato's original Allegory, when the escaped prisoner tries to do exactly that, the still-chained prisoners refuse to believe her and threaten to kill her if she tries to free them. Perhaps it's the Stockholm syndrome? Nonetheless, I'm confident that the "prisoners" you'll be freeing—in particular the board and the compliance department—will react much more positively, welcoming their enlightenment, empowered and ready to hold management accountable. The shadow-masters, however, including the CEO, the CFO, and possibly the general counsel, will probably be less thrilled.

Before we get into the meat of the book, let me take a minute to introduce myself and to explain what I'll be covering.

From the time I was five until I turned ten, my dad used to call me "happy-go-lucky," something he didn't exactly mean as a compliment. I grew up in a family of really smart and talented individuals, but I just wanted to play. I was carefree and happy.

I have an older brother and younger sister, and, like the stereotypical middle child, I got the least attention—and the most hand-me-down clothes—of anyone in the family. But I didn't mind. From kindergarten through high school and even into college, I wasn't extraordinary—at

---

2   Including employees who raise integrity concerns/issues, otherwise known as whistleblowers.

least not to my parents, teachers, and peers. Not surprisingly, people including my parents tended to underestimate me. But rather than hurting me, I think being underestimated actually made me stronger. Maybe being "happy-go-lucky" was a blessing after all.

So why, in a book about corporate compliance & ethics, am I telling you about being an overlooked, underestimated, middle child? Well, for one thing, I've always thought that middle children are the best! But there's another reason: like middle children, compliance & ethics officers (whom I'll usually refer to as "compliance & ethics" or "C&E" officers) are often underestimated by their employers, sometimes pigeonholed, or perceived as "non-value added," "costly overhead," "bureaucratic," or just plain "useless." I'm not making this up—those are actual quotes from business executives and chief financial officers I worked with over my career. Clearly, not a very enlightened bunch.

As a result, compliance & ethics functions tend to get the least attention and receive what feels like a hand-me-down budget—unless something goes terribly wrong, like a violation of law, regulation, or code of conduct. At that point, as with many middle children (and stepchildren like Cinderella), the C&E officer goes from being an afterthought to being the first one to get blamed (like that imprisoned compliance officer or board member who escaped Plato's cave). I didn't like that as a kid, and I liked it even less as a grown-up C&E officer. You shouldn't either.

At times like these—and there were more of them than I care to remember—I never crawled into a hole or cave, and I never dwelled on the unfairness of the situation. Instead, like underestimated underdogs everywhere, I dug in my heels and figured out a way to overcome it. My strategy was simple: I would succeed by exceeding expectations.

As you might expect from someone with forty years of experience as a regulator and chief compliance officer, I view the compliance & ethics function as crucial and "critical essential," as defined by the US Department of Homeland Security, not only for COVID-19 pandemic purposes in our current world, but also in the long run, across multiple industries. What makes compliance & ethics so important?

- An effective C&E program—led by an effective chief compliance officer (CCO)—enables the company's executive management and employees to successfully meet (and/or exceed) stakeholders' expectations as well as guidelines (and laws) imposed by legislators, regulators, and others.

- That, in turn, enables the company's board of directors to fulfill its fiduciary duties of care and loyalty to shareholders (don't worry, I'll explain those terms as we go through the book), and, more broadly, to other stakeholders and society as a whole.

- At their core, effective C&E programs help protect employers and their boards of directors from legal liability. C&E officers also help strengthen and protect their company's reputation. Conversely, ineffective programs, can ruin a company's reputation in nanoseconds.

- Bottom line: More needs to be done to support C&E officers and strengthen compliance programs to both protect the board and hold management more accountable.

It's OK to be underestimated as a compliance & ethics officer, but you need to remain confident in who you are, have conviction and courage to assert yourself when it matters, collaborate with others, yet remain independent so you can clearly and promptly escalate issues and solutions to management and the board of directors. Ultimately, that's what this book is about. And throughout, I'll show you exactly how to achieve that goal.

A Note on Structure

As you've probably noticed, this book is divided into two distinct parts. In part 1, I'll talk generally about compliance & ethics, often through personal and professional stories and metaphors. These will illustrate important lessons I've learned over my 40-year career, from my early days at the Federal Reserve (before compliance was a well-known function) through my years as a chief compliance officer for some of the biggest companies in the world. My goal is to enlighten board members, as well as current, and especially, future compliance & ethics officers. We'll also talk about leadership do's and don'ts (the famous "soft skills" we hear so much about these days).

In addition, I'll discuss culture, behavior, and ethics. That's because, ultimately, compliance is all about human behavior. Whether you believe that people are inherently good or bad, human decisions are what drive corporate culture. And it's the culture that shapes an organization's short- and long-term objectives and successes.

In part 2, I'll go into greater detail about the compliance & ethics function and how it should operate in an enterprise-wide manner to be effective and sustainable for the long run. In the last section of part 2, I'll lay out six recommendations—concrete, tangible steps that you and your company should take to restructure and/or strengthen your C&E function, not only to ensure more efficient implementation, but also to protect the company, its employees, its board, and, of course, yourself.

Some of these recommendations will be controversial and provocative. That's by design. This book is not only meant to prompt discussion, but also to be a catalyst for fundamental change. The status quo is broken and the root causes aren't being addressed. The only way to change the culture—which, in turn will clean up organizations and protect our customers, markets, and society—is to call out those who need to be held accountable. If some feathers get ruffled in the process, I'm okay with that.

My Parents, Chess, and Sports as the Great Equalizer

My mom as a teenager

I was born in late September, in Princeton, New Jersey. My mom was Japanese, and my dad was a native Taiwanese. They were a non-traditional 1950s couple, even for Asians, given the history of the fifty-year Japanese occupation of the former Formosa (today, Taiwan). My parents met in the United States in the 1950s, where my dad was studying for his PhD at the Princeton Theological Seminary and my mom was working on her master's degree at a university in Virginia. My paternal grandfather was a devout Christian pastor in Formosa, and my maternal grandfather was a scientist.

As immigrants in the United States, my parents faced many obstacles and plenty of anti-Asian prejudice and discrimination. But they overcame it all, largely because they believed in themselves and persevered. As trite as it sounds, I learned from them that anything is possible if you put your mind to it.

My parents were polar opposites of each other. He was extroverted, arrogant, confident, proud, and always loved to entertain. She was introverted and cerebral. She preferred to be at home raising a family or sketching with her pencils, and generally stayed under the radar. But despite their differences, they loved each other very much. My parents always spoke to each other in Japanese and raised my siblings and me in that culture, with a strong belief in family, faith, academics, and an equally strong sense of doing the "right thing."

My dad in 1958

After receiving his PhD in theology from Princeton, my dad proceeded to earn a second PhD, this one in political science and East Asian studies at Columbia University in New York. While he was at Columbia, my siblings and I used to play on the campus and I'd wonder whether I'd end up studying there myself.

Over the course of my dad's career, he ultimately became a trusted advisor to Japanese Prime Ministers, CEOs of Japanese multinational corporations, members of the US Congress, and even advised a US Ambassador to Japan. And in partnership with a US Congressman, he developed economic opportunity zones in the Mid-Hudson Valley of New York. In recognition of his lifetime's work for Japan and the westernized Asian economies, he was awarded a highly coveted medal of honor from the Japanese government. As a family, we couldn't be prouder of him.

Eventually, my dad became a professor of political science at the State University of New York (SUNY) at New Paltz, a small, beautiful village about 75 miles north of Manhattan. Academics are traditionally a prestigious profession in Asia, but teaching in the United States didn't seem to be held in as high esteem. Consequently, my dad found teaching students to be a unique yet stressful experience—especially during the volatile 1960s.

The Vietnam War; the assassinations of John F. Kennedy, Martin Luther King, Malcolm X, and Robert F. Kennedy; nation-wide riots and student protests on college campuses across the country; and, of course, the Watergate scandal combined to put everyone on edge, and the country felt like a tinder box. Every evening, my dad would watch the CBS news with anchor Walter Cronkite, and he'd shout out loud, "demagogue!" whenever clips of the US Senators giving their speeches during the Watergate hearings came on screen. (Funny how history repeats itself; I find myself doing almost the same thing when watching the "news" today.)

Source: Who is Danny/Shutterstock.com

To de-stress, my dad spent time with his family and, among other things, taught me how to play chess. I loved it. I was fascinated by the history of the game, its mental challenges, and the need to think five to ten steps ahead of your opponent, anticipating his or her every move and counter move. But best of all, playing chess gave my dad and me a wonderful opportunity to get to know each other better. While we were playing, he was my mentor, not just my dad. And I became his mentee and protégé, not just his "happy-go-lucky" disappointment. During our chess matches—and until the day he died, in May 2015—he'd tell me lesson-filled stories from his life, including his regrets, disappointments, and, of course, his proudest moments.

In 1972, when American Bobby Fischer defeated the Soviet Union's Boris Spassky in the World Championships, chess suddenly became an international sensation. Although at twelve years old, I wasn't going to be a grandmaster, I was good enough by age fifteen to join my high school chess team and compete against other schools. I was the #3 ranked teammate (out of five—always the middle child), but as in my other passion, tennis, the difference in skills between #1 and #3 is wide and deep.

Sports

I'm not sure why, but my local school had me skip kindergarten and advanced me straight into the 1ˢᵗ grade a year early. Consequently, I was always the youngest in my class, the shortest, the least mature, and the most naïve growing up. Ultimately, I graduated high school at sixteen and Columbia University at age twenty.

Growing up in a town with only three Asian families out of a total population of roughly 10,000, I was often teased.[1] And the fact that I started high school at twelve and was barely four feet tall just made things worse. Of course, everyone gets teased and called names, and although it annoyed me, I didn't let it affect me, nor did I allow bullies to physically beat me. I overcame it by being myself, but also by excelling as best I could in school sports.

I grew up at a time when three New York sports teams were winning championships at the same time (which other than the NY Yankees and football NY Giants) they've rarely won since then. The 1968 American football Jets, the 1969 baseball "Miracle Mets," and the 1970 and 1973 basketball Knicks. That said, in 1969, my favorite American football team was—and still is—the Minnesota Vikings, because they played in the snow and mud, as American football should be played—and as effective compliance & ethics (C&E) officers should too—in the trenches.

Me pretending to be Mets great, Tom Seaver

Sports was my passion and my calling. Every day, I'd go to the local basketball court, pretending to be one of my favorite players: Walt "Clyde" Frazier, Earl "the Pearl" Monroe, Lew Alcindor (who became Kareem Abdul Jabbar in 1971), or the always-hurt-but-still-great Willis Reed. Or I'd spend hours throwing an orange sponge ball—either left-handed or right-handed—against an outdoor wall of our house,

---

1   "Asian" is, of course, a euphemism for the much-worse terms I encountered.

pretending to be Tom Seaver, Jerry Koosman, or Nolan Ryan (wild pitches included), pitching in the World Series.

All that practice paid off. I was short, but fast and unrelenting. On the basketball court, I had a laser-like jump shot (swish) and an unortho-dox-but-effective combination left-handed hook/lay-up from five feet away (don't ask), that consistently banked off the backboard and straight through the net. And in street football games, I was as fast as a rabbit and liked to think that I had the hands of an all-pro wide receiver. All I ever wanted to do was score points and help my team win games, whatever the sport was. And slowly but surely, I earned the respect—and genuine friendship—of my teammates, even the star players, based on my skills rather than on skin-deep perceptions. Just as a compliance & ethics officer should.

I also like to think that I inherited my dad's work ethic and my mom's courage, strength of character, and sense of calm and confidence. She used to tell us stories of what life was like during the war (World War II), being on the receiving end of whistling American bombs that rained down upon her village in Japan. She was a survivor with a great poker face, and my siblings and I never quite knew what she was thinking.

Looking back, I think that my mom possessed the traits that would make her a great compliance officer! She stayed under the radar and always remained calm and collected in the face of chaos. She was "CCO-ic," as in "stoic."

Lessons Learned

- Like my dad, good compliance & ethics officers persevere, regardless of obstacles, challenges, pressure, discrimination, or the perception of impossibility. Yes, it takes strength of character to overcome the odds. But throughout, you must have faith in yourself, faith in the friends and family who support you, and faith in those who mentor and guide you. That ability is what defines me and what should define any effective C&E officer, and especially a chief compliance officer (CCO).

- Compliance, like chess, has plenty of rules and requires strategic thinking. But don't be afraid to explore creative, out-of-the-box ideas and solutions, so long as you stay focused on keeping your company within the legal and regulatory lines.

- As a C&E officer, you must train yourself to:

  - "See" the full scope of the "chess" board (even if the line of sight is hidden or blinded)

  - Have an overarching strategy as well as multiple micro-strategies

  - Anticipate your opponents' moves (also known as "emerging risks")

  - Defend against existing attacks (risks and losses)

  - Understand the purpose, role, and utility of every piece (society, the board of directors, management, businesses, and staff).

- The biggest difference between compliance and chess is that in compliance, your goal is not a kill-the-king victory, it's a win-win, where all sides—compliance, the business, the board, and regulators—are happy with the end-result of risks which are properly identified, prioritized, and managed to satisfactory levels so that the firm can grow safely and responsibly. The only thing you're losing is the possibility of committing legal or compliance violations, but that's a sign that your C&E program is working. And since you're in compliance, that's your goal, right?

- Sports are a great equalizer. If you work hard, learn your craft, and let them see you shine, people will respect you for your perseverance, knowledge, skills, courage, results you achieve for the team, and your ability to keep your fellow employees safe and the company thriving. In other words, they'll value you for who you truly are, as opposed to what you look like, sound like, where you went to school, or anything else.

- Like any good US (or international) football player, a C&E officer must be prepared to get into the trenches and fight for his or her team. You can't be defensive or cower when others try to intimidate or gang up on you. Your job isn't to be the most popular or to be Mr. or Ms. Nice Guy or Gal. You must remain independent from management, but still collaborate with your colleagues.

Culture Meets Strategy Over Breakfast

Source: mamanamsai/
Shutterstock.com

In May 1980, I was twenty years old and had just graduated from Columbia University with a degree in economics. A month later, I joined the Federal Reserve Bank of New York as a supervisory banking applications analyst. I arrived "bright eyed and bushy-tailed" and armed with a fundamental understanding of both macro- and micro-economic principles. And thanks to my chess experience, I also had a pretty good handle on strategic thinking.

My job involved reviewing "foreign banking applications," which were filed by major US banks seeking Fed approval[1] to expand overseas, and by foreign banks seeking Fed approval to enter and/or expand within the United States. What a fantastic way to learn about and understand the expansive business strategy of major international banks! At that time, some US banks were incredibly aggressive in their efforts to expand

---

1 Back then, a lot more applications required formal approval by the Fed. The process has been streamlined since then, often only requiring after-the-fact notification.

internationally, and they pushed, punched, dragged, and kicked the regulatory envelope, presuming that they had the authority to engage in any activity as long as it wasn't explicitly prohibited in writing by law or regulation. (We often heard from these banks—and regulators still hear—comments like, "Show me in writing where it says I can't do it.") They believed that they could expand their businesses in terms of seemingly impermissible activities (products, geography, or clients) because their legal counselors had advised them that such expansion met the *letter* of the law. Our busiest "customers," we used to say, were Citibank and Citicorp,[2] as they were the most aggressive in exploiting regulatory loopholes. Lawyers representing these banks would even visit our offices to review other banks' regulatory proposals (which were available under the US Freedom of Information Act (FOIA)—with the proprietary sections redacted) just to see what other banks were strategizing and filing similar applications to stay competitive. Smart.

Having an adequate balance sheet and capital strength was an important part of the banks' application, but that wasn't enough for Fed approval. The banks' biggest challenge was to convince us that in addition to having the financial "sources of strength" (resources) to support their proposed new activities, they also had to have in place the necessary management controls to fully comply with US and local laws and regulations. Banks looking to establish a new or expanded presence in the United States also had to show a record of satisfying the needs and expectations of the local communities they currently served. Plus, they had to concurrently demonstrate to the US Department of Justice that their activities were not anti-competitive—a topic that's just as important today as it was back then.

At that time, in deciding whether or not to approve a bank's application, we used a six-factor rating system called CAMELS, which stood for:

---

2   Today known as Citigroup, Inc.

- **Capital** adequacy: Does the bank have sufficient capital now and in the future?

- **Assets**: In addition to the quality of the bank's assets, what are its investment and loan policies and practices?

- **Management** capability: How does the institution's management identify, track, and respond to risks?

- **Earnings:** How stable are the bank's return on assets, margins, and future earnings prospects?

- **Liquidity:** In a worst-case scenario, how liquid are the bank's assets?

- **Sensitivity**[3]: How much would the banks and its assets be affected by changes in interest rates, market pricing, and other factors?

Each factor in the CAMELS system was rated on a 1-5 scale, with 1 being the best and 5 the worst. While it was generally pretty easy to put a number to C, A, E, L, and S, coming up with a numerical score for M was more of a challenge. That's because we had to assess "softer" issues, such as management's style, goals, ethics, and values—in other words, "corporate culture."

Recalibrating Drucker

This is what triggered my awareness of and lifelong fascination with the interdependence between a bank's (and more broadly, any company's) business strategy, its culture, and its compliance with laws and regulations. Each is important and all three are necessary for success. In other words, to grow successfully, the company must also be compliant with the law and have a corporate culture that demands the right ethical behavior from its employees—and whose management support and encourage such compliance.

---

3   The Sensitivity rating was added in 1995.

I also became aware at that time that banks (and the individuals who run them) often don't behave rationally or predictably.[4] Fast forward over twenty years to 2006. This is when well-known management guru Peter Drucker is known to have said: "Culture eats strategy for breakfast." As you'll read on about my career, you'll see why I amended this world-famous statement to:

"Culture *meets* strategy *over* breakfast."

In other words, culture and strategy must work hand-in-hand. Culture drives strategy; and a poorly executed strategy is a reflection of a poor culture, which in turn could result in reputational ruin.

The Lemmings

Nearly every day, one of our most senior Fed executives over bank supervision would rant down our aisle of workstations, arms outstretched, screaming about "those lemmings!", complaining about the irrational proposals from financial institutions that continued to pour in from all directions. (Lem-

mings are small rodents, which, according to legend, occasionally commit mass suicide by jumping off cliffs, one after the other after the other. To non-lemmings, their behavior seems completely irrational.)

"Lemming Effect" (1980)
Source: Lizzillustrations/Shutterstock.com

Following the money, major banks were seeking Fed approval to establish international banking offices and subsidiaries in US financial centers to engage in international

---

4   In 2002, Daniel Kahneman was awarded the Nobel Prize in Economics for his work on what later became an entirely new offshoot of economics, "behavioral economics."

private banking especially in Latin America, along with relatively high-er-risk energy and commodity financing businesses. Others sought to expand aggressively into overseas markets to engage in activities not explicitly written in the law.[5]

Dozens of others would soon follow, typically smaller, less-capitalized, less financially stable institutions with less-sophisticated management (i.e., the lemmings) thinking that if one aggressive bank proposed entering into a new market, product, or client-base, they must too. Too often, these weaker banks wouldn't have conducted the necessary research and due diligence to assess whether their system of internal controls would be sufficient to support business as usual let alone expansion.

The Fed approved most of these strategic proposals because the applicants met the *letter* of the law. These were the protocols at the time. Unfortunately, as invariably happens with lemmings, less than five years later, a lot of those smaller, less-capitalized banks suffered massive credit losses and fell off the proverbial cliff. Eventually, even the big banks, like Citibank, Chase, Bank of America, Chemical Bank[6], JP Morgan, and Bankers Trust[7] were hit hard too.

The period from 1982 to 1989 became known as the "lost decade"[8] for bankers. This moniker was derived in part from the fact that many Latin American borrowers defaulted on their loans, and also because even more American banks either suffered major losses or went out of business as a result. Much of the damage could have been averted had the lemmings/banks in question not been in such a hurry to follow each other off the Latin-American lending cliff.

---

5   Our senior manager used to also ask us, prophetically, why investments and the establishment of international offices required Fed approval, but the lending of money by these banks and banking offices didn't.
6   Ultimately merged with Chase and now all a part of JP Morgan.
7   Since acquired by Deutsche Bank.
8   Federal Reserve History, "*Latin American Debt Crisis of the 1980s (1982 – 1989).*" https://www.federalreservehistory.org/essays/latin-american-debt-crisis. Retrieved November 21, 2020

Lessons Learned

- If you're a compliance & ethics officer, ask yourself the following: Is your institution's business strategy financially and managerially sound and fully compliant today? Will your current strategy and C&E program enable your company to thrive tomorrow, as you grow organically, or through mergers and acquisitions? Does your company's corporate culture support and encourage your C&E program? These questions apply whether you work for a bank, a broker dealer, an insurance company, in energy, tech, healthcare, or pharma, or whether your company is publicly traded or private, big, or small.

- If you're a board member, CEO, or CFO, do you truly understand the spectrum of risks (including, of course, compliance risks) that your company faces? And is solely meeting the letter of the law today sufficient to address the anticipated risks of new markets, changing clients, and pandemics of tomorrow?

- Skilled CEOs, CFOs (and CCOs), among others, should never make strategic projections assuming rationality and predictability. Instead, anticipate whether your competitors' most likely moves are disruptive or simply a lemming strategy from a risk-management perspective, including compliance and reputational risks. Don't follow others only to fall off that cliff!

- The Fed was, and still is, a fantastic training ground for entry- and mid-level C&E officers, risk officers, and those seeking a longer career in compliance and risk management. So are other public-sector regulators, such as the New York State Department of Financial Services (DFS), US Department of Treasury Office of the Comptroller of the Currency (OCC), US Securities and Exchange Commission (SEC), or Financial Institutions Regulatory Authority (FINRA). The same is true of other international regulators, whether in Hong Kong, Australia, London, Paris, Brussels, Tokyo, or anywhere else.

- If you're thinking about a career in compliance & ethics, there's no reason to limit yourself to finance or banking. The US Department of Health and Human Services, Federal Energy Regulatory Commission, Food and Drug Administration, Federal Trade Commission, Homeland Security, Federal Communications Commission, and of course, the US Department of Justice are all great places to start.

- If you're a CCO, how can you help navigate compliance risks so that lemmings within your organization or industry don't take the firm's reputation over the cliff? Will you, have the stature and authority to shape and manage new emerging risks?

- Lemming-like behavior never seems to go away. In the 90s, banks were falling all over themselves to get into derivatives; in the 2000s (continuing through today), everyone was launching products designed to reach high-net-worth clients. As happened in the 1980s, many lemming-like institutions failed, in part because they didn't have the appropriate risk-management and compliance infrastructure in place. I predict we'll see more of the same as banks and fin-techs line up, hoping to cash in on the cryptocurrency trend, and end up following the leaders off a cliff and into oblivion.[9]

- Poor culture often leads to poor strategy because the firm as a whole will go astray.

---

9   If you're interested in the gory details of some of the best-known lemming stories, see: Hays, Laurie, "Ex-Bankers Trust Official Is Fined in Derivatives Case." *The Wall Street Journal*, June 12, 1996. https://www.wsj.com/articles/SB834536362903833500. Retrieved May 13, 2021; Report of The President's Working Group on Financial Markets, "Hedge Funds, Leverage, and the Lessons of Long-Term Capital Management." Report to the Speaker of the House, US Congress, April 28, 1999 - https://www.cftc.gov/sites/default/files/tm/tmhedgefundreport.htm. Retrieved May 13, 2021; Stulz, Rene – "Credit Default Swaps and the Credit Crisis", Journal of Economic Perspectives, Volume 12, Number 1, Winter 2010. https://www.jstor.org/stable/25703483?seq=1. Retrieved May 13, 2021; Glazer, Emily, Farrell, Maureen and Patrick, Margot. "Credit Suisse's Exposure to Archegos Investments Grew to More Than $20 Billion." *The Wall Street Journal*, April 21, 2021. https://www.wsj.com/articles/credit-suisses-exposure-to-archegos-investments-grew-to-more-than-20-billion-11619045988. retrieved May 13, 2021; and US Department of Justice Press Release and Order. "Goldman Sachs Charged in Foreign Bribery Case and Agrees to Pay Over $2.9 Billion", October 22, 2020. https://www.justice.gov/opa/pr/goldman-sachs-charged-foreign-bribery-case-and-agrees-pay-over-29-billion. Retrieved May 13, 2021

If You Can't Stand the Heat, *Don't* Get Out of the Kitchen

For eleven years after graduating from Columbia University, I lived in a tiny closet of a room within a three-bedroom flat on the upper west side of Manhattan. The room had become available when the prior occupant suddenly and mysteriously disappeared. I'll refer to him as "Bob," since he always listened to Bob Dylan. About a year after I moved in, Bob reappeared and moved back in, just as suddenly and mysteriously as he'd disappeared.

At first, Bob seemed like a nice enough guy. He'd often spend his evenings sitting alone in the dark by the open kitchen window, listening to Bob Dylan[1] or Hank Williams, Sr.[2] songs and staring wistfully out at the bustling Broadway street corner below us. We got along fine for a year or so, but I gradually realized that Bob was slowly but surely creating a stressful situation (or a culture of hostility). He'd invite strangers to stay

---

1   Usually, *Just Like a Woman* over and over
2   I *Can't Help It If It I'm Still in Love with You*

with us and throw late-night parties, sometimes for weeks at a time. He never washed his dirty dishes and he had trouble paying his share of the rent and utilities (or maybe he just didn't feel like paying).

Being the naïve and nice guy that I was, I regularly ended up washing all his dirty dishes because I thought it was the right thing to do. I'd also pay his half of the rent, phone, and other utility bills—even though I was still struggling to pay my own bills. I mistakenly assumed that he'd pay me back when he had the money, like any responsible person with a shred of integrity would. There were no Zelles, Cash Apps, Paypals, or Venmos in the early 1980s—all we had was checks and cash. And I never knew when Bob would be around the apartment, as he was always mysteriously disappearing for days at a time. After a year of covering my roommate's rent and expenses (yeah, I was *really* naïve), I realized that Bob had no intention of ever paying me back. In fact, when I finally confronted him, he confessed that he was trying to make things so uncomfortable for me that I'd move out, leaving the whole low-rent three-bedroom apartment to him. "If you can't stand the heat," he said, "get out of the kitchen.[3]"

I had no intention of getting out of the kitchen or the apartment. Despite my friends and family urging me to leave, I decided to stay. However, I immediately stopped washing Bob's dishes and paying his half of the utility bills, knowing that our power would be cut off (it was). I also stopped paying his share of the rent, even though that likely meant eviction. Draconian measures, but it seemed like the only way to get him to take responsibility.

Taking responsibility and being accountable are themes I'll return to throughout this book.

Even though I'd done everything right and Bob was the at-fault party, our landlord got completely fed up and took us to court to evict us because even though I'd paid my share, Bob hadn't. I was ready to tell the judge my side of the story, but Bob's lawyers were clever, jumping up and

---

3   A favorite phrase of US President Harry S Truman.

claiming to the judge that they needed more time to prepare their case. That triggered an automatic delay of a few weeks, giving Bob more time away, during which he brought in a succession of strangers who declared themselves to be "Bob's legally allowable guest." I got to know some of them, and they eventually admitted that Bob had brought them in with the express purpose of "cranking up the heat" so I'd move out.

Bob's legal team achieved three more court delays but the fourth time, I had my chess hat, anticipated their move, and preemptively announced to the judge that we were, indeed, ready to proceed. I knew that going to trial as "co-defendants" could result in eviction, but enough was enough: I was willing to take the risk. Unfortunately (and predictably), we lost the case and were evicted. But after much discussion, the landlord and his sons—who knew that Bob had been the source of the rent problems—allowed me to sign a new lease under my own name, and I returned to *my* kitchen.

A few weeks later, Bob came by the apartment to collect his things. He was working at a fish market and held a large meat hook in a rather threatening way. Talk about a stressful situation! Crossing paths in the narrow hallway between our bedrooms, the reality sunk in that I was the one who'd withstood the heat in the kitchen and that Bob was the one leaving. Despite the presence of the meat hook, a physical altercation seemed imminent, but at that very moment I felt like the underestimated kid in me could have defended myself—and prevailed—if he'd attacked. He saw the look in my eyes and backed away.

Lessons Learned

- In your work and personal life, there's a good chance that you'll come across people who don't hold up their end of bargains (written or unwritten), shirk responsibility, refuse to be accountable, and don't pull their own weight, whether financially, morally, or compliantly.

- Sometimes, compliance & ethics officers must take draconian measures to force first-line businesses—or even management—to clean up their act, take responsibility, or assume accountability.

- Don't do *their* work for them, because it's *their* responsibility and accountability.

- Too often, the acts of an allegedly guilty party can affect an innocent party. And sometimes people get dragged down by things they had nothing to do with. C&E officers feel this way when they're blamed for the misconduct of executives and managers who aren't held accountable.

- When the heat starts to build and you begin to feel the pressure to get out of the kitchen, it's important to do the right thing. C&E officers have a duty to stand up to bullies or managers or anyone else who's suspected of (or actually is) violating the law or conducting themselves improperly.

- Escalate your concerns and/or suspicious about these infractions to the appropriate level, including the board of directors, given their fiduciary duties of care and loyalty to their shareholders. We'll talk more about these duties in part 2.

Managing Change Means Managing Culture and Strategy

Three Years or Thirty Years

Source: hafakot/Shutterstock.com

At the Fed we used to say, "I'll work here either three years or thirty years." Of course, there's no right or wrong amount of time to stay with an employer—it all depends on one's work-life balance and career objectives. That said, I left the Fed after three years to join JP Morgan Chase & Co.[1] (Chase) as a junior compliance officer. It was February 1983, about six months after Chase had suffered two major financial losses. One of them involved Penn Square Bank, a small, aggressive Oklahoma-based energy lender (which failed in July 1982). The other involved Drysdale Government Securities, Inc., a thinly capitalized dealer (which failed in May 1982).

---

1   At the time known as The Chase Manhattan Corporation.

Both losses were highly publicized in the press as being the result of poor risk management, unanticipated accounting challenges, weaknesses in Chase's overall system of "internal accounting controls," lack of accounting guidance as to how government securities interest is calculated, and operational questions over collateral management.[2] As you can imagine, the damage done to Chase's reputation was significant.

Chase's Cultural Recognition

At this point, you may be asking, "Why on earth would he leave a perfectly good job at the Fed to work for a bank that was clearly in reputational trouble?" The answer is simple: I embraced the fact that Chase recognized that, culturally, it needed to strengthen its "internal accounting controls," including developing stronger policies and procedures over the controls they'd benchmarked against the books and records section of the US Foreign Corrupt Practices Act of 1977 (FCPA). At the same time, Chase was, quite wisely, looking to beef up its corporate compliance[3] program. Accordingly, I applied for the job immediately and got the job as a junior regulatory compliance officer.

My initial responsibilities included identifying and reviewing regulatory changes that affected all of Chase's products, services, and business lines across the world, including their compliance as an employer, taxpayer, pension manager, broker dealer, and overseas branch or subsidiary.

Since the internet, smartphones, and laptops didn't exist yet in the 1980s, every day, my colleagues and I would read, cover to cover, paper versions of a daily US government magazine called *The Federal Register*, which published proposed or final rule changes to federal laws and regulations.

---

2   For example, Rowe, James, L., "Chase Loses $16.1 Million In 2d Quarter." The Washington Post, July 21, 1982.- https://www.washingtonpost.com/archive/business/1982/07/21/chase-loses-161-million-in-2d-quarter/937bb7d7-a731-4c6b-9d27-91341a230d72. Retrieved November 22, 2020
3   "Compliance" wasn't a familiar term or job title in the 1980s (unlike "lawyer" or "accountant"), so people who wanted to know what kind of work I did would look at me as if I had three heads when I told them I was in compliance. My mom used to think I handled customer complaints. I guess that's partially true!

If we found something that was applicable to Chase, I'd analyze and communicate the impact of the rule to the affected business or function, and enter the proposed or final rule into a registry and centralized inventory of laws and regulations that we shared with our legal department. We'd then work with the impacted Chase business or operational units to consider what processes and systems we would have to modify to deal with the rule change's potential or actual operational impact. Years later, regulators would view this disciplined process as an expected practice, known as "regulatory change management."

I also helped draft Chase's comment letters responding to the regulators' proposed rule changes based on work with our technology and operations teams. These letters were signed by our vice chairman and sent to the regulators who were issuing those proposed regulatory changes. This may seem like a rather mundane task, but it was a fantastic way to learn how a bank (or affiliate or any corporate entity) operates and how a change in a law or regulation can affect a company's strategic objectives. Anticipating these changes helps keep the company prepared.

Access to the Very Top of Chase

Early in my Chase career, my boss gave me the tremendous access to—and multiple chances to work with—our senior-most executives, including our group chairman. I was quite amazed at the opportunity I had to help shape Fed views or drive cultural and control changes from the very top. This was an early indicator of the importance of having direct access to our board of directors. More on this in coming chapters.

If Regulations Change, So Should the Cultural Fabric of a Company

Over my career, I've continually been amazed at how some regulatory expectations for control processes never change (nor should they). At the same time, I've been disappointed that some institutions lack a robust, continuous, automated improvement process to maintain an inventory of laws and regulations and/or a process to identify, analyze, assess, and operationalize regulatory changes that impact their business, products, clients, and regulatory compliance. Some firms just don't get it. If the external environment changes, shouldn't the firm's cultural mindset adjust accordingly?

During my time at Chase (1983 to 1994), our compliance unit was tasked with producing corporate-wide compliance policies and procedures. These included certain tax withholding compliance laws, transactions with affiliates, anti-money laundering, loans to insiders, and a series of consumer bank protection laws and regulations, each with subsections issued by multiple regulators at the US federal, state, and international levels. Monitoring and codifying the legal and regulatory changes and requirements in the form of written controls across every single one of Chase's activities and operating entities on a consolidated basis, are key elements (together with compliance risks assessments, training, monitoring surveillance, testing, and reporting) of what would eventually be called "enterprise compliance risk management." We'll talk extensively about this throughout part 1 as well as in part 2.

Lessons Learned

- Having a regulatory change management process is critically important for banks—and any other company, regardless of industry. It enables them to remain aware of and prepared for the operational impact of changes and to assess whether and/or how their compliance risks have changed.

- Maintain an inventory of laws and regulations and link it to a methodical compliance (and operational) risk assessment process to determine which laws and regulations need to be prioritized based on the levels of inherent and residual risks vis-à-vis the firm's risk profile and underlying activities, products, clients, and geographic footprints. Today, this is all part of a robust "governance, risk, and compliance" (GRC) framework.

- Close coordination with your legal and legislative liaison colleagues as well as the business and technology and operations departments are essential. This is just as true today as it was in the 1980s.

- Change means opportunity. It can also mean increased risk, particularly if you're not aware that change has taken place, either internally or externally. Being blind to change is a major symptom of a deficiency in your compliance culture.

The Importance of Written Policy Controls

Source: Monkey Business Images/Shutterstock.com

When I was in high school, I had a job working in an ice cream and sandwich shop down the street from our house. I was a combination busboy, dishwasher, janitor, and client-facing waiter/ ice cream scooper. One day, a customer came in and asked for a banana split—my first one ever. I spent a lot of time carefully arranging the ice cream—one scoop each of vanilla, chocolate, and strawberry—and beautiful, symmetrical mountains of whipped cream, artistically sprinkled the nuts, and finished it off with a perfect cherry on top. Quite proud of myself and my creation, I handed it to the customer. Thirty seconds later, she returned to the counter and asked, "Where's the banana??!" Oops!

I was reminded of that little episode when I was assigned by my boss to write Chase's policy on Section 23A of the Federal Reserve Act: Transactions with Affiliates,[1] a high-level law that restricted banks from using

---

1   12 USC 371c

(and risking) their FDIC[2]-insured, taxpayer-funded deposits to fund riskier non-banking activities by their non-bank affiliates. This could include involving the bank's affiliated broker-dealer in underwriting or dealing securities for its own account or other non-banking activities, which both Congress and the Fed view as posing an "unsafe and unsound banking" risk to those taxpayer-supported bank deposits.

Section 23A—and a few years later, its sister law, Section 23B—would ultimately be implemented by the Federal Reserve under its "Regulation W."[3] Violating these rules was considered a "cardinal sin" for two reasons:

1. Violation threatened the sanctity and safety net of federally insured deposits by exposing them to higher-risk non-banking activities.

2. Regulation W (including Section 23A) was the Fed's cornerstone law and regulation. It was their requirement to ensure that banks operated safely and soundly. It wasn't until more than 20 years later—before, during, and after the financial crisis of 2007–2010— that we learned precisely how important the world's confidence in our banks and payments system is to almost everything in our lives, regardless of who we are, where we live, and what we do for a living.

Today—and tomorrow—Regulation W will likely play a key role as more nonbanks blur the line of banking. Big Tech firms like Amazon and Google, "fintech" companies (which are essentially mobile apps designed by technology engineers), cryptocurrency, and digital assets all pose risks which we haven't yet even fathomed to our global payments system and to small retail customers.

Anyway, Chase wanted to strengthen its existing Section 23A controls. And my manager asked me to draft our policy because of my prior Fed

---

2   Federal Deposit Insurance Corporation
3   The Fed's Regulation W (12 Code of Federal Regulations/CFR 223) became effective April 2003.

experience and because I'd already established a level of credibility with Chase's management. In addition, I'd proven on a number of prior projects that I had a firm grasp of complex regulatory requirements and could translate them into operational language that businesses and others would be able to understand and, more importantly, to implement.

Naturally, I said, "Sure." After all, the Fed had trained me to understand how multiple laws and regulations, including Section 23A, impacted banks and their parent bank holding companies (BHCs) such as Chase. Furthermore, as a Fed analyst, I had learned that before 1978, foreign banks operating in the US were often "grandfathered" which meant they were operating at a competitive advantage vis-à-vis US banks such as JP Morgan, Chase, and Citi. The Fed would therefore impose "conditional approvals" requiring that many of these grandfathered or otherwise competitively advantaged foreign banks seeking to operate in the US to subject themselves to the very same prohibitions and restrictions of Section 23A as US banks. That's how important Section 23A was and implementing Regulation W continues to be.

Just as with my first, magnificent banana split, I was so proud of myself when I completed the first draft of my Section 23A policy. To me, it beautifully summarized in plain English the essence of the law. It was neatly organized, and the cherry on top was a complete absence of typos or grammatical errors. A few minutes after distributing it to my colleagues for their comment, Ron Mayer, our regulatory counsel approached me. "Great summary of the law," he said with a wry smile. "But where are the written controls?" Oops! As I gained experience over time, I learned that all policies must have the banana, that is, controls with responsible owners clearly defined.

The Importance of Teamwork

I loved working with my colleagues at Chase, especially during my first three years, when we were a cohesive, "start-up" unit of eight, taking

Source: Monkey Business Images/Shutterstock.com

on Chase's regulatory compliance and internal accounting controls. Our manager at the time was a former Navy veteran—tremendously disciplined, organized, and focused—a true gentleman who cared for his team. The others were seasoned experts with a variety of experience: one had an auditing and tax background; another was a former Fed regulator like me. We also had a former airline industry compliance officer, an attorney who worked closely with our in-house attorneys and had a focus on consumer banking laws, and two junior compliance officers, including one who became a successful attorney after he left Chase and one who later became—and still is—a fantastic leader (now in Human Resources) at an energy company. And then there was me.

I felt like we were the 1970 and 1973 New York Knicks basketball champions, a close-knit team and family. We occupied an open office space with our Navy vet manager sitting at the back and the two most junior compliance officers up front, next to our administrative assistant. All my teammates were incredibly patient with me as the new kid, and I tried to absorb as much as possible.

From the beginning, I felt like I could be myself with my team, and that feeling deepened over time. If any one of us needed help, we knew we could rely on one another. At the same time, we had fun and saw ourselves and each other as individuals, not just as FTEs or accounting expenses. It was exactly the kind of environment I needed, since things in the "home kitchen" were beginning to heat up with Bob, the meat-hook-loving roommate we met back in chapter 3.

Lessons Learned

- Policies and procedures are more than summarized versions of laws or regulations. You need to understand the process, people, and technologies[4] involved and map them out so you can see where and how a particular law or regulation impacts the business, operation, accounting, customers, and other stakeholders as well as the interaction (that is, the flow) of money and information.

- Once that's done, you need to establish firm controls and make sure that they're documented, agreed upon, and codified into your policies and procedures with clear roles and responsibilities. Then you need to train your team and affected businesses and operational units and assign the responsibility for enforcement to the most appropriate person or department. Otherwise, it's a banana-less banana split! This is especially true for transversal formal policies (ones that cut across the whole enterprise) that require board and/ or executive management approval.

- You also need to link your controls to and from the compliance risk assessments[5] (see chapters 1.12–1.17 and part 2), as well as to online and in-person training. Without this linkage, your company runs the risk of slipping on the banana peel for lack of controls, lack of awareness, and violation of law.

- Ultimately, the controls will need to be monitored and tested to assure that what's written is actually being followed, evidenced by a documented audit trail. Demonstrating this is a good manifestation of the right corporate culture of compliance.

---

4   In 1992, these became known collectively as a "system of internal controls." We'll discuss that in detail in part 2.

5   As well as other credit, market, operational, and other risk assessments. For purposes of this book, I'll focus predominantly on compliance risks.

- Whether as a manager or teammate, treat all your colleagues with respect—and that respect will be mutual.

- Where possible, at least for smaller units, work together as a family. But, like a fast-moving basketball team, understand one another's roles, pass the ball to the teammate who's got the best shot, and jump in to help when necessary. Always play defense and bring in specialists to effectively anticipate and manage your risks. But always return to your defined role and responsibility.

On Special Assignment

Source: alphaspirit.it/Shutterstock.com

By 1984, Chase's compliance department was formally transferred into the Internal Accounting Control department, headed by George Mah,[1] who held the title of vice president. One reason for the transfer was to move compliance out of a revenue-generating domestic institutional banking business and into the independent finance function, under Chase's chief financial officer (CFO), to whom George reported. In hindsight, having joined Chase's compliance department as part of a first-line business should have raised red flags. Transferring our department into the finance function made us truly independent, with stature and authority. The C&E function must not be hired, fired, or evaluated for bonuses by the 1LOD business. Otherwise, there's an inherent conflict of interest and a high risk that compliance & ethics officers will be suppressed or compromised when

---

1   George reported directly to Chase's CFO, who in turn reported to the chairman and CEO of all of Chase.

identifying and escalating major compliance issues. For example, thirty years later, Wells Fargo Bank's risk and compliance officers were found to lack independence because many of their compliance officers had reported into the branch/retail business executive. This was the business which, over many years, created millions of fake customer accounts to generate fees and maximize share price so that Wells' CEO and executive management could "earn" big bonuses. Risk and compliance failed to escalate their concerns independently because of their reporting lines. Unfortunately, many of these whistleblowers (which we'll discuss more in part 2) were fired. Meanwhile, although I hate to admit it, compliance & ethics officers can go rogue themselves if tempted or if they feel that they've been "Stockholm-captured" by the businesses unit to curry favor with the business leaders and the CEO.

Because compliance is responsible for measuring, monitoring, and reporting on the effectiveness of the 1LOD businesses, taking compliance out from under a revenue-generating unit gave Chase a strong "second line of defense" (2LOD).

It was quite uncommon in the banking industry at that time to have a formal compliance department or function with transversal authority across all businesses, subsidiaries, products, services, and locations, which is why we reported to finance. As a result, I learned the importance of working closely with our corporate and management accounting and global chart of accounts colleagues, and how to utilize our financial controllers and the operations and technology managers as an extended network of "compliance officers." Even though these controllers (and ops and tech staff who reported to the chief ops & tech executive) were dedicated to specific business lines, they too were centrally paid by the Chase's CFO and/or the executive over operations and technology.

Despite what you may have heard elsewhere, compliance is *not* about how to interpret the law, but how to safely and responsibly *operationalize* it to fit the strategic and cultural needs of the organization and, within the law, to contribute to the value of the business, the enterprise, its shareholders, and longer-term stakeholders such as the community, employees, and society. That process typically starts with money. Understanding how money flows (and, by extension, how people behave when driven by money) within a banking or non-banking organization—as well as into and out of it—helps enable compliance officers to understand the compliance risks they're likely to encounter. For that reason, we always started with debits, credits, payments, settlements, and computer programming code. Only then did we delve into the laws and regulations.

Project Fox

I'm not sure whether it was because George and I are both Asian, because I worked hard and delivered results, or the combination, but either way, he took me under his wing and was my professional mentor throughout my Chase career. With George, recognition for having done a good job was never a "thank you"; instead, it was another assignment. And on those occasions when he wasn't happy with something I'd done or said, he'd say to me in his baritone voice, "young man...." and then yell at me for whatever he wasn't satisfied about.[2]

Early one morning in the spring of 1985, George walked into the compliance department and pulled me aside. He quietly told me that he wanted me to report directly to him on an incredibly confidential project for which I wouldn't be able to seek administrative support, would have to do all the photocopying and binder production myself,[3] and couldn't discuss with any of my colleagues. No conversations at all, except with George, his boss (Chase's group CFO), the group general counsel, the chief auditor, and the head of our Investor Relations department. Naturally,

---

2   Like my prior manager, the Navy veteran, George was former military—in his case, an Air Force veteran. To this day, I support the military and believe that veterans make excellent managers and employees, given their discipline, code of honor, and respect for the chain of command.
3   At that time, there was no Microsoft PowerPoint or Microsoft Office Suite. We had to produce hard copies of everything, and slides were typed and then photographed.

I accepted the assignment enthusiastically, and that's how Project Fox was born.

For the next six months, I got to the office at 7am and didn't leave until 10pm, six days a week. Before heading home each evening, I was required to deliver multiple sets of tabbed, hard-copy binders which I produced with new information relating to the proposed corporate governance and actions by the board of directors involving the "business judgment rule," super-majority votes, and "staggered boards," as well as information and definitions and corporate industry practices around "greenmail," poison pills, shareholder rights, entrenched management, and "shark repellants."

This was the age of corporate raiders like Ivan Boesky, Carl Icahn, and others who would be the inspiration for the movie *Wall Street* (and its main character, Gordon Gekko) a few years later, or even *Pretty Woman* three years after that, where the major characters were activist shareholders seeking to acquire enough voting shares of a company to influence the composition of the board of directors, corporate strategies, and intense expense management in order to maximize short-term profits and shareholder value. Quite often, that included breaking up the corporation into multiple pieces, because such sales would unlock hidden assets and unrealized value. In other words, the parts were greater than the conglomerate whole. This was short-term shareholder capitalism at its height, unlike the trend these days towards long-term stakeholders and "environment, social, and governance" or ESG focus (which we'll discuss in greater detail in chapter 2.8).

Of course, all my hush-hush work on Project Fox was in addition to my day job as a junior compliance officer, which meant that by the time I got home (usually around 11pm), I was exhausted. To unwind, I'd watch the syndicated television comedy series, *The Honeymooners* with Jackie Gleason so I could fall asleep with a laugh. Then I'd get up at 5am and do it all over again.

The stress of basically working two jobs slowly caught up with me (I'll talk about that more in an upcoming chapter). But I loved the pressure, the challenge and responsibility, and the opportunity Project Fox gave me to work and interface with Chase's most senior executives. Those working relationships, in particular with the CFO, corporate secretary, general counsel, and chief auditor taught me a huge amount about corporate governance, a board's fiduciary duty of loyalty, and shareholder and proxy voting.

All of that came together as we crafted a strategy to preempt a potential hostile takeover of Chase. There were no such rumors, at least that I was aware of, but I was fascinated by the design and execution of Chase's strategic plan to implement these measures well in advance.

Ultimately, we were successful, and Chase's shareholders voted on a series of management proposals to stagger its board of directors and trigger a super-majority approval of 75 percent of shareholders when certain conditions were met, including unwanted or hostile attempts against Chase.[4] I'm very proud of having been a part of the end result and honored to have been given the opportunity at the age of 26. For me, Project Fox was extreme and intense; for Chase's brand and management, it was a tremendous victory.

Most importantly, Chase's management and board of directors proved prescient, as only one year later, the Bank of New York launched a hostile takeover bid of Irving Trust Company, one of the oldest banks in the US.[5] Hostile takeover bids were common among non-banks such as energy companies and multinational conglomerates, but Project Fox proved that knowing your industry and understanding emerging risks can prove strategically quite important to management.

---

4   https://www.latimes.com/archives/la-xpm-1986-05-18-mn-21291-story.html
5   Bartlett, Sara. "The Clumsy Quest for Irving Bank," *The New York Times*, September 18, 1988. https://www.nytimes.com/1988/09/18/business/the-clumsy-quest-for-irving-bank.html. Retrieved November 30, 2020

Lessons Learned

- Regardless of whether you're in the banking, financial services, healthcare, energy, or any other industry, work with your accounting and finance colleagues to assess whether and/or how regulatory changes would impact your regulatory and financial reporting, accounting policies, global chart of accounts, management profitability reporting, and your operational and technology processes and controls.

- Start learning about how money flows to, from, and within your company, operationally, technologically (in terms of business, the people inputting, and checks and balances) to demonstrate that these money flows ultimately are reflected with integrity in the company's financial statements and are compliant with applicable laws and regulations.

- Today, of course, a "thank you" to an employee goes a long way. That said, the true reward for a job well done is often more work with more responsibility. Take this as a compliment.

- With encouragement, mentorship, self-initiation, and the pursuit of the greater good (as George liked to say), to this day I believe that nothing is impossible, no matter how steep, how high a climb, or seemingly insurmountable a challenge might be. Chase's executive management had a vision and a strategy, but it still needed to be executed with precision and timeliness.

Should I Stay, or Should I Go?

Source: Andrey_Popov/Shutterstock.com

One autumn day in 1986, George Mah approached me to see whether I'd be interested in a special project in our London offices. George had reorganized the compliance department and promoted me to be the head of corporate compliance across all of Chase's global businesses and offices.[1] However, I had never spent any time overseas, not even to visit my grandparents in Japan or Taiwan.

The London project's mission was to identify and enable Chase's United Kingdom investment banking businesses to meet regulatory deadlines, which were rapidly approaching, in order to comply with the newly enacted UK Financial Services Act of 1986 (FSA Act). This law was the "most comprehensive overhaul of investor protection legislation for 40 years."[2] Not obtaining authority under this new UK law would have

---

1 Today, these roles are called chief compliance officers (CCO), or Chief Ethics and Compliance Officers.
2 David Barnard, NY Office of Linklaters & Paines. "The United Kingdom Financial Services Act, 1986: A New Regulatory Framework," *International Lawyer, vol 21 (1987) (issue 2).*

meant conducting investment business[3] illegally. The pressure was on and I was excited about both the opportunity and the challenge!

This was the "deep end of the pool," and George was encouraging me to dive in, to manage a dream team of experienced players in New York and London while having a functional network of financial controllers and operations and tech managers serving as compliance officers across the globe.

However, I had to weigh two options. Option one: Stay in New York and enjoy a promising career at Chase's Head Office as well as post-college life in New York City with my Columbia friends. Plus, I was dating someone in New York who would eventually become my soulmate (and my wife). I was also mentally and physically exhausted because we'd just completed Project Fox, successfully. Option two: Parachute like a Navy SEAL into one of the great financial centers of Europe and lead the mobilization of the bank's London forces, a mission that was supposedly for only "a few weeks."

Two songs from one of the great bands of the time, The Clash, kept running through my head: *London Calling* and *Should I Stay or Should I Go*? So, I did what today would be called crowdsourcing and asked some close friends for their thoughts. One of them said, "Are you, nuts?!? How often do you get the opportunity to live and work in London?" My future (and always pragmatic) wife simply said, "Go. It would be a good experience for you."

In the end, I said yes, and arranged to bring one of my teammates with me. Don, who had a background in aeronautic engineering and operational controls at Chase, was incredibly calm, had a great sense of humor, and worked well with others. We arrived in late September 1987 and immediately set about mobilizing the London businesses and control functions. Our first task was to quickly but thoroughly identify,

---

3   Today, investment business includes brokerage, dealing, trading in securities, certain wealth management and asset management businesses and funds, and advisory activities.

designate, and apply for regulatory authorization from the UK securities regulators—all by the end of November. Those who had to be deemed "fit and proper" by the UK securities regulators[4] were individuals, legal entities, and businesses conducting "investment business." Interestingly, the application for authorization process was quite similar to the banks' strategic proposals I'd analyzed years earlier, when I was at the Fed.

In addition to Don and me, the rest of George's SWAT team included Chase's chief securities counsel at Head Office, the Chase UK general counsel, the local head of credit risk, and the country manager/CEO. Plus, one of our strongest teammates was our administrative assistant from New Zealand. We met regularly to identify gaps, priorities, timelines, owners, and status reports. I'd also send daily updates to New York, particularly when we needed to call in reinforcements (say if a particular business or function or individual wasn't cooperating. I was granted wide authority to escalate and address those who passively or otherwise resisted. Chase had neither the time nor the luxury to waste time. Strategically, too much was at stake).

One of our first jobs was to assess the number and skill sets of our UK compliance staff. Some were former UK regulators, and each was quite knowledgeable about local rules and requirements. Yet the new FSA Act was uncharted territory to everyone in the UK. Fortunately, our US experience helped, because the FSA leveraged many of the United States' securities laws and regulatory frameworks—with which we were already familiar—to protect investors.

Our London team quickly coalesced into a well-oiled (and at the same time, enjoyable and fun) machine. If ever Don or I needed local prioritization by a London businessperson, the local head of credit risk would enable it. And our local general counsel was incredible. He was not only decisive and fearless, but also incredibly accessible and human—qualities that enhance any professional. This was one of the

---

4   Which themselves were newly established.

best compliance-legal partnerships I've experienced. Another fantastic compliance-legal partnership in the US was with our senior regulatory counsel in New York, Ronald C. Mayer, who was always accessible and patiently and consistently explained the why's, not just the what's. To this day he remains a close friend.

After five months in London (interrupted by one brief trip home to New York for the holidays), we completed our mission and received UK regulatory approval to have Chase's investment businesses authorized by at least five self-regulatory organizations (SROs), including the primary supervisory regulator (then known as the Securities and Investment Board, SIB) and the Securities Authority (TSA, now known as the UK Financial Conduct Authority, or FCA).

Lessons Learned

- Just do it. If you ever have the opportunity for an international assignment, particularly if you're early in your compliance or professional career, jump at the chance. You won't be able to fully appreciate what you have in your own country unless you experience the cultures (both corporate and human) in other countries.

- Mobilize teams internationally and keep the vision and strategic objective cohesive and transparent. Escalate issues to Head Office and local executive management concurrently. Sometimes, teams from Head Office have to be parachuted in to assist local teams. However, as I'll describe in later chapters, sometimes having too much Head Office involvement can be disruptive and counterproductive.

- My wife always reminds me that without health and family, there is no work. Work must not come first. Health, then family, then work. Health, then family, then work. I have to keep reminding myself. I was prioritizing work over health and even told one of my staff in the 1990s that "I live to work." He looked at me as if he didn't understand me and replied, "I work to live." He was right; I was wrong.

Two Cornerstones — Getting Married and the US Sentencing Guidelines

Source: painting by author

Don and I shared a single office in London, and we'd take the Tube (subway) to "The City" six days a week. With so little time before our regulatory deadlines, we worked from 7 or 7:30am to 10pm every day. We agreed to take only one day off per week, so by the time Sunday rolled around, we were so exhausted from the week's work that we'd usually retreat to our respective flats to unwind or simply to sleep.

On an occasional Sunday, I'd venture alone into London's Hyde Park, which was literally across the street from our Kensington neighborhood, not realizing at the time that Kensington South was one of the more upscale locations in London. To enter the park, I'd cross Kensington High Street, remembering to "look right" before crossing the street.[1]

Source: Google Maps (my flat was *not* Kensington Palace)

Wandering through the park, I'd always walk by an especially large, beautifully manicured house, not really thinking about what it was or why it was in the middle of Hyde Park. I imagined that it contained offices of the employees who maintained the park, or maybe there were stables behind the house, like those that once housed the carriage horses in New York City's Central Park. I was usually so exhausted from the week's work that I'd simply walk past it, meandering aimlessly, wanting nothing more than to unwind and take in the fresh London air. Years later I discovered that that house, only a seven-minute walk from my flat, was Kensington Palace, the home of Princess Diana and Prince Charles. I wasn't aware then that that was their residence, but whenever I think back to my time in London, I smile but then am saddened with the memory of Princess Diana.

Two Letters a Day

Meanwhile, my future wife was sending me two letters every day. Keep in mind, this was all happening at a time (1987) when there were no iPhones, iPads, FaceTime, Skype, Zoom, or even laptops to send emails. The flat's landline phone was always full of static, as if it were a World War II "wireless," which, ironically, is what they called radios at the time. The phone even looked like a relic from World War II.

---

1   Anyone who's survived into adulthood in the United States or most of Europe knows to look left then right before crossing the street. But in England, where they drive on the other side of the road, that could get you killed. Fortunately, the British are nice enough to have painted "Look Right" on the street at many intersections. I'm sure those words have saved countless lives.

My soulmate's letters kept me sane and laughing. And knowing how much we missed one another helped me stay motivated and positive. One of her letters was a greeting card of a young girl and her dog (see the picture at the top of this chapter), clearly missing whomever they were waiting for. Years later, I did a painting of a similar image, because I'd never forgotten the expressions of the girl and dog or how much my future wife and I missed each other.

Another "Thank You"

Ultimately, our Chase SWAT team achieved both of our major regulatory deadlines, one in November, and the most important one the following April. Had it not been for our core team of legal, credit risk, our UK CEO, and our Head Office management in New York, Chase's European strategic growth plans would have been hopelessly stalled—with major compliance consequences. We succeeded because of how well we worked together as a team, and because we had the right corporate culture from the top (starting with our executive management in New York and local executive management in London). Culture *meets* strategy *over* breakfast!

I returned to New York, hoping to pick up my day-to-day duties where I'd left off, but instead, was asked by George and our chief securities counsel to dive straight into yet another major project, this one involving the compliant separation of our commercial and investment banking businesses, which by law at the time (the US Glass-Steagall Act), had to remain segregated. Once again, the recognition for a job well done wasn't a "thank you"; it was more work—and I loved it!

Sadness and a Purpose to Fight Financial Crime and Terrorism

Throughout 1987 and 1988, I frequently returned to London to complete the re-engineering of the UK compliance department, eventually hiring a well-known, highly respected external candidate to be the UK chief compliance officer (CCO).

Even after Project Fox was finished, I had to fly to London several times a year for follow-up meetings. Most of the time, I flew there on Pan American World Airways (Pan Am) flight 100, and back to New York on flight 101 or 103. In the winter of 1988, I arrived in London after Thanksgiving and returned home a few days before Christmas. I don't remember the exact date, but it was before December 21, 1988, the day that Pan Am Flight 103 was destroyed by a terrorist's bomb over Lockerbie, Scotland, killing all 243 passengers and 16 crew. Among the passengers was one of Chase's senior executives, who had transferred to London from New York. He was heading home for the holidays and in fact, had to change flights because of a last-minute meeting.

Rest in Peace. God bless him and his family.

Combatting terrorist financing is one of the most important responsibilities of a dedicated compliance & ethics officer, and this was one event among many that reaffirmed my commitment to a career in compliance. September 11, 2001 was of course, another defining moment, as have been the numerous acts of terrorism around the world since then.

Have Faith in Yourself, Your Loved Ones, and for Some, the Beyond

This book isn't intended to be religious. However, both my wife and I were raised in families where faith was—and remains—very important. I firmly believe that to succeed in anything in life, one must have faith in oneself (that is, self-confidence). That said, throughout your personal and professional life, you'll find yourself needing to have faith in other people, whether it's your life partner, your children, your friends, your team, your colleagues, or even your bosses. And for those who believe, faith in your God (or some other higher power) can help you realize that everything will be okay.

As a compliance & ethics officer, I've experienced what it means to live in a dog-eat-dog world where complying was an afterthought and violations incurred little more than a slap on the wrist. (The attitude was, "Just write a check and let's move on.") But that began to change in 1991, when the US Department of Justice issued its very first Organizational Sentencing Guidelines, which elevated the stature of C&E officers and departments—and put corporations on notice. The Guidelines raised the consequence of violations to more than just slaps on the wrist or "simply the cost of doing business." We'll talk much more about this in part 2.

Life is so precious, and it can turn completely upside down in a split second. That's why, in February 1993, my soulmate and I chose to get married in The Lady Chapel in St. Patrick's Cathedral in New York City. She is the cornerstone of my life, my purpose, and compass. She keeps me grounded and humble, is my toughest critic, and my biggest fan. She often tells me that, "if you get cut, I bleed." From the moment we exchanged our vows and rings, we became—and continue to be—one.

Lessons Learned

- Take breaks. Breathe in the fresh air, appreciate your surroundings, and recharge your batteries.

- Life's too short. Have some fun—even at work. Don's and my desks faced each other and sometimes, to lighten the mood during one of our super-long days, we'd crumple up paper and shoot "baskets" into each other's trash cans. Keep your eye on the goal. Meeting that regulatory deadline can enable strategic growth.

- Life is precious. Believe and have confidence in yourself, embrace those who love you, and have faith, period.

Taking the Leap of Faith for Growth

Source: Christos Georghiou/Shutterstock.com

By the fall of 1993, George Mah had been my mentor for almost ten years, throwing me into the deep end of the pool multiple times, and guiding me along the way. The times with him were intense but wonderful. Throughout the day, he'd bark orders at me or his other direct reports, and if he didn't need my services that day, he'd simply ignore me. I didn't exist. But that was his style and it suited me fine. For the most part, George treated me like a son, and was my "career dad," even though my own father mentored me equally well. Having two mentors was an incredible blessing for me. Both at work and after, George taught me a lot about career management—and life in general. He loved to tell stories about Chase and how to navigate across an organization. He also reminded me that no matter how senior an executive is, whether it's the chairman, the president, or anyone else, they're still human. Treat them as humans (don't be afraid), and they'll treat you the same.

He'd sometimes invite me to join him after work at the nearby, underground sushi bar on the corner of Nassau Street and Maiden Lane in New York City. I've forgotten the name of the place, but I do remember the very first time out with George and his other directs, because I ended up getting sick in the trash can right outside the bar. Too many Kirin beers for me. Ever since, I've been a nurse-one-or-maybe-two-beers kind of guy.

One afternoon, he stormed into my office, visibly upset but I wasn't sure why. Bellowing at me in his baritone voice (he sounded like Alec Guinness as Obi-Wan Kenobi in *Star Wars*, but with a foreign accent), he said, "Luke...."[1] "Young man, you have to think about your career."

"Thank you," I said. He continued his bellowing: "I mean *strategically*. Where do you want to be in five to ten years and beyond?" I later learned that George had once again seen others get promoted before him. George was a troubleshooter for Chase, the go-to guy whom the CFO and other executives asked to identify and address weaknesses around internal controls, including internal accounting controls.

But to some, George was Darth Vader. As a proxy for the CFO, George had significant authority across the bank and he operated through fear.[2] If George knocked on your door, you knew there was a serious issue to address. Quite often, in the wake of his visits, people would be transferred, or entire departments restructured. As you can imagine, this didn't make him terribly popular. I don't think George cared very much about what other people thought of him. He did, however, care quite a lot about Chase and its well-being. And for years, he'd delivered at the highest and most intense levels and with the greatest sense of urgency.

George should have been promoted to senior vice president years earlier, and why that hadn't happened was a mystery—at least to George and me. But for whatever reason—whether it was a lack of promotion positions, discrimination against Asians, and/or corporate politics—George

---

1 Just kidding!
2 Culturally, that was a more acceptable practice at the time.

was upset with Chase. And perhaps because he saw something of himself in me, he decided to think strategically about *my* career.

But like George, I loved Chase. At 33, I was still happy-go-lucky Eric, global head of corporate compliance at one of the largest international banks in the world, completing incredible missions, and with what seemed to me to be a wonderful path to future success. Plus, I had also just married my soulmate, so life was incredibly good. And "comfortable." I had no intention of leaving Chase. Headhunters called me constantly, asking whether I was interested in this or that opportunity, and 99.99 percent of the time, I'd say, "thanks, but no thank you," and try to give them a referral to someone I knew outside of Chase. I always believed that doing good for others (paying it forward) is the right thing, and that one day, good will happen back. At the same time, my mentor was being anything but subtle in hinting that I needed to reevaluate my career at Chase. So, I did.

One late afternoon, right before the Christmas holidays of 1993, I was packing up to leave for the day and the phone rang. It was a recruiter. I almost brushed him off, but I could hear George's voice in my head: "Luke…." The recruiter described for me a compelling opportunity at the Canadian Imperial Bank of Commerce (CIBC), which was looking to hire a chief compliance officer for their US business operations. The recruiter told me that CIBC was on the cusp of a major strategic expansion and needed someone who could re-engineer their existing compliance program up to a sustainable level of regulatory health and newly aligned corporate culture, which in turn, would enable them to execute their new capital markets expansion strategy, globally.

In short, they realized that they couldn't expand strategically unless they were regulatorily healthy in a sustained manner. Right up my alley! After many discussions with both the recruiter and my wife, I agreed to explore and pursue the opportunity. By the end of January, I had completed multiple rounds of interviews in New York. I then asked to meet with their Head Office compliance management in Toronto so that I could better understand CIBC's corporate culture and commitment to compliance, and to confirm what kind of authority the US CCO would have relative to the Toronto headquarters. I also wanted to find out to whom I'd report in the United States, and to assess whether CIBC was considering bringing me in because they simply wanted to address any control weaknesses in the US or because they truly wanted to transform themselves into a very successful investment bank, ultimately in the same league as JP Morgan, Goldman Sachs, and Morgan Stanley.

Being Comfortable vs. Taking the Leap of Faith

Like my New York-vs.-London dilemma, I once again heard the Clash song, *Should I Stay or Should I Go?* Stay comfortable with a promising career at Chase or take the leap of faith to a new job, where I could design, execute, and sustain my own compliance program, which would enable the bank to succeed magnificently in its global capital markets expansion?

CIBC at the time was a relatively small corporate and treasury bank in the United States, with US headquarters in New York and satellite agencies or branches in Chicago, Houston, and San Francisco. I didn't mind their much smaller size in the US or the relative anonymity of the CIBC brand. It was the second or third largest bank in Canada, which had only five or six major banks in total. And it was beginning to integrate its corporate and investment banking businesses in Canada, something that was prohibited at the time in the US.

Banks as Utilities, Plus Canadian ESG Ahead of Its Time

Culturally, Canadians view banks differently than we do in the US (and other places)—at least as of the 1990s, but I don't think it's any different today. If a Canadian bank were to have made a billion dollars in annual profits (a lot at that time), Canadian society would have been outraged, because they saw (and possibly still see) banks more as long-term "utilities" that prudently serve the public and the communities in which they operate. With a handful of banks operating as an oligopoly (which, in economic theory, can control markets, pricing, and therefore drive profits) Canadian banks' earnings were small compared with their American, European, and Asian counterparts. Canadian banks were twenty years ahead of their time.

One popular topic today—and a challenge for many firms—is ESG (environment, society, and governance) and the importance of a board of directors having a long-term fiduciary duty of loyalty to stakeholders regardless of the cost, rather than a short-term duty to maximize profits and shareholder return. The idea is that companies should serve society as the larger good. I'll discuss this in more detail in part 2.

The Evolving Importance of Compliance

Just a few years earlier, Congress enacted the FDIC Improvement Act of 1991,[3] and embedded within that law, the Foreign Bank Supervision Enhancement Act,[4] which for the first time required foreign banks in the United States to be supervised—and audited—by the Federal Reserve. Until then, each state's banking department had supervised foreign banks.

The rationale was to ensure that foreign banks operating in the US would be subject to the same rules and compliance expectations as US banks. Until then, foreign banks had been allowed to engage in activities beyond those permitted of US banks, which gave them a competitive advantage. However, many foreign banks weren't ready for these audits. And CIBC, like other foreign banks, wanted to have business credibility and satisfactory results, which was the path to strategic expansion.

Eventually, the recruiter and CIBC convinced me to take the leap of faith to join the bank as their US chief compliance officer. And so, in mid-January 1994, I submitted my resignation to George, letting him know that I'd be leaving Chase. George was surprised. And angry. He

---

3   12 U.S.C. 1811
4   12 U.S.C. 3101

asked me why I was leaving and told me that he needed me to continue as head of corporate compliance. Now it was *my* turn to be surprised. I reminded him that just three or four months earlier, he himself had told me to think about my career.

"I didn't mean now! I meant that for the long term!" he shouted.

My recruiter had warned my wife and me that Chase would apply intense pressure to get me to stay, and he was right. Each day, for the rest of January, either George or the global head of HR would seek me out with multiple counteroffers: increased responsibilities, higher pay, and so on. More importantly, they asked me what they'd have to do to keep me at Chase. I told them that they should promote George, and I asked whether I'd ever be promoted to that level, and wondered out loud why it had taken my resignation for them to offer me more responsibilities. In the end, despite Chase's best, and well-intentioned counteroffers, I was ready to join CIBC.

Although George was angry that I was leaving, I think he was happy for me. Like any good mentor, he'd encouraged me to think strategically and non-linearly and to look out for myself and my family. And without overtly saying so, he'd also opened my eyes to possible "ceiling" limitations for Asians within Chase.[5] Thus, after eleven wonderful years with Chase and a fantastic team and colleagues, I joined CIBC.

Eighteen months later, Chemical Bank Corporation (Chemical) acquired Chase, paying $10 billion and retaining the better-known Chase name. The six months preceding the acquisition were also marked by intense cost-cutting pressure by one of Chase's largest shareholders, Michael F. Price, an investment manager known to have shaken up companies he considered "complacent."[6] I wonder, in hindsight, whether those Project

---

5   There's some question as to whether today's JP Morgan Chase may still have work to do when it comes to promoting Asians. Just take a look at their board of directors and executive management team: https://www.jpmorganchase.com/about/our-leadership
6   "Banking's New Giant: The Deal: Chase and Chemical Agree to Merge in $10 Billion Deal Creating Largest U.S. Bank." *New York Times*, August 29, 1995

Fox "poison pills" would have mattered, as shareholder activism had become a demand to maximize short-term earnings.

As Chemical appeared to be the clear driver of the merger, most of the leadership positions went to Chemical alumni. Twelve thousand out of the combined 75,000 employees were slated to be cut, and the morale among Chase personnel was quite low. Some of my former colleagues who survived the merger said that "it would have actually been better to be cut, than to have survived."[7]

---

7   The first thing I did when I heard about the merger was call my wife and then the recruiter who brought me over to CIBC to thank them for convincing me to take that leap.

Lessons Learned

- Don't be afraid of the unknown. Often, leaping out of your comfort zone and into a discomfort zone is the best way to learn. Personally, I believe that being comfortable is, professionally, a negative. It leads to complacency.

- Do your homework. I researched and analyzed CIBC in multiple ways, as if I were still a Fed analyst. I thought about their strategic growth plans and how (and whether) compliance could enable them. It did.

- Ask questions of both your current employer and any potential future employer. How will the decisions you make now impact your long-term strategic plans, your overall career path, and, most importantly, your values?

- Don't make big decisions on your own—or in haste. Get input from trusted friends, advisors, loved ones, and mentors. And make sure you listen to dissenting voices as well as those who support your possible move.

- Understand the corporate culture of your current and future employer. Does it feel right now? Will it feel right later?

- If all the pieces are in place, take the leap! Have faith!

The Voicemail—and the Important Relationship Between Compliance and Marketing

Source: EtiAmmos/Shutterstock.com

I'm not going to say where I was working when the following incident took place, but it's a true story.

Early one morning, as I was organizing my day, reading my emails, and multi-tasking as usual, I punched the button on my phone to play my voicemails. Some were unsolicited vendors. Others were short and sweet: "it's Sam, Tuesday at two is fine." Or, "Hi Eric, when you can, please call me about ABC or XYZ." But while listening to the next voicemail, I had to stop in my tracks because I'd suddenly heard a loud, guttural, top-of-the-lungs-let-me-tell-you-what-I-really-think war cry: "FUUUUUCCCCCK YOUUUUUUU"!!! (with an even louder emphasis on the word "you").

I looked up, tilted my head quizzically like a dog hearing a dog whistle, and wondered whether the voicemail had been intended for someone else.

But after I replayed it about a thousand times (just kidding!; maybe five times), there was no question that it was meant for me, and that it was from the head of marketing and communications. The voicemail started uneventfully, quietly and calmly, almost monotonous, and politely listed a series of pros and cons in response to recommendations I'd made on draft language of some advertising literature, which from a regulatory perspective needed to be precise. I understand that marketing language tends to be creative and customer focused, with the goal of creating brand awareness and purchasing (as opposed to compliance's objective of crafting language to protect customers' interests by avoiding confusion).

Anyway, after about 60 seconds of politely listing objections on the voicemail to me, the marketing head clearly thought they'd hung up. But the line was still live—and recording—a "hot mic" so to speak. (Office phones, especially when on speaker, sometimes stay connected unless you press the "close" or "end" button.)

I've always known that compliance & ethics officers are the subject of jokes, sometimes anger, disrespect, and even underestimation. But I'd never before experienced such a passionate expression of "dissatisfaction" over a draft marketing document. We'd had "artistic differences of opinion" before on language but not to the point of expletive expression.

Immediately, I forwarded the voicemail back to this individual with my own voicemail stating, "Hi it's Eric, I'd like for you to hear what *you* sound like." Kind of like adding one more stanza to the song, *Positively 4th Street* (by Bob Dylan) about wishing that for just one time they could stand inside my shoes... and what a drag it'd be ... to "*hear their own voicemail.*"[1] Of course, Mr. Dylan didn't end that or any of his other songs with, "FUUUUUCCCCK YOUUUUUUU," but that classic song certainly would have allowed the marketing head to hear what I had.

---

1   One of my favorite songs, the lyrics actually read, "I wish that for just one time you could stand inside my shoes...You'd know what a drag it is to see you."

Later that day, I received a call from the marketing head, sheepishly apologizing and explaining that they'd dropped a cup of coffee on themselves and screamed the expletive. I replied, "That's funny, when someone drops a cup of coffee on themselves or their desk, they'd usually say 'OHHH F...', not 'F... U,' with an emphasis on the U."

A few months later, the marketing executive was replaced. I'm not suggesting that it was because of that angry-warrior voicemail, but perhaps because I wasn't the only person who'd been on the wrong end of this teammate's hostile war cries and conduct.

The relationship between the marketing/communications and compliance departments is a complex but important one. Ultimately, the objectives of both are the same: enhance and protect the reputation of the firm. However, the means by which each department achieves those objectives aren't necessarily identical and don't need to be. That said, alignment and meeting in the middle is essential.

Fortunately, that was the only time I've encountered such an extreme reaction from my marketing and communications colleagues. Ninety-nine point nine percent of my career interactions with that department have been collaborative, quite productive, and enjoyable.

Lessons Learned

- Marketing and compliance can—and must—co-exist. Creative marketing and advertising and regulatory compliance are not mutually exclusive.

- Making profits and managing C&E risks aren't mutually exclusive either, because companies are in the business of managing risks, not eliminating them (unless identified in your compliance risk assessment that zero risk is the only acceptable risk).

- Always keep your voicemails, emails, and other communications professional, and ensure that you fully disconnected them at the end. I always hang up the phone and then turn on the speaker to ensure that the dial tone returns. It's not easy to remember, but essential.

Compliance, Baseball, and Corporate Strategy

Baseball pitcher (P) throwing the ball to the catcher (C)

Source: Will Hughes/Shutterstock.com (edits by author)

I love baseball. Yes, many folks think it's a slow and essentially boring game of catch: back and forth between the person on the hill (the pitcher) and the crouching person in the mask (the catcher), while a third person (the batter, who's holding a piece of wood) tries to hit the ball before it reaches the catcher. Meanwhile, there are seven other players just standing around behind the one throwing from the hill to the one in the mask.

I get it. But there's much more to this wonderful, classic, and historic game. Each pitch and each throw has a specific, strategic purpose. And to hit the ball effectively, the batter (let's call him or her a risk factor) needs to anticipate each pitch and adjust accordingly. The defensive *controls* (all those individuals seemingly standing around behind the pitcher) therefore need to anticipate the risks posed by each batter as well as those posed by the batter's teammates (baserunners—whom we'll call *unanticipated risks*). And, of course, everything has to be done in a way that doesn't upset the umpires (regulators who enforce compliance).

Although some baseball players excel in the "five tools"—speed, throwing, defensive fielding, hitting for average, and hitting for power—most specialize in only one or two. Some, such as relief pitchers, are so specialized that they might come into a game to pitch to a single batter or even to throw just one or two pitches, after which they leave the game and are replaced by yet another highly specialized pitcher.

One of the most underrated and underappreciated roles in baseball is the catcher (whom we'll of course, call the chief compliance officer or CCO). Like most of the other defensive players, catchers usually play the whole game. However, unlike the others (except the pitcher), the catcher is involved in *every* pitch. In addition, he or she has to be ready to throw out opposing runners (unexpected risks) who are trying to steal bases, and acts as a backup on routine plays executed by other defensive players. By the way, catchers are also expected to perform well on offense, as hitters.

The baseball diamond itself provides a nice visual. As illustrated below, when playing defense, all the players—except the catcher—are facing the same direction, towards the batter and are responsible for managing specific risks posed by the batter. For example, if the batter hits to left field of financial risks, the left fielder must be prepared to manage those financial risks. If the batter hits to the credit risks of second base, then the second baseman must manage those credit risks. And so on.

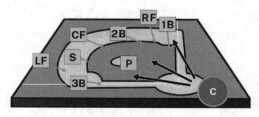

Source: LAUDiseno/Shutterstock.com (edits by author)

Like his or her teammates, the catcher/CCO also sees the batter and is concerned with managing the risk posed by the batter. However, unlike the rest of the defense, the catcher/CCO must also see the *entire field of play* (enterprise) and provide guidance to the rest of the team on how to deal with all risks. That means suggesting specific pitches for the pitcher to throw at the batter, repositioning defensive players (finance, operations, technology, risk, legal, human resources) to better defend against the various risks the batter might present, and implementing strategies sent in by the team's manager (CEO) who is overseen by the general manager (board of directors) on behalf of the team's/company's owners. The catcher's/CCO's global, enterprise-wide approach allows all the other risk specialists and players to focus on what they do best, knowing that the catcher will be there to back them up.

Moving from the Major Leagues to the Minor Leagues

After eleven years of playing in the major leagues as Chase's CCO/catcher, surrounded by a top-notch team of experienced, full-time compliance, finance, technology, operations officers, and lawyers, I joined CIBC's team in February 1994. It was a very different experience. With their much smaller headcount, narrower scale of businesses, not-yet-fit-for-purpose derivatives infrastructure, and the lack of a full-time compliance staff, CIBC in the US was in no way ready to pitch, throw, catch, or hit in the major leagues of global capital markets.

My mandate was to put together a team that was capable of transforming itself from a minor league club into a "ready-for-prime-time," major league-global-capital-markets-and-investment bank. To do that, we would have to prove—to our stakeholders, including our regulators such as the Fed and New York State Banking Department[1]—that CIBC'S strategies were sound, run prudently, and equipped to manage our growth and new risks.

---

1   Today known as the Department of Financial Services (DFS). Both the Fed and DFS could be viewed as the banking equivalent of Major League Baseball's Commissioner). Indeed, so could the US Treasury Comptroller of the Currency, the Consumer Finance Protection Board, or non-US regulators such as the UK Financial Conduct Authority or Hong Kong Monetary Authority.

We had about nine months to design, plan, grow, and/or acquire major league talent; construct a holistic infrastructure of people, technology, and processes; and implement controls fit for purpose to support CIBC's existing—and expanding—new US and global businesses. To help execute this objective, I was charged with upgrading our compliance and broader risk-management and infrastructure controls, including leading the regulatory examination management process. Culturally, I was pleased that our management linked the successful strengthening of our controls with our growth strategy.

Lessons Learned

- Whether you're a new compliance & ethics officer or have been in that role for years, take the lead. Be your team's catcher to lead your fellow specialists on the field to win the game, whether that means achieving effective compliance or satisfactory exam results. The net result is a green light to grow.

- Think strategically, and, like a catcher, be involved in all aspects of your organization's initiatives and decisions.

- Play defense, offensively. In other words, instead of only reacting to crises, proactively evaluate existing risks, anticipate emerging risks, communicate that information (your compliance risk assessment) to the teammates who will most likely be called upon to deal with those risks, and direct the flow of resources.

- Understand what league your company is playing in and honestly assess your understanding of the rules of the game. Do you know your competition? What's their current strategy versus their future strategy, and what's yours? Does your company have what it'll take (including chemistry, teamwork, and the right corporate culture) to get from where you are now to where you want to be? If not, what will it take?

Mind the Gap: Lessons Learned About Compliance Risk Assessments from Subways and Trains

Source: StudioTheo2020/ Shutterstock.com

"**M**ind the Gap." That was the announcement that echoed continuously in London's Tube (subway) stations. Similar announcements are heard and seen in subway stations in Toronto, New York City, Hong Kong, and around the world. These important announcements repeatedly remind riders of the spatial gap between the train door and the station platform. And Don and I heard it daily as we commuted from Kensington Station to London's "City," where Chase's corporate banking offices were located at the time.

Falling Through the Gap as a Type of Compliance Risk Assessment[1]

To commuters, the risk of falling through the gap was (and still is) perceived to be relatively low, especially when compared to the more significant,

---

1   Because Compliance Risk Assessments (CRAs) are so important, I'll be touching on them a lot over the next few chapters.

perceived risk of falling (or being pushed) in front of an arriving train. People (and companies) utilize a "compliance risk assessment" to weigh whether an "inherent" risk (defined as a possibility of loss or injury) in terms of *likelihood* and/or *severity if the event actually occurs*. A risk assessment matrix (or heat map) typically looks like the chart below, which measures the likelihood of a risk versus its severity, and graphically shows a total level of risk for each possible combination.

Severity

Likelihood		Negligible	Minor	Moderate	Major	Catastrophic
	Almost certain	5	10	15	20	25
	Likely	4	8	12	16	20
	Possible	3	6	9	12	15
	Unlikely	2	4	6	8	10
	Rare	1	2	3	4	5

Source: konstakorhonen/Shutterstock.com

One might think that the severity of injuries sustained when falling through the gap would also be lower than getting hit by a train. In fact, with hundreds of thousands of people entering and exiting trains all day, the likelihood that at least one person will fall through the platform gap is actually far higher than the likelihood that someone will fall (or get pushed) in front of a moving train. Sadly, most regular commuters ignore the constant "mind-the-gap" warnings, leaving them with a false sense of security and misperception of low risk leading them to behave carelessly. As a result, the *actual risk* to rushing commuters of injury or even death from falling into or getting one's foot or leg trapped in the gap is very real. For example, only months after his father, US President Abraham Lincoln, had been assassinated in 1865, Lincoln's son, Robert Lincoln's legs were caught in the gap between an outdoor train and the platform.

Ironically, the person who pulled him from the gap and saved his life was John Wilkes' Booth's[2] brother, Edwin.

More than 120 years after Robert Lincoln's mind-the-gap experience, Don and I had our own experience, illustrating how easy it is to ignore perceived benign or low risks. It was mid-November 1987, and we were heading back from Chase's office to Kensington South station when we smelled smoke at one of our regular transfer stations. Not seeing any smoke billowing or emergency crews, we assumed that a newspaper or some other trash thrown onto the tracks had accidentally caught fire. Based on that perception, the risk that it was more serious seemed low. But the following morning, we found out that that very evening, a fire had started at King's Cross St. Pancras tube station, killing 31 people and injuring 100. Based on a public inquiry, the London Underground was strongly criticized for their major underestimation and attitude toward the risk of underground train fires. Staff were complacent and had been given little or no training on how to deal with fires or conduct evacuations.

As the London inquiry showed, human beings tend to discount or ignore the possibility that unlikely events can happen (like a cyberattack about which many in management might foolishly say, "it can't happen here!"). Sadly, when one of those unlikely events does happen, the consequences are often far more severe. For example, around the world, there have been a total of 56 notable subway fires, including one in New York City in March 2020.

In the compliance world, compliance gaps are gaps in any company's ability to effectively and sustainably comply with laws, regulations, compliance policies, and/or codes of conduct or ethics in which there is a risk of violation, material impact on the company's capital and/or its reputation. Some of these risks are "business-as-usual" gaps, which are taken for granted but nonetheless require regular mind-the-gap reminders

---

2   The assassin who fired the shot that killed Abraham Lincoln.

of the potential hazards (e.g., employee safety reminders which tend to be routinely ignored—at least until the COVID-19 pandemic of 2020–21).

Extraordinary gaps are dangerous risks—and harsh lessons which, unfortunately, are typically embraced only after the fact. These lessons learned must be studied and used to prepare for and, hopefully, avoid future threats of reputational damage, severe regulatory enforcement, penalties, and personal liability.

Unanticipated risks (the things "we don't know that we don't know," or didn't anticipate, or more likely, have simply been complacent about) are often the most catastrophic. In a matter of mere (socially viral) nanoseconds, months or years of successful growth strategy and decades of brand building and goodwill can be undone, causing disastrous damage to the company's reputation and its bottom line.

To properly identify, prioritize, and manage all these risks, methodical and documented compliance risk assessments (CRAs) must be conducted regularly (at least annually, if not quarterly, or continuously if automated and embedded in the business process). We'll explore the evolution of compliance risk assessments, at least as it's happened over the course of my career, in coming chapters.

Lessons Learned

- Mind the gap. Anything—whether glaringly severe and obvious or seemingly benign and routine—might lead to dangerous complacency and severe consequences.

- Risk assessments, particularly compliance risk assessments, enable gaps to be identified, controlled, reassessed, and prioritized. The execution of robust controls (people, process, and technology) will reduce a high inherent risk (uncontrolled risk) into a more manageable residual risk. Indeed, the absence of robust controls warrants the assignment of higher residual risk ratings than should be the case.

- Don't wait for the corporate equivalent of the King's Cross Subway fire to spur you (after it's too late) to start paying attention to safety measures, notice red flags, and avoid complacency. More on this in the following chapters.

The Rubik's Cube of Compliance Risk Assessments

Source: gd_project/Shutterstock.com

Throughout my career, I've kept a collection of baseballs, tennis balls, and other objects in my office. I'd often grab or throw these objects around with my team members to lighten the mood when discussing a particularly challenging matter. My favorite item was a Rubik's Cube, a visual reminder of the importance of seeing and addressing many sides of complex, sensitive risks or issues—especially compliance-related ones.

Every chief compliance officer must manage a company's compliance risks and compliance risk assessment like a Rubik's Cube. That's because a company is a dynamic combination of people, process, technology, and corporate sub-cultures that flows through the company's legal entities, divisions, products, and services across multiple geographies and jurisdictions. This is equally true for a bank, hospital, energy or technology firm, or producer of food. Every company must also be aware of external risks and multiple changes to their industry or environment.

Source: Committee of Sponsoring Organizations of the Treadway Commission – Enterprise Risk Management visual; COSO.org

With so many moving parts both internally and externally, the inherent compliance & ethics risks are both complex and fluid. By managing a company like a Rubik's Cube, the CCO can help the CEO and the board of directors understand the complexities of C&E risks and the difficulties of getting all sides of the "corporate cube" or issues resolved. As we'll learn in part 2 of this book, a major misalignment of cultures within a company and subsequent mismanagement of compliance and ethics risks could ultimately doom a company and its board of directors.

Unfortunately, too many CEOs and business leaders claim to have solved their corporate Rubik's Cube of compliance & ethics issues, offering as proof the fact that they've upgraded their controls. But in most cases, management hasn't solved the whole cube—only one side of it. Or worse, instead of solving even one side, management has simply "painted" the appropriate color on each face of the cube, creating the false impression that everything is perfect or completed, while leaving the underlying chaos in place.

In the short term, the paint job can give management a false sense of comfort and allows them to convince themselves, the board, shareholders, regulators, and other stakeholders that all is well. But in the long term, that false sense

Source: Kenishirotie/iStockPhoto.com

of security makes them ignore risks or foolishly take even greater ones (in the same way that people ignore mind-the-gap warnings). Eventually, the paint will chip, and it will become clear that the problems they'd covered up have only gotten worse.

Compliance Risk Appetites and Risk Assessments Enable Prioritized Allocation of Time/Resources

The good news is that it's not necessary to solve the entire Rubik's Cube all at once, achieving perfect alignment or eliminating all compliance risks. Instead, the most important goal is to manage each risk to a residual risk level that complies with the board's approved "compliance risk appetite" for what's acceptable, manageable, and sustainable in a way that the board can understand the risks in a thematic, story-telling manner.

In part 2 of this book, we'll get into the details of exactly how to manage compliance risk, including times when you might need to eliminate all risks, and the importance of proper documentation, books, and records.

Lessons Learned

- The Rubik's Cube is an excellent metaphor for a large, small, simple, or complex corporate organization, which is a combination of many moving external and internal parts.

- Try to align the legal entities, business divisions, internal controls, and corporate culture of your enterprise-wide cube. But be careful that you (or worse, your executive management) don't create a false sense of security by "painting" the sides before you achieve truly sustainable alignment and effective compliance.

- Your corporate Rubik's Cube doesn't have to be perfectly aligned all at once, because the purpose of an enterprise, at least a for-profit one, is not to *eliminate* all compliance risks whether legal, regulatory, or code of conduct, but to *manage* those risks in a prioritized manner so that the organization can be profitably (but safely and compliantly) run while protecting shareholders and other stakeholders, including customers, employees, society, and the community in which the organization operates. That said, there are some risks which must be eliminated. For example, the risk of terrorist financing or bribing a foreign government official.

- A compliance risk assessment that is methodical, documented, and linked to your policies, training, monitoring, testing, and reporting program is essential to prioritizing your risks so that they can be properly managed to acceptable levels.

Achieving Regulatory Exam Readiness — Without the Drama

Source: Ivan Cholakov/Shutterstock.com

I love old war movies, particularly those made during or shortly after World War II. Many of those old classics, such as *Twelve O'Clock High*, *Strategic Air Command*, and *Dive Bomber* were full of propaganda designed to boost morale for the strategic war effort or post-war recovery. Many of those movies had scenes (or triumphant endings) in which American fighter planes were heard and then seen, bursting through the clouds and roaring into the sunset towards the front to engage the enemy (with dramatic music in the background). Those scenes became so clichéd that one famous movie critic's 1969 review of *Battle of Britain* made a point of skewering them:

> *"Remember the obligatory scene of the dashing young pilots lounging around the officers' club? Suddenly the attack alarm sounds, and they*

all dash out into the night, leaving the fire burning and a few chairs overturned… and then the roar of airplanes is heard overhead as our boys fly off to engage…."[1]

Nevertheless, I loved those old war movies. And I thought about them a lot as my CIBC team and I roared into action in advance of our annual regulatory exams and internal audits, ready for battle. The difference was that the regulators and auditors were *not* our enemies. In fact, they were our allies, the ones who would help us help ourselves, enabling us to execute our global growth strategy. But we still had to be "battle ready" and "battle tested," and my regulatory readiness updates for Head Office and our US general manager, said that we were.[2]

How did we know we were ready? Because I'd created our Compliance Risk Assessments (CRAs, which I'd then called "exam readiness assessments"), based on publicly available regulatory examination manuals issued by the Fed, the Federal Deposit Insurance Corporation, and the US Treasury Comptroller of the Currency. These exam manuals have always been rich in detail and publicly available, and describe wholesale and retail products, underlying risks, along with "internal control questionnaires" and exam procedures. To this day, they remain accessible on the web, and thoroughly describe what regulators expect of financial institutions with respect to systems of internal controls, regulatory compliance, satisfactory risk management, and expected controls to enable accurate books and records. These regulatory examination manuals were (and still are) the quintessential "open-book tests" for institutions preparing for a regulatory examination. At the same time, they were a blueprint that helped us execute a firm-wide business and compliance risk management strategy for our individual businesses to operate safely and profitably.

---

1   Review of "Battle of Britain," November 3, 1969. RogerEbert.com. Retrieved July 28, 2020
2   I wasn't the only one who was channeling WWII movies. One day, after we'd proudly satisfied one of our regulatory exams, my boss, the global head of compliance, wrote to congratulate us and mentioned that he'd been visualizing those planes flying overhead into the sunset!

Today, directors, compliance & ethics officers, the CEO, and his or her executives should view the US Department of Justice's June 2020 "Evaluation of Corporate Compliance Programs" as an open-book test. This DoJ directive is formatted into a series of questions that can help companies self-evaluate and assess gaps against DoJ expectations and determine whether their compliance program is effective and sustainable in view of continuous changes in risks and therefore, continuously improving in effectiveness.[3]

With the complete support of our US general manager, business heads, US and global general counsels, and the global head of compliance, I'd distribute exam readiness binders and matrices for each business and function to complete before our regulatory exams. Weekly, I'd meet with our executive management, business leaders, and functional heads to assess the status of gaps and planned actions to close them based on priority with target dates and owners. Between meetings, I'd follow up with each of them on the areas requiring closer supervision.

That's how I mobilized and aligned our first- and second-line functions as CIBC's US regulatory exam coordinator and US CCO. Everyone knew the strategic stakes: If we didn't pass our regulatory exams, we wouldn't be able to expand aggressively into global capital markets. It was an incredibly arduous process, not only for me, but also for the organization. But it kept us focused and demonstrated our commitment to align, prioritize, and complete our twin objectives of satisfying our examiners and enabling CIBC to grow strategically. This rigorous exercise also shaped our corporate culture and affected our productivity and overall attitude in a consistent, positive manner.

In order to make the transition to the "major leagues," CIBC had to meet and/or exceed the open-book test expectations of the Fed and New York State with respect to our current and future businesses, particularly

---

3   "Evaluation of Corporate Compliance Programs" (updated June 2020). US Department of Justice Criminal Division. https://www.justice.gov/criminal-fraud/page/file/937501/download. Retrieved December 5, 2020

our new global capital markets derivatives and proprietary trading activities. We also had to demonstrate that we understood and managed both known and unknown risks; that we would continue to comply with the Fed's multiple regulatory limits, restrictions, and prohibitions; and that we knew how to extract trade data into our financial subledgers, general ledgers, and risk management systems for regulatory reporting, consolidated financial statement reporting, or risk management purposes.

Each year, so much of our global strategic growth was at stake because we were required to achieve supervisory expectations satisfactorily (which we did). And each year thereafter, we succeeded again. At first, it was with our "propeller-engine, legacy planes" roaring overhead, but over time, as our technology investments and capabilities increased, we upgraded to advanced jet engines and added new business lines every year: a full range of derivatives trading and sales (1995); high-yield bond underwriting (1996); US government securities dealing (as a Fed "primary dealer," 1997); full-service equities; fixed-income brokerage; research; alternative investments; and hedge funds (1998 and beyond).

Lessons Learned

- Regulators and auditors are *not* the enemy. They are your allies in your battle against excessive risks, money laundering, fraud, terrorist financing, misconduct, market abuse, bribery, cybercrimes, and corruption.

- Be truthful with your regulators and auditors. Credibility is essential, and ultimately they will assist the firm. Culturally, sometimes it's your CEO and C-suite that may be your worst enemy, particularly if they don't invest in the needed infrastructure and controls for a sound culture as well as the robust technology to monitor and test for a compliant and ethical company.

- Open-book tests are incredibly difficult but fulfilling. If you can extract from publicly available regulators' websites their expectations and control objectives, questionnaires, examination procedures, and enforcement actions, you'll know the answers and be able to learn from the mistakes others have made that resulted in major penalties and reputational damage. The challenge is to get management, your board of directors, and business leaders to understand that utilizing open-book tests not only gets them exam ready but also helps manage your risks and will result in growth, safety, and profitability. Our goal, as compliance & ethics officers, is to get management to understand this duality: that effective compliance leads to strategic success.

Do the Math to Better Evaluate Residual Risks

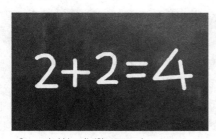

Source: bakhistudio/Shutterstock.com

I've always been fascinated with numbers, particularly if they involve the numbers three or one. Not necessarily because legendary New York Yankee Babe Ruth wore the number three, and I certainly didn't have the ego to expect to be viewed as number one. What I'm drawn to are the digits themselves. I was third-ranked on my high school chess team, third-ranked on my high school tennis team, and am one of three children. I also believe in the "three-legged stool" of legal, compliance, and audit, where all three legs must be strong. One wobbly leg can topple the whole foundation of a company. The same applies to the triad of risk management, compliance, and human resources; or technology, operations, and finance. And in my faith, the Trinity is paramount.

I also loved my high school trigonometry class. *Trigonometry* comes from the Greek word *trigōnon* (meaning triangle) and metron (meaning measure) and studies the relationships between side lengths and angles of triangles. The "corporate accountability pyramid," as you'll see in part 2, is an illustration of the relationship between the personally liable board of directors, the liable CCO, and unaccountable management, whose actions or inactions lead to regulatory violations and major reputational damage.

The Number 1

Then there's the number one, which, for some bizarre reason, always seems to be popping up for me. For example, I often look up randomly for the time of day and it will inevitably be 1:11am or pm or 11:11am or pm. One cold night in 2009, even the weather pop-up on my laptop seemed to have had a preference for 1s, like the time when the temperature was 11 degrees at 11:11pm and the wind speed was 1 mile per hour (see exhibit below):

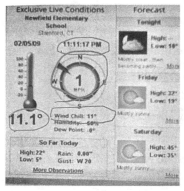

Source: my computer screen in 2009

Sometimes, though, the number one can be more troublesome, such as on the Friday morning in November, when an HR person called me (from her hotel in Beijing!) to advise me that I was being restructured out of my position. Needless to say, I was quite upset. Not because the HR rep was telling me such bad news in a phone call, but because I was actually transferring! Guess what the date was when I received that infamous phone call. November 11, 2011 or 11/11/11.

The Meaning of Numbers — Particularly Compliance Risk Assessment Numbers

My point? There are many ways to interpret numbers. They need to be put into context, particularly for Compliance Risk Assessments (CRAs). And numbers (data) have to be applied in a way that's user-friendly, sustainable, and tells the story you must tell to your board of directors. In other words, numbers and data are a means to an end. What do the numbers mean? What actions should you take based on numbers, particularly in the context of a CRA?

Over my career, I've seen CRAs evolve tremendously—particularly in the eyes of banking (and other) regulators and the US Department of Justice—from the mind-the-gap exam management self-assessments in the 1990s, to incredibly complicated compliance risk matrixes, in which every law, product, client, location, and regulation needs to be calculated, weighted, and populated on a 1,000+-line Excel spreadsheet.

Keep it Simple and Sustainable — Don't Turn Your Compliance Risk Assessment into Calculus

Source: MIKHAIL GRACHIKOV/Shutterstock.com

Since one of the major objectives of a CRA is to prioritize potential company actions based on the likelihood of a particular risk happening, the severity of the risk, and the ability of existing controls to meet a legal or regulatory requirement, completing thousands of lines of spreadsheet based on a numeric weighting of each of these components will quickly become unsustainable. This is especially true without automated tools. Inputting thousands of variables into an excel spreadsheet risks human error, inconsistent input and output, stale data, and misinterpretation of the results instead of the meaningful set of compliance risk analytics and themes that your board members need.

Running the numbers is actually just the first step. Remember the risk assessment matrix (heat map) that I introduced in chapter 1.12 (and is pictured on the next page)? Again, it's a visual way of measuring the likelihood of any given risk versus its severity. When you plug in your list of priorities and the associated risks, you'll have a very basic picture. But what about specific actions that have to be taken to mitigate risks,

Severity

	Negligible	Minor	Moderate	Major	Catastrophic
Almost certain	5	10	15	20	25
Likely	4	8	12	16	20
Possible	3	6	9	12	15
Unlikely	2	4	6	8	10
Rare	1	2	3	4	5

Likelihood (vertical axis label)

Source: konstakorhonen/Shutterstock.com

timelines, assigned owners for each item, and how they're going to be monitored to ensure compliance? That's a lot of variables to ultimately identify residual risks and to resolve them to the point that they are within the board's risk appetites.

Regulators, however, expect to see those numbers and will scrutinize them to determine whether your calculations are methodical, documented, and show actions, timelines, and who is responsible for executing the actions. These actions should include training and policy creation and/or amendments for the coming year, as well as readjusting surveillance, monitoring, and testing priorities. In addition, a compliance risk assessment's calculations should be used as a basis for allocating compliance resources for the coming budget year in the form of an Annual Compliance Plan (which I'll discuss in more detail in part 2) to be presented to and approved by your board of directors.

As you can imagine, at some of the firms where I was CCO, the combination of an overly complex compliance risk assessment process and methodology without the appropriate compliance technology tools left us vulnerable to regulatory and audit criticism, because the Excel spreadsheet process would be untimely, vulnerable to human error, and overly simplistic—or maddeningly complicated. Excel doesn't cut it anymore.

Compliance risk assessments must be forward-looking and include "predictive analytics," not solely a point-in-time "guess" based on high level data. My staff frequently complained that there were far too many internal and external variables (including literally hundreds of regulatory requirements) to accurately maintain and track. In addition, each regulatory agency (and often, each individual within a particular agency) had its own expectations as to which compliance risks would be assessed and how.

Lessons Learned

- Keep it simple. Trying to calculate risks on a line-by-line basis for every product, business, geography, and client, cross-referenced for every law and regulation is unsustainable. It's also a nightmare for the people responsible for closing the control gaps identified by the risk assessments.

- Regulators expect risk assessment calculators to have data integrity.

- Compliance risk assessments are more than simply calculators of risk, but the technology needed to run and predict compliance risks is often missing (usually because of inadequate or non-existent investment). CRAs are meant to be a means to an end, helping you identify and prioritize actions, resources, and owners. That, in turn, should lower the residual compliance risks to a manageable level for the board and management, thus ensuring that the company as a whole will be able to operate safely and profitably.

- Support for executing CRAs has to come from the top ("tone at the top" is often assessed by the DoJ and other regulators). At the same time, the corporate culture has to enable an understanding of the risks that management and the company face, not only to reap the rewards, but also to manage those risks in order to avoid the fallout from not addressing them, or worse, from not anticipating them in the first place.

- An Annual Compliance Plan enables you to prioritize your limited budget and resources to your higher risks. This should be based on a set of four or more compliance risk categories. Don't use the standard three-category scale (high, medium, and low) because it's too easy to default to the medium category. Having too many mediums will result in too many resources being allocated to medium risks—and not enough devoted to higher priority, more catastrophic risks, especially black swans.[1] A four- (or more) point heat scale can help.

1   *Black swan* is a term popularized by Nassim Taleb in his book, *The Black Swan: The Impact of the Highly Improbable.* According to Investopedia, "Taleb describes a black swan as an event that 1) is so rare that even the possibility that it might occur is unknown, 2) has a catastrophic impact when it does occur, and 3) is explained in hindsight as if it were actually predictable." Small world: Nassim was one of the options traders I oversaw at CIBC in my capacity as CCO.

The Trader and the Compliance Officer's Kneecap — Underestimating Risks

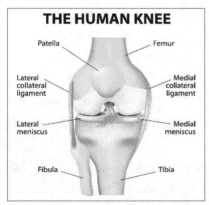

THE HUMAN KNEE

Patella

Femur

Lateral collateral ligament

Medial collateral ligament

Lateral meniscus

Medial meniscus

Fibula

Tibia

Source: Designua/Shutterstock.com

Achieving US regulatory success led to transformative capital markets growth at CIBC from 1995 to 1999. It was the perfect case of strategic success and aligned corporate culture being driven by regulatory compliance. That, in turn, not only produced a much-improved control infrastructure and a productive enterprise-wide culture of compliance, but also paved the way for John Hunkin, our newly promoted CEO, to promote me and others who'd contributed to our success, to global heads for all of CIBC.

John likely also remembered me from our very first meeting, in July 1995, when he was then our Investment Banking President and had visited our NY headquarters. Everyone on our US executive team was there, dressed in what was then the corporate uniform of suit and tie. Except me. I showed up on crutches, wearing a forest green Lacoste tennis shirt and khaki shorts, which revealed a plaster cast from my right ankle up to the hip.

After the meeting, John introduced himself to me and asked about my khaki-and-plaster wardrobe. I explained that I'd had an accident while playing on CIBC's inter-bank divisional softball[1] team a month earlier in a game against Bankers Trust.[2] (Stay with me—this is about underestimating risks through compliance risk assessments—I promise!)

I'd joined the team the season before, as a way to get to know my fellow players, since most of them worked on the trading floor. As described in this book's introduction, I've always believed that sports are the great equalizer, and I wanted to be treated and respected as their teammate, not just as their compliance officer watching over them.

As our team's starting pitcher my first year, we did relatively well. In my second season, though, our captain Dave lost confidence in me—with good reason. That year I couldn't hit, struck out often, and was error-prone when playing the infield. As a result, I spent a lot of time on the bench, pleading, "Put me in coach, I'm ready to play," as if I were John Fogerty singing his hit song, "Centerfield." But my pleas were futile unless the team didn't have enough players, which is exactly what happened on that fateful day (June 8, 1995).

We were losing 9-0 in the last inning of the game and I was playing second base[3] when the Bankers Trust batter hit a short fly ball between the infield and center field. (As a quick aside, the first "compliance" principle in baseball or softball is that the infielder must *always* yield to the outfielder, since he or she—running forward—has a better, more consistent view of the ball than the infielder, who's running backwards.)

---

1   For those of you readers outside the United States, softball is similar to US baseball, but played with a larger sized ball. The rules are virtually the same.

2   Yes, the same Bankers Trust (BT) that was being sued by two major corporate clients. These clients triggered what ultimately cost BT irreparable reputational damage because they had allegedly structured and sold complex derivatives to unwitting clients (allegedly), which caused major financial losses by these clients (exactly the same type of business CIBC wanted to expand into).

3   As kids, the worst player on the team was usually the catcher (ironic, since the CCO is the most strategic player. But in adult games, the worst player often ends up at second base).

Time out! Let's do a quick compliance risk assessment, starting with the inherent risk of a collision between me (the infielder) and the centerfielder (my trading floor colleague, who was built like a US football linebacker):

- **Likelihood: Very low.** After all, it was the last inning of a 9-0 blowout and the infielder is always supposed to yield to the outfielder.

- **Severity: Potentially high.** The math of two forces, each running at 15–20 miles per hour, crashing into each other head on is pretty basic: ($F = m * v^2 / (2 * d)$), where F is the average impact force, m is the mass of an object, v is the initial speed of an object, and d is the distance traveled during collision. But you don't have to crunch the numbers to see that the chance of serious injury is high.

Meanwhile, I did my own risk-reward analysis during the play, discounting the potential severity of a head-on crash. The worst that could happen, I thought, is that one or both of us would end up with a slight headache. The reward, however, could be significant: I'd make a great Derek Jeter-type acrobatic circus catch. I said to myself, "I've done it before, and I can do it again," and I'd redeem myself in the eyes of my teammates. So I put my head down and ran full speed for the ball!

What I didn't take into account was that captain and centerfielder Dave, was charging full steam ahead and had no intention of yielding to me. Seconds later, C-R-A-S-H!!![4] Our foreheads collided and we were sprawled on the ground. Dave was cursing as the ball rolled into the outfield. Something about my right knee looked off, so I knew not to move.

Another risk assessment: strangely (and I guess thankfully), I felt no pain at all in my knee or leg. Therefore, I thought it was a simple knee

---

4   Years later, one of my teammates told me he was standing on the sidelines about 75 yards away and could *hear* the crack of the bones as Dave and I collided!

dislocation. Although a dislocated knee is worse than a bruise, it still seemed pretty minor and could be popped back in like we've seen in the movies. Or so I thought.

I was laying on the ground and players from both teams surrounded me while someone called an ambulance. When the emergency medical technicians (EMTs) arrived, they discovered that the end of a bone was protruding out the right side of my thigh, which lead to a flurry of "Oh my God"! "Ewwww," and "Geez!" from the players.

The EMTs popped the bone back in, allowing me to cling to the idea that I'd only dislocated my knee, as they loaded me into the ambulance. At the hospital emergency room, x-rays revealed my severe "residual risk" reality: my lower kneecap had shattered into 23 pieces and a ligament that connected the knee to the surrounding muscle had torn and had to be reattached. I needed reconstructive surgery, which they scheduled for later that week.

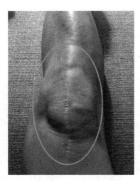

My knee, half a kneecap and my 8-inch surgical scar

A concerned Dave, with whom I'd collided, dropped by the hospital with his wife to see how I was doing and gave me a book entitled *"Compliance Officers Can't Play for Shit"* (just kidding! I honestly don't remember the name of the book). He and his trading floor teammates were also quite gracious and welcoming when I returned a couple weeks later in my cast and crutches. They even presented me a "Most Valuable Player" trophy—with the right lower leg sawed off!

Fortunately, my personal and professional objectives kept me focused. In the office, the traders and even management teased me, yelling out loud that if I didn't watch it, they'd send in another trader to break my *other* kneecap. We'd laugh, but I wanted to show everyone (including myself) that no matter what, we had a lot of risk, compliance, and control infrastructure work to get done to meet our regulatory expectations and enable strategic growth. Nothing was going to stop me—and nothing did.

Net Residual Risk and Remediation

Clearly, I'd made a series of poor risk assessments and calculations. First, I underestimated the *likelihood* of crashing into my teammate. Second, I underestimated the *severity* of that risk—especially since the person I was going to collide with was twice my size. And third, even after having suffered damage, I insisted on believing that my injuries were minor. That made it nearly impossible to fully prepare for the full year of three-times-a-week, scream-inducing torture sessions with physical therapists to break scar tissue and literally re-learn how to walk and go up and down stairs, let alone once again play softball, basketball, and tennis.

At home, my wife, with all of her love, kept me sane and kept my spirits up by always making me laugh. She made me really, really appreciate what true love and devotion is and gave new meaning to the phrase from our wedding vows, "… in sickness and in health…."

Underestimating Compliance Risks at Blue Bell Creameries. Net Result: Greater Director Risk of Personal Liability

Fast forward to 2019, when Blue Bell Creameries pleaded guilty to charges that they'd sold contaminated ice cream products.[5] They paid more than $19 million in fines and the CEO faced criminal charges. What does ice cream have to do with softball injuries? You'll see some interesting parallels.

If the rule in softball is that when chasing a fly ball, the infielder should always yield to the outfielder, the rule in any kind of food service is to always ensure that your facilities meet or exceed the highest sanitary and safety standards. I willfully disregarded the softball rule, thinking that the

---

5   Chorney, David, A. "Three Things to Learn from Delaware Supreme Court's Opinion on Board of Director Oversight Duties. Marchand v. Barnhill)", Mintz. https://www.mintz.com/insights-center/viewpoints/2146/2019-07-three-things-learn-delawaresupreme-courts-opinion-board. Retrieved June 28, 2021

risk was small. Similarly, Blue Bell's CEO and other executives willfully disregarded the safety and sanitary rules as well as the results of a test that found the presence of *listeria*, a deadly pathogen. They also tried to cover up the contamination, presumably thinking (or hoping) that the risk of anyone dying was small.

Once I crashed into my teammate, I insisted to myself that the problem was minor and that I'd be back on my feet in no time. Eventually, I had to face reality. Similarly, Blue Bell initially treated *listeria* as a minor problem, but eventually had to face reality when several customers died. In my case, reality convinced me. In Blue Bell's, not so much. The company continued to lie and cover up the truth.

Obviously, there are major differences between my story and Blue Bell's, not the least of which are that in the grand scheme of things, my miscalculations, were fairly minor. Dave was, thankfully uninjured, and I eventually recovered fully, returning to the softball diamond a couple years after that outfield crash.

Blue Bell, however, ignored warning signs, covered up negative results, misled their customers and investigators, and people died as a result. More about Blue Bell and the major impact on the personal liability of corporate directors, in part 2.

Lessons Learned

- Take your risk assessments seriously, especially factors concerning the likelihood that particular events might happen as well as the severity of the event should it happen (even if it's unlikely).

- Be realistic when assessing your current situation. What if things are worse than you think they are? What will you have to do to mitigate damage that's already done?

- Practice what you preach. If the first principle is to yield to the outfielder, then yield no matter what. Similarly, if the first-line businesses need to yield to the compliance officer, they must yield.

- Set an objective, no matter how steep. Then meet it. Whether it's remediating a risk assessment rating of red (indicating the highest level of risk and severity), or re-learning how to walk, you can do it!

CRADs and TIGRs

Source: Carol Boalin/Shutterstock.com

I n five short years (1994 to 1999), CIBC grew from having a sleepy corporate lending and treasury funding operation in the United States to a major North American capital markets and corporate banking institution with an international presence. CIBC's US balance sheet, client base, and profitability had all expanded by multiples. At the same time, the control infrastructure in the U.S. was stronger, because we were also upgrading controls to support our new business platforms, through new people (with the right capacity and skills), processes (which were better understood and documented), technology infrastructure (which could capture the transaction flows more effectively and efficiently), and overall system of internal controls (to address the Fed's and New York State's supervisory expectations for risk management).

Having officially made it to the "major leagues," the next strategic objective was to scale CIBC's US success to the rest of its worldwide business, especially across Canada for its retail and small business banking and wealth management (including notably retail brokerage), as well as for our institutional trading, sales, and corporate and investment banking.

Linking Business Strategy and Risk and Control Effectiveness

To achieve that objective, the CEO, John Hunkin, selected an "architect," Wayne Fox, CIBC's vice-chairman and head of treasury and balance sheet management (who would shortly thereafter also be given responsibility for risk management and take on the role of chief risk officer or CRO). Wayne assembled and led a group of senior executives, supplemented by several consultants for industry perspective, to design a global firm-wide governance framework focused on ensuring that balance sheet, risk, and capital resources were optimally allocated to businesses and functions and demonstrated proper risk management and controls in order to maximize the Bank's returns on equity and to shareholders (this was known as the Balance Sheet Resource Allocation Process). Wayne's chief administrative officer (CAO), Mike Shapiro (who, after Wayne became CRO, became global head of operational risk), was chosen to lead a group of executives (including me) to execute the chosen design. In the meantime, my task as global head of compliance & ethics (C&E) was to assess our compliance program, focusing initially on Canada.

I spent the first 90 days meeting with business executives and leaders of each of CIBC's major business lines. I wanted to find out what they expected of the compliance function and whether the existing teams were fulfilling those expectations. I also wanted to articulate and execute my own vision of compliance, which was to integrate and centralize all C&E officers into a single function, paid out of a central budget. That would demonstrate that we were completely independent and not beholden to any other department that might otherwise have been able to determine or influence a C&E officer's salary, bonus, or performance evaluation.

I discovered that we had nearly identical C&E teams across and within each of our three main business lines: wealth management, investment bank (also known as CIBC World Markets), and retail and small business banking. By definition, these compliance units were not independent because they were paid by the businesses. We also had a centralized "Corporate Center" which supported our business unit compliance officers and handled centralized, corporate-wide matters. These included reporting compliance-related issues on a consolidated basis to the board of directors and executive management. I found this federated or decentralized compliance structure to be not only duplicative but indeed, quadruplicate. I saw (as did our head of HR and general counsel) an opportunity to consolidate all those disparate functions into a single, centralized department—in my case, the C&E department and function. Ultimately, I streamlined and de-layered the team, reducing our headcount significantly. However, unlike other banks, which simply vaporize the cuts, I reinvested the cost savings into new technologies and developed or hired more skilled individuals both internally and externally so that we ended up with a solid group of full-time, fit-for-purpose, independent C&E officers.

Executive Management and Governance Reorganization to Link Strategy and Risks

Upon the advice and recommendation of the senior executive group led by our CRO, the CEO revamped the existing governance structure to enable a direct governance reporting and escalation process between CIBC's independent board of directors and senior executives, as well as between those executives and the major businesses and functions they managed. The CEO established a revised Senior Executive Team (SET), comprised of: the major business leaders, the CRO, the CAO (of the bank), and the CFO. Once the SET was in place, we established two overarching subcommittees to support it:

- The Capital and Risk Committee (CRC), which focused on quantitative balance sheet and capital and risk issues governed by the previously referred to quarterly Balance Sheet, Risk and Capital Resource Allocation Process. The CRC was chaired by the CRO.

- The Operations and Administration Committee (OAC), which addressed qualitative control and operational issues. The Wealth Management business leader (a member of the SET) chaired the OAC and I was Secretary. Mike Shapiro and I served as voting members of the OAC and regularly attended the CRC to ensure cross-committee synergy.

The division of labor and executive sponsorship between the CRC and the OAC was functional and logical: The CRC oversaw activities of capital-intensive businesses such as corporate, commercial, small business and retail lending, investment banking, and securities underwriting and dealing. These businesses triggered a large proportion of CIBC's credit and market risks and therefore consumed significant balance sheet and capital related to these financial risks. The OAC oversaw activities that were less capital-intensive and more operational, such as wealth and asset management and elements of retail banking (like credit cards and mortgages), where operational risks like fraud are prevalent. These businesses triggered comparatively more operational risks.

In creating these two subcommittees, our CEO's and CRO's objectives were both straightforward and somewhat ahead of their time: Shape and drive a strong risk-and-control culture linked to the strategic planning and budgeting process. The better the risk management and control effectiveness of a major business line or infrastructure/governance function (such as finance, operations, technology, risk management, and C&E), the more balance sheet, risk, and capital resources would be allocated to that business or function. Conversely, the weaker the controls and culture across the business or function, the lower the budget allocation. They'd have to re-earn the trust and confidence of the SET based on the views and recommendations of the CRC and OAC.

Source: dangdumrong/Shutterstock.com

CRADs and TIGRs

At the heart of this were two parallel control programs: Comprehensive Risk Assessment Document (CRADs[1]) for CIBC's businesses, and The Infrastructure Group Reviews (TIGRs)—a sibling risk assessment program for functions. In both cases, the unit in question would make an annual presentation to a joint meeting of the CRC and OAC, in which the business or function leader would discuss his or her strategic business and budget plans. More importantly, they'd offer a self-assessment of the type and status of their inherent and residual financial (credit and market), non-financial (operational) and other (reputational) risks, the effectiveness of current controls to address and manage those risks, and remediation plans to address self-identified, compliance, audit and/or regulatory exam findings.

Executives at CIBC not only had to "talk the talk" typical of many firms' annual strategy and budget planning sessions, but also "walk the walk." The CRADs and TIGRs achieved these objectives. During these presentations, committee members would effectively challenge the business/function and budget plans as well as the risk assessments and remediation plans. The goal was to enable the units being questioned to better understand—and thereby minimize—their inherent and residual risks, as well as to implement better controls.

Real, Tangible Dividends of the CRADs and TIGRs: Getting It or Not

One of the major benefits of the CRAD and TIGR presentations was that they gave everyone involved a deeper understanding of the unit's

---

1   We originally planned to call these the "Comprehensive Risk Assessment Programs," but calling them CRAP didn't seem appropriate.

underlying people, processes, and technology (since corporate functions were often transversal across businesses) which in turn, helped all of us get to know our enterprise-wide risks and controls. At the end of each CRAD or TIGR presentation, each committee member would express his or her concurrence or, in a few instances, non-concurrence to the assessment of risks and controls presented. Businesses/functions that "got it" (meaning that they not only understood their risks, but also continuously demonstrated to the committees that they weren't recidivist in audit or regulatory findings, and in fact, minimized such risks) received a pathway to formally request access to incremental levels of balance sheet, risk, and capital resources that would enable them to lend, underwrite, advise, design, sell, or trade at the CRC as part of that committee's quarterly process (which in turn the CRC would review and ultimately recommend to the SET).

Conversely, businesses and functions that we felt didn't get it, were recidivist, or culturally unfit within CIBC's overall corporate culture, would be constrained through a higher operational risk capital allocation. That resulted in moving them down in the pecking order for access to credit and market risk resources, meaning that they had to generate more revenue with fewer of the balance sheet resources to support that revenue—at least until they remediated their deficiencies and controlled and reduced residual risks to tolerable levels.

Carrot and Stick (Incentive and Consequence)

To be clear, the rewards and constraints were quite transparent. Units that got it received larger annual budgets and were able to expand their activities (assuming the right controls and processes). Those that didn't get it, risked losing funding, which could translate into staff reductions and more difficulty in achieving the revenues needed to continue meeting their budget plans. The trickle-down impact of not having access to those balance sheet resources was, in certain instances, a drag on employee incentive compensation, since in the case of challenging financial markets revenues are sometimes hard to generate. Since banks generally compensate their producers (at least partially) based on the revenue they bring in, one can see how remediating internal control issues quickly became something that moved to the top of business leaders' priority lists.

CRADs and TIGRs also identified—and inventoried—historic and anticipated losses, thus increasing our ability to prepare for unanticipated events and risks and losses, which was driven by international "Basel Committee" operational risk standards.[2] Overall, by linking business objectives, risk processes, and control effectiveness, CRADs and TIGRs demonstrated the economic value of strengthening controls rather than weakening them and proved conclusively that it's possible to achieve strategic growth by managing risk and complying. Since the findings of our CRADs and TI-GRS were seen by the highest levels of senior executive management, the presentations and underlying documentary support drove and aligned the right corporate culture. For example, exception-based summaries of high residual risk matters were provided to the board and our US and home office Canadian regulators supported the CRAD/TIGR process, noting it as indicating a good tone-at-the-top culture.

Of course, not all businesses or infrastructure units quite got it or wanted to adapt. For example, a large, full-service US subsidiary, which we'd recently acquired, wanted to remain autonomous. Its local management team continually resisted integrating itself into the CIBC culture, and that resistance began spreading to other business units. Finally, one of our major external stakeholders had to remind us that CIBC was the acquirer (not the target company) and that they expected CIBC's culture to envelop the subsidiary's, not the other way around. Suffice it to say, it did—in fairly short order. No business or function, including this subsidiary, was exempt from the CRAD/TIGR process.

---

2   Basel II Advanced Measurement Approach-Compliant Operational Risk Program

Lessons Learned

- Align business culture through CRAD- and TIGR-like processes by making risk assessments meaningful and linking them to incentives and consequences that motivate internal control and compliant behavior, budget, and strategic business objectives. Business leaders depend on budgets and revenues to drive their businesses. Formal and top-of-the-house risk assessments owned by the business and functional leaders and governed by executive management, worked tremendously well in aligning business, risk, and corporate culture.

- Reward businesses and functions that get it and constrain those that don't until they ultimately do.

- Culture and strategy can be driven by incentive but more importantly, by consequence—particularly if monetary. Linking strategic objectives to a consequence of monetary hurdles and capital creates a logical and financial link between corporate culture and strategy.

Corporate Culture and the Role of Compliance & Ethics

Source: Production Perig/Shutterstock.com

"Corporate culture is an organization's values, ethics, vision, behaviors, and work environment. It is what makes each company unique, and it impacts everything from public image to employee engagement and retention. If employees share a company's ethics, vision, and other cultural elements, it can positively affect a company's bottom line. Companies with good corporate culture often have high workplace morale, and highly engaged, productive staff."[1]

"Walk the walk." "Tone at the top." Clichés, yes, but these and other similar sentiments are widely expressed by CEOs, business gurus, HR leaders, and even me. Each phrase tries to express the idea that corporate culture spreads throughout organizations from the top down. The same applies to the organization's record of compliance and ethical behavior. At the same time, we've all heard equally clichéd responses, like

1   "What is Corporate Culture." Indeed.com. Retrieved August 7, 2020

"talk is cheap," which express the idea that what's said is too often not what's practiced, particularly the further down one happens to be in the organizational chart.

Lack of Accountability and Unclear Roles Lead to Corporate Cultural Breakdowns

Sub-cultures, management silos, and corporate politics driven by internal business competition or personal animosity often delay key decisions and/or make goal setting (let alone implementation) nearly impossible. Dysfunction results and little gets done.

Employees, in turn, grow frustrated because problems that could (and should) be easily solved get bogged down by politics, red tape, endless management discussions, approvals that never happen, or people who simply don't talk to one another. And when conversations actually do happen, how many times have we walked away thinking we've reached an agreement on a plan of action only to find out later that the person on the other end of the conversation decided to do something completely different? Other times, it's paralysis by overanalysis: weeks and months of furious debate over simple decisions that ultimately fall apart because of internal politics or turf wars. Besides being infuriating, it's also dangerous and expensive, in terms of hard costs (lost business, legal fees, and regulatory fines) and reputational damage.

Not all negative corporate cultures are the result of bad communication or misalignment of goals. In some cases, communication is excellent and goals are perfectly aligned, but the overall tone (again, starting at the top) is poisonous, driven by greed, and completely lacking in empathy for (or protection of) customers or employees (think, for example, of the decades-long Wells Fargo fake account scandal). And the results, much as with dysfunctional cultures, are nearly identical: increased risks, regulatory enforcement actions, and reputational suicide. Over the next few pages and chapters, I'll talk about the correlation between corporate culture and compliance risk assessments, since these are two important pillars of an effective compliance & ethics program.

Corporate vs. Geographical and National Cultures

Despite the stress and the challenges, my ten years with CIBC were incredibly enjoyable and fulfilling. As Global CCO, I consolidated, re-engineered, integrated, and led a truly centralized, authorized, and independent compliance function. The major driver of our success was not only the corporate culture driven by our senior executive team, but also the national culture of Canada. At the risk of over-generalizing, I found my Canadian colleagues (and friends) to be incredibly collaborative, with a shared goal of making business decisions by consensus. Although sometimes the decision-making process would take longer than desired, the ability to socialize, synthesize, and ultimately reach a group decision was both effective and transparent.

The Weekly Commute to Canada and 9/11

Being the Global CCO based out of Toronto, Canada also meant a weekly commute between New York City and Toronto for five years. I didn't mind the three-hour door-to-door-trip in each direction because I loved CIBC, the Canadian people, and Toronto's cosmopolitan culture and cuisine. However, on the morning of September 11, 2001, my whole world changed (as it did for everyone else) when two planes flew into the World Trade Center towers, a third into the Pentagon, and a fourth crashed in a field in Pennsylvania. For one thing, I was in Toronto while my wife was alone in Manhattan. And none of us at CIBC could fly home or even take the train, since all travel was locked down. It took days to finally arrange a car to drive me and my New York-based colleagues the eight hours from Toronto to New York.

I suddenly realized that my life's priorities were completely wrong. I'd let work control my life, rather than the other way around. But once the post-9/11 dust had settled (literally), I went back to my old ways, commuting between Toronto and New York, preoccupied with work as the days, weeks, and months flew by. Meanwhile, my wife remained alone in Manhattan, working only blocks away from Ground Zero, smelling (and breathing) the residue of death and terror.

Eventually, I knew I had to make a life- and professional change. So, in 2004, when a recruiter contacted me about a job as Deputy CCO for the Investment Banking Americas division of UBS, the giant Swiss bank, I jumped at the chance.

CIBC gave me a lovely send-off, with heartfelt speeches by various members of the executive team, including the CEO. One of them even gave me a slap on the shoulder and congratulated me on a "nice trade-up to UBS." He was right. As of 2004, it seemed as if CIBC was playing in the major leagues of global capital markets. But UBS was like the 1927 New York Yankees.[2]

Moving to UBS seemed, at the time, to be a major professional and personal win for me, but it was not without its challenges. When a friend of my wife's family—a banker who worked for a major investment banking competitor—found out about my move, he remarked, "Eric was a big fish in a small pond at CIBC; now he'll be a small fish in a huge ocean."

Migrating from an Integrated Canadian Corporate Culture to a Siloed New York/Swiss/British One

Based in Zurich, Switzerland, UBS was (and still is) one of the largest banks in the world, and was ranked #1 at the time for foreign exchange (FX) and equities trading. In 2004, UBS IB Americas' Stamford, Connecticut headquarters was home to the largest trading floor in the world—the size of two US football fields—and housed 5,000 trading and sales staff. What an ocean for me to swim in. Was I a minnow or a tuna? Or maybe

---

2   Led by half a dozen future Hall-of-Famers, including Babe Ruth and Lou Gehrig, the '27 Yankees are widely considered to be one of the best teams in baseball history. Other candidates include the 1939 Yankees, and the 1970 Baltimore Orioles.

a salmon swimming upstream against the waterfall or just one in a large school of compliance officers?

Regardless, at least for the first year, I simply enjoyed the commute. Working out of the New York office, I no longer had a four-hour, door-to-door commute (up from three hours each way thanks to all the post-9/11 increased airport security). Instead, I had a relaxing 20-minute walk from my home on the east side of Manhattan to the office on East 49th Street. I'd also commute once or twice a week (45 minutes by train) to UBS's regional headquarters in Stamford, Connecticut.

A Culture of Really Smart, and Seemingly Nice Colleagues

What impressed me the most about UBS—at least initially—was how smart and nice everyone seemed. They were articulate, focused, truly deep subject matter experts, whether in management, business, legal, or compliance. That said, joining UBS was my first major challenge with a truly "matrixed management" organization. Not because I was new to matrixed organizations (most, if not all large firms have them), but because I was hired to wear three distinct hats, each of which required me to execute major compliance restructuring and/or upgrades, quickly to prevent regulatory criticism.

1. As Americas Head of the UBS Investment Bank's (IB) anti-money laundering (AML) function, I was asked to staff up the department because virtually the whole AML department had left to join other organizations.

2. As deputy CCO of UBS Americas IB region, I had to juggle broker-dealer regulators from the SEC and FINRA, commodities regulators, the Federal Reserve, and state regulators from both Connecticut and New York.

3. As head of the financial holding company and bank regulatory compliance for the New York Branch of UBS, I had to manage

relationships with regulators from the Fed and the New York State Banking Department (now known as the Department of Financial Services or DFS) and had to recreate this unit as if it were a start-up, because it was responsible for coordinating the regulatory exams led by the Federal Reserve Bank of New York.

Culture and Reporting Lines

As if having three different jobs at the same time wasn't challenging enough, I also had seven different bosses, spread out among four locations. As a foreign banking organization (FBO) operating in the US, major management and budget decisions were made at UBS's Group headquarters in Zurich. Adding to the complexity was the fact that, like many FBOs with major, global investment banking operations, the investment bank was headquartered in London. Here's an overview of my seven bosses (for a visual summary, see the illustration on page 112):

1. I was hired by the UBS Americas IB chief compliance officer (Boss #1) to be his Deputy CCO. This included Canada, the United States and Latin America (Mexico and Brazil). However, I didn't discover until after I arrived that Boss #1's other compliance direct reports in the Americas weren't fully aware that I had been hired as his deputy, which technically gave me functional authority over each of them.

2. Boss #1 reported to the UBS Americas IB general counsel (Boss #2), who in turn reported into the UBS IB global general counsel (Boss #3), both of whom were based in New York. Since US Boss #1 was based in Stamford, I took more management direction from Bosses #2 and #3 in New York.

3. As head of anti-money laundering compliance (AML) for UBS IB Americas, I also reported on a matrixed (or "dotted line") basis to UBS IB's global AML head (Boss #4), based in London.

4. Boss #4, in turn, reported to Boss #5, UBS IB's Europe, Middle East, and Africa (EMEA) region, who also reported to UBS IB global general counsel (Boss #3).

5. Since money laundering and sanctions risks (financial crimes) are a global, cross-border issue that transversed UBS' multiple business lines, I also had a functional reporting line into the UBS group (Head Office) AML head. (Boss #6), who was based in Zurich.

6. As with most CCOs, there must also be a partnership and functional reporting line into the regional business head. In my case, as UBS IB Americas head of AML, that line went to the CEO of the UBS IB Americas, Boss #7.

Seven bosses, one of whom was a solid line (based in Stamford). The other six were indirect and/or functional and based in New York, Stamford, London, or Zurich. If you're overwhelmed just reading about it, imagine what it was like to go to work there every day. By the way, I was not informed that I'd have so many bosses during the interview process.

Matrix Management - Seven Bosses at UBS

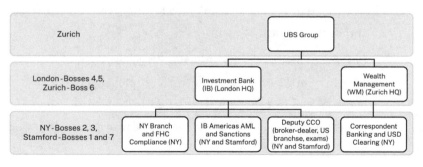

Source: Eric Young

Matrixed Organizations Are a Reality

Organizations can be structured in a variety of ways. Historically, one of the most common—and most problematic—has been the siloed structure, where individual departments or divisions are run like separate businesses, each with its own sub-culture, and people in those units tend to communicate only with each other.

Problems arise when a decision has to be made that involves multiple units. Siloed organizations often fall apart because fingers are pointed, responsibility and accountability are avoided, and communication breaks down. If the issue isn't resolved quickly, it can spiral out of control, starting with decreased efficiency and profitability and ultimately leading to reputational damage. I'll give an example of this in a moment.

Because the weaknesses of the siloed structure can have severe, negative consequences, many companies have reorganized, opting instead for a matrixed or cross-functional organization, where individuals may have more than one boss (although very few have as many as I did), depending on the projects they're working on.

While switching to a matrixed structure may sound like a great way to cure the siloed mentality, it has plenty of drawbacks (including many that overlap with silos), which I'll get into below. As George Bradt put it recently in *Forbes* magazine, "Sometimes, *not often*[3] but sometimes, a matrix is actually the right way to organize."[4] In fact, people have been talking about reorganizing corporate structures for a long, long time. Nearly 2,000 years ago, back in 65 AD, Gaius Petronius, a Roman governor and advisor to the Emperor Nero took this rather dismal view: "Every time we were beginning to form up into teams, we would be reorganized. I was to learn later in life that we tend to meet new situations by reorganizing… and a wonderful method it can be for creating the illusion of progress while producing confusion, inefficiency, and demoralization."[5]

---

3   Italics mine
4   Bradt, George. "In Praise of Matrix Organizations." *Forbes*, October 9, 2020. Retrieved August 13, 2020
5   Ibid.

As I hinted above, one of the biggest problems with a matrixed structure has to do with decision making. Generally speaking, everyone wants to make decisions. The right decision can increase your visibility to management, resulting in promotions and increased opportunities to shine. However, if there's even the slightest chance that something could go wrong, people are a lot less interested in making decisions. It's a lot easier to take a step back, let someone else take the risk, and then point fingers when they fail.

This is true not only for managers of individual business units or departments, but also for the multiple levels of management above them. For example, who's supposed to approve budgets, hirings and firings, key technology and infrastructure requests, and other major plans that might affect more than one department? The bottom line is that sometimes there are too many cooks in the kitchen, all competing to get credit for the *soup du jour*. Other times, there aren't any cooks and the soup ends up getting made by the dishwasher or some other unqualified person.

When a Matrixed Organization Works Well

Before I arrived at UBS, key members of the compliance staff had resigned from UBS and my bosses had backfilled the team with three independent contractors. Excluding those contractors, the full-time UBS-IB compliance department, consisted of an administrative assistant who took on some part-time compliance duties, a full-time compliance officer, and me. Clearly understaffed, we needed to significantly increase the size—and skill sets—of the compliance team.

Given that I reported to seven different people, re-engineering the UBS-IB compliance program could have been a huge challenge. But I was able to successfully navigate the matrix (which I sometimes called the labyrinth), in large part because Bosses #s 1, 2, and 3 allowed me sufficient autonomy to design the AML program and to significantly increase the headcount as needed.

Within 18 months of my joining UBS, my financial crimes compliance department had grown to 50 AML officers, comprised of a team of Know Your Customer staff (also called the Client Vetting Unit) who would identify, verify, or re-certify the identifies of new clients under the USA PATRIOT Act; AML advisors, who were typically legally trained compliance officers supporting key UBS businesses; and AML and Office of Foreign Assets Control (OFAC) surveillance specialists responsible for monitoring unusual or suspicious activities and filing suspicious activity reports (SARs) with the US government.

Building and re-engineering effective compliance programs has always been my specialty, and often involves changing the status quo, encountering and overcoming resistance to change, and advocating for and receiving approval for larger compliance budgets. I recognize that at UBS, none of that would have been possible without the support of my bosses, especially, Boss #3,[6] who to this day is still one of my mentors. For that, I will always be grateful to him.[7]

When a Matrixed Organization Could Have Been Disastrous, and How I Overcame It

One of my few remaining legacy compliance officers introduced me to a small New York-based wealth management business unit, that, instead of being supervised by anyone in the US, was being supervised by their Zurich-based management team. As such, this unit didn't technically fall under my compliance responsibilities. The problem was that remote

---

6   In President George W. Bush's administration, he was general counsel at the US Treasury Department, but later was a key author of the USA PATRIOT Act, which was enacted shortly after the 9/11 terror attacks.

7   One of the reasons Boss #3 supported me dated back to my first month at UBS in a meeting with him, our CEO, Boss #7, and our COO. During that meeting, the CEO tried to convince me that the Client Vetting Unit should remain within the business unit. I disagreed and explained that the Fed would criticize us severely if we did that. I convinced the CEO, which gave me instant credibility with Boss #3. What I hadn't known at the time was that the debate over whether compliance should take over Client Vetting had been brewing between our bosses in London. After several weeks of debating roles and responsibilities, they reached the same conclusion that I had in 15 minutes, based solely on a regulatory/risk perspective.

supervision of a business unit creates supervisory, operational, and regulatory risk, particularly if the unit in question engages in inherently high-risk activities. One of the most glaring examples of this problem is the case of Nick Leeson, a former English derivatives trader at Barings Bank, the United Kingdom's oldest merchant bank. Leeson was able to hide significant trading losses out of Barings' Singapore office for a long time because he wasn't supervised locally and was responsible for both the trading itself, as well as the settlement of his trades.[8]

The compliance risks and reputational damage that come from failing to supervise remote locations are not limited to financial institutions. Indeed, the biggest challenge of complying with the US Foreign Corrupt Practices Act (which I'll discuss in part 2) is the difficulty of supervising sales and other staff—directly or indirectly through third party agents—who are in remote locations. Unless remote employees are supervised closely by the Head Office or region, the compliance risks and reputational damage can be incredibly expensive and embarrassing, if not reputationally fatal.

OFAC Sanctions as Regulatory Playbook

In 2005, state and federal bank regulators sanctioned a Dutch bank, ABN Amro Bank NV, $80 million for violating anti-money-laundering rules under the Bank Secrecy Act, which at the time was headline news.[9] Regulators said that, among other things, the bank violated trade sanctions against Iran and Libya and didn't properly detect suspicious shell companies with connections to Eastern Europe that were transferring money via ABN Amro's North American regional clearing center. ABN Amro

---

8   That's a fundamental internal-control no-no, because those two functions, particularly in trading, are supposed to be handled by two separate individuals with separate reporting lines to ensure a proper segregation of duties and checks and balances. Given the size of Leeson's losses, he's often blamed for bankrupting Barings in 1995. For further details see, Smith, Elliot. "The Barings collapse 25 years on: What the industry learned after one man broke a bank." CNBC.com, February 26, 2020. https://www.cnbc.com/2020/02/26/barings-collapse-25-years-on-what-the-industry-learned-after-one-man-broke-a-bank.html. Retrieved June 28, 2021

9   Today, headline enforcement actions and penalties can reach billions of dollars, e.g., Goldman Sachs' $5 billion fine for bribery and corruption over Malaysia's 1MDB fund.

had already failed to correct a 2004 order over its correspondent banking and dollar clearing businesses. As with most enforcement actions, ABN Amro's reputation was damaged at the time because the regulators publicly announced the details of the bank's violations, the types of weaknesses, and the required corrective action.

For years after Amro, busting companies for violating trade sanctions against Iran and other US-designated enemy states and specially designated nationals became a major regulatory play, which regulators successfully ran against major (and smaller) industrial and commercial firms.

Taking a Courageous Stand Based on Others' Enforcement Actions

Throughout my career, I've used public enforcement action announcements as playbooks to assess whether similar weaknesses in controls exist within my own organization and to outline the actions we'd need to execute, along with timelines, owners, and specific controls to be created.

When I escalated my concerns about that unsupervised New York Wealth Management unit to London-based Boss #4, he informed me that that unit wasn't within the investment bank compliance department's responsibility. "It's not our problem" (or as I sarcastically like to say, "I'm glad that leak isn't on *my* side of the rowboat!").

Technically, Boss #4 was correct. However, from personal experience, I knew that when it comes to weaknesses and violations—especially AML and OFAC—regulators don't care in the slightest which division the offending unit is in. They're concerned about the overall legal entity and enterprise operating in the United States (and globally); in this case, UBS.

Therefore, together with my deputy AML head, I escalated the issue to my US Bosses (#s 1, 2, 3, and 7) and to Boss #6 in Zurich. We proceeded, over a series of weeks, to coordinate with the group head of wealth management, who was responsible for the NY-based correspondent banking business, to engage in a consulting agreement with a Big Four accounting firm. That firm worked with us to design and implement a series of AML control upgrades, including a significant investment in surveillance technology, policies, procedures, and training programs, and an account "look-back" to assess whether existing accounts posed a risk to UBS in the United States.

Along the way, we documented and executed all major remedial and preventative steps. We also disclosed to our US regulators our self-identified supervisory and potential regulatory weaknesses based on our analyses of other firms' regulatory enforcement actions—and what we learned from them. Our goal was to proactively minimize the risks (not to mention the significant reputational damage) that our serious unsupervised wealth management AML gaps could have caused, even though Boss #4 insisted that it wasn't "our problem."

Lessons Learned

- Understand your matrixed reporting lines (who they are, how much authority they have in general, and how much they have over you). That will determine how much authority and autonomy you truly have.

- Consider the impact that multiple and non-aligned matrixed reporting lines have across the organization and the potential for misalignment. Is it the corporate culture? Tone at the top? Or lack of coordination across siloed business units?

- Review regulatory enforcement actions to learn from the industry (or major audit findings from within the organization), and conduct gap analyses, asking yourself, "Could it happen here?" If the answer is Yes, escalate and lead a prioritized remediation plan to identify and address control weaknesses with timelines, owners, and action plans.

- Recognize, escalate, and underscore the US regulatory risk and severity if your matrixed head-office management doesn't understand the US environment or regulatory risk, and escalate to others if the risk is being ignored or minimized.

- Always raise a flag if you encounter a business or other unsupervised unit in the United States (or elsewhere).

Building—but Then Sadly Dismantling— an Effective Compliance & Ethics Program

HOUSE CONSTRUCTION PROCESS

Source: Golden Sikorka/Shutterstock.com

Cliché: Building organizations is like building a house, particularly one with a strong foundation. But to create a high-quality and durable compliance & ethics program, a better analogy would be building a skyscraper or a sports stadium.

As I noted in the last chapter, I was recruited in 2004 to completely re-engineer an effective compliance & ethics program for UBS's: US branches, US financial holding company, and Americas regional invest-ment banking anti-money laundering and financial crimes compliance department. Collectively, let's call my domain of responsibilities the "Fed-focused" compliance program.

It was clear that I had a huge task ahead of me: With $2 trillion in total assets as of the end of 2004, UBS was ten times larger than CIBC and had many more products, services, and business lines. UBS was managed out of financial hubs across the world (e.g., equities run globally out of one financial center, such as London; fixed income out of another financial center, such as New York or Hong Kong.), creating many more autonomous management siloes and fragmented cultures across their three main businesses: the investment bank, asset management, and wealth management. And each had their own control infrastructures.

And because virtually all of my "Fed-focused" compliance staff had already left UBS before I'd arrived, I essentially had to re-build the compliance skyscraper or stadium from the foundation up. There I was, the "happy-go-lucky kid," trading in his Canadian baseball glove to re-engineer and build a Swiss behemoth as architect, carpenter, electrician, plumber, and any other construction-related job you can think of. All at the same time.

Here's my Fed-focused, enterprise-wide skyscraper construction checklist:

1. Your skyscraper needs a strong foundation, engineered to support the weight of the building (known risks) as well as to withstand a spectrum of external dangers (unanticipated risks of earthquakes, tornados, floods, and continuous regulatory changes) and internal hazards (reorganizations, new products, illegal, or unethical behavior).

2. You'll need safe and effective plumbing, heating/cooling, and electrical systems (this is your technology and operations) for occupants on every floor (business divisions) and in every room (teams and individual employees).

3. Your building and its systems must also accommodate future business and employee growth.

4. Security measures, fire sprinklers, and a maintenance department which are properly maintained and updated (regulatory changes), with safety features (internal controls) continually upgraded to protect the building's inhabitants externally and internally.

5. Constructing your skyscraper (and an effective compliance & ethics program) requires foresight, planning, and pre-construction zoning (regulatory) approvals. Once those are in place, you have to hire the right project managers and operators with the right skill sets to build in logical, safe, and coordinated stages.

6. Clearly defined and documented designs, project plans, and status reports are mission-critical to articulate how you'll monitor, test, and report to ensure that the building will be vibrant and secure for a very long time.

7. You'll need a manager to keep the building running effectively, efficiently, and securely (tone at the top and corporate culture).

8. Most importantly, to monitor and govern each of the steps listed above, there needs to be appropriate corporate governance/oversight; strictly defined and documented internal controls so that expenses, accounting, and transactions are properly recorded and authorized; and a system that ensures that all activities are conducted in compliance with laws, regulations, and codes.

Autonomy to Execute an Effective Compliance Program

Fortunately, UBS management[1] granted me the autonomy and authority to execute the enterprise-wide compliance & ethics program upgrades that I knew would be expected to meet Federal Reserve, State of New York, and State of Connecticut banking department expectations. That meant building a program unlike anything previously attempted by UBS—particularly in the US: an enterprise-wide compliance risk management program as expected under the Department of Justice US sentencing guidelines. If we succeeded, my next goal would be to scale it for the rest of UBS Americas compliance, including its US broker-dealer and capital markets operations in the United States, Canada, and Latin America.

---

1   Putting aside for a moment, which of my seven UBS managers.

Thankfully, we already had a Big Four accounting firm on premises to "back-fill" the compliance staff on an interim basis, since the full-time staff had already left. And fortunately, I already knew most of the interim Big 4 team from my Fed and CCO experience with Chase and CIBC. Smart and very experienced, we were ready to execute our new UBS compliance & ethics skyscraper.

UBS as Multiple Rubik's Cubes

The biggest challenge was that UBS globally and across the Americas region were a massive collection of separate, siloed legal entities and business divisions—multiple Rubik's Cubes to solve simultaneously. And while there were individual laws and rules for specific risks to address money laundering, terrorist financing, bribery and corruption, insider trading, capital and lending, and many others, there were no written rules or regulatory expectations (by federal-, state-, or non-US regulators) that applied to the entire enterprise-wide high rise. That's when I remembered what my mentor, George Mah at Chase had previously taught me. "(Close your eyes and) use the Force, Luke…." Translation: focus, work as a team to hit the target no matter how impossible it might seem or how much management resistance you encounter, to build an enterprise-wide compliance & ethics program.

Fed Governor Bies' Speech and Enterprise Compliance

Fortunately, by 2004, the internet was a well-established tool, so I tracked down the text of a 2003 speech given by Federal Reserve Governor Susan Bies. Entitled "Strengthening Compliance through Effective Corporate Governance,"[2] it was eloquent and remarkably aligned with George's (and,

---

2   "Strengthening Compliance through Effective Corporate Governance." American Bankers Association, Annual Regulatory Compliance Conference, Washington, DC, June 11, 2003.
I recalled when Governor Bies' speech was published, a collective virtual applause—strike that—standing ovation was heard globally across the compliance industry. Finally, an advocate for compliance officers and enterprise-wide compliance risk management programs!

therefore, my) compliance philosophy, which focused on the important linkage between corporate governance, internal controls, and regulatory compliance at the firm-wide level. That made it the perfect blueprint for building an effective, enterprise-wide compliance & ethics program, including the need for an active, independent board of directors. Here are a few important excerpts (emphasis mine) from Governor Bies' groundbreaking speech, which focused on the accounting scandals of Enron and WorldCom and the continuous compliance violations of banking institutions:

> "[W]e all have been shocked by the headlines announcing corporate governance or accounting problems ... 'What were the underlying deficiencies in the *internal control processes of these companies that rendered their [board] governance practices ineffective?* ... they exemplify breakdowns in fundamental systems of *internal control.*

> "[T]hese companies lost track of the *basics* of effective corporate governance—internal controls and *a strong ethical compass.* While most companies have effective governance processes in place, these events remind all of us of the importance of doing the basics well.

> "[T]he need to return to *focusing on the basics* becomes clear. [I]nternal control [is] a process, effected by an entity's board of directors, management, and other personnel, designed to provide reasonable assurance regarding the achievement of:

> □ Effectiveness and efficiency of operations
>
> □ Reliability of financial reporting
>
> □ Compliance with applicable laws and regulations.

"The basics *of internal controls* for *directors and managers* are simple. Directors (must annually) focus their attention on… high-risk and emerging-risk areas… *Regulatory compliance is one of these risk areas.*

"… (B)oards… have *the responsibility to understand the organization('s) compliance function and… its effectiveness* and to identify the emerging compliance risks. "The challenge for compliance officers is to ensure that their staff has *the expertise and ongoing training to meet the specific and changing risks* of the organization.

"… To be effective, *compliance risk management must be coordinated at various levels* within the organization. In any control or oversight function, there are *common elements of a successful compliance process* that each organization should exhibit. While the diversity, size, and business mix of the organization will affect the specific aspects of an effective process, *every financial institution should consider* these elements.

Voila![3] Collectively, Governor Bies's speech, with the Foreign Corrupt Practices Act (in particular its requirements to maintain books and records), the Department of Justice's Corporate Sentencing Guidelines, the FDIC Improvement Act, and the COSO Internal Control Guidelines,[4] became the framework and foundation that helped me build UBS's C&E skyscraper effectively. Each are derivatives of one another.

---

3   French for "there it is."
4   The Foreign Corrupt Practices Act, Sentencing Guidelines, FDIC Improvement Act and COSO are discussed in part 2.

Source: critterbiz/Shutterstock.com

"If You Build It, (They) Will Come"[5]

In chapters 2.12 – 2.18, I'm going to talk about *how to* "clean" an organization/company using my Compliance Hexagon©, in order to (re) build an effective compliance & ethics department and function. But as I conclude this chapter, let's talk a little more about the *why*. To do that, I'm going to use another building metaphor, this one from one of my favorite movies, *Field of Dreams*. In the movie, Ray Kinsella (played by Kevin Costner) sees a vision of a baseball diamond and hears a voice telling him that, "If you build it, he will come." Thinking that the "he" is "Shoeless" Joe Jackson, an old-time baseball player Kinsella's dad loved, Ray ignores the financial cost and plows out a large portion of his profitable corn field to build the baseball field and diamond.[6]

Building a baseball stadium involves many of the steps I outlined at the beginning of this chapter, with the goal of having strong corporate governance, a system of internal controls, and a continuous commitment to compliance & ethics. How well you achieve that goal can be the difference between enhancing or damaging your company (or baseball team) and its reputation. History—whether we're going back centuries or just talking about the 40-year span of my career as a CCO—is full of examples of both well-built (effective) and poorly built (horribly ineffective) structures and programs that either enable the right culture of ethics and compliance—or don't.

In *Field of Dreams*, the character played by the great James Earl Jones sums up the importance of proper construction. I've translated some of his words into compliance-speak in parentheses.

---

5   From "Field of Dreams." Universal Pictures, 1989
6   By the way, the "he" in "he will come" ends up being Ray's dad, who is the team's catcher, a position, which, as you may remember from chapter 1.11 is a wonderful metaphor for CCO.

"The one constant through all the years, Ray, has been baseball (*internal controls and compliance*).

"America (*countries, industries, and eco-systems around the world, especially during the COVID-19 pandemic*) has rolled by like an army of steamrollers. It's been erased like a blackboard, rebuilt, and erased again. But baseball (*effective compliance and internal controls*) has marked the time.

"This field, this game (*this corporate governance led by the board to challenge management with escalation of issues to the board by the CCO*)—it's a part of our past, Ray. It reminds us of all that *once was good, and it could be again.*

"Ohhhhhhhh, people will come, Ray. People (customers) will most definitely come (because of the strong reputation and right compliance and ethical culture of the firm)."

And Thus, We Built the Compliance & Ethics Field of Dreams

From 2004 to 2006, my interim team of Big Four colleagues, a growing number of future all-star compliance & ethics officers, and I collectively rebuilt both UBS's AML/financial crimes compliance and bank regulatory compliance department into an effective Compliance & Ethics Field of Dreams that would be fit for purpose to meet our inspectors' expectations and enable regulatory health and safe, responsible business growth. One of my closest interim teammates was a star college baseball pitcher in addition to being a lawyer, former CCO, and consultant. He was a total team player: supportive, smart, wise, thoughtful—and fun! My two other interim teammates were both former Fed examiners, incredibly insightful and tireless, who drafted compliance inventories of laws and regulations; user-friendly compliance risk assessments (including documented methodologies); a compliance manual readily accessible for businesses and compliance staff; and developed a monitoring, surveillance, and reporting process. Together we created an enterprise-wide compliance & ethics program that was comprehensive and effective, and would satisfy even the toughest regulators.

"Say It Ain't So, Joe!" The Field of Compliance & Ethics Dreams Dismantled, Before the First Pitch Was Even Thrown

Sadly, despite having initially supported my efforts to build a robust compliance skyscraper at UBS, some of my own bosses who were focused on (or knew only how to manage) their silo-focused broker-dealer compliance worlds, ultimately decided to dismantle my enterprise-wide compliance & ethics program, citing, among other reasons, the need to cut costs.[7] Cutting costs and not understanding the Fed's (and other regulators') expectations proved counterproductive in multiple ways, which of course, ended up costing UBS significantly. Proving the point that you get what you pay for, as a result of dismantling my program, UBS ultimately paid much more in remediation costs, and their reputation was negatively affected by a number of regulatory enforcement actions.[8]

7　In the movie, it was Ray's *bankers* who were insisting that Ray stop utilizing the Field of Dreams

8　Violation Tracker – UBS. https://violationtracker.goodjobsfirst.org/parent/ubs - last retrieved June 28, 2021. See also, Corporate Research Report, "Corporate Rap Sheet – UBS" - https://www.corp-research.org/UBS. Retrieved June 28, 2021

Lessons Learned

- When building or re-engineering your compliance & ethics program, think of building a skyscraper or a sports stadium. Much more complex than a simple house, you'll start with a strong foundation, but you'll also need the right plumbing and wiring, back-up generation in the event of a power outage, basic maintenance systems, protection against external and internal dangers, and clearly defined ways of testing, measuring, and maintaining all of the other systems.

- Whether your field of dreams or skyscraper enables your company to grow and thrive or comes crashing down on your heads, causing irreparable damage depends on regularly maintaining and upgrading your skyscraper.

- If you build it right (so that it meets or exceeds regulators' requirements), maintain it to a sustainable and nimble level (with an effective system of internal controls), continually update it, and staff it with committed all-star players, your skyscraper will withstand the test of time—no matter what, and no matter why or by whom.

Compliance: Fish out of Water or Amphibious Evolution?

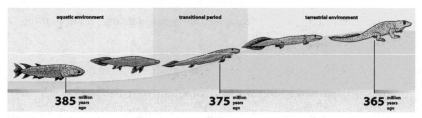

Source: EreborMountain/Shutterstock.com

One day in 2006, I received a call from a major recruiting firm asking if I'd be interested in a CCO position with a retail bank in California. My wife and I had no plans at the time to relocate to California (or anywhere else), but I was intrigued for three reasons:

1. As CCO of a retail bank, I'd focus *solely* on consumer compliance issues. Until that point, my twenty-five years of regulatory compliance & ethics experience had been either at the enterprise level including consumer banking, and/or predominantly covering wholesale banking and capital markets products and activities.

2. To continue to grow and learn as a compliance officer, I wanted to dive deep into consumer products. I purposefully wanted to feel

like a "fish out of water" (not just a small fish in the Chase or UBS ocean or a big fish in a smaller CIBC pond). In this case, I'd be protecting millions of consumers and small businesses, particularly in California, where the well-being of individuals and employees is paramount (over that of corporations and employers).

3. I'd be working for a Japanese bank based in California. During my sophomore through senior years at Columbia in New York, I worked as a summer and winter intern, analyzing Latin American economic developments at the Japanese multinational trading company, Mitsui & Co, Inc. But I'd never before worked for a Japanese company as a compliance officer.

I was interested in the California position, yet a bit hesitant about relocating, particularly because both my wife's and my own parents were elderly. But my interests and intrigue outweighed my geographic hesitation and I agreed to meet the recruiter at their 200 Park Avenue offices, also known as the Met Life Building, but perhaps more famously known as the former Pan Am Building.

Pan Am and a Compliance Officer's *Raison d'Etre*

For those of you familiar with the New York City skyline, the Met Life/ former Pan Am Building is, in many people's view, the heart of Manhattan, sitting directly above the landmark Grand Central Station, where (prior to the COVID-19 pandemic) millions and millions of commuters converged to start or end their workday. Even though Pan Am went out of business 30 years ago, I'll always think of that building as the Pan Am (and not the Met Life) Building. And to this day, seeing the building brings back wistful and sometimes painful memories.

That's because the Pan Am Building will always remind me of the fate of Pan Am Flight 103. As I noted in chapter 1.8, I flew home on Pan Am 103 from London to New York in December 1988, *about a week before* a

Source: 360b/Shutterstock.com

terrorist bomb exploded aboard the fateful Pan Am 103 over Lockerbie, Scotland. I thoroughly believe in fate and that it wasn't God's will to put me on that doomed flight. But what happened to Pan Am 103 and its passengers, and then in 2001 with the 9/11 attacks, only strengthened my resolve and essentially became my *raison d'etre* (my main justification, reason, or purpose for existing) as a compliance & ethics officer. In fact, I think the following should be the *raison d'etre* for *all* compliance & ethics officers:

- Countering the financing of terrorism
- Combatting money laundering and other proceeds of crimes
- Preventing any direct or indirect acts of bribery, corruption, and/or collusion (including price-fixing)
- Knowing our customers (and third parties), thoroughly
- Managing and preventing anti-trust violations in all forms
- Executing US economic sanctions policies against enemy states and designated agents of Iran, North Korea, Libya (at the time), as well as any other hostile actors or terrorists
- With others, preventing and detecting cyber-crime and fraud
- Working closely and independently with the board of directors to hold management accountable

But back to my meeting with the recruiter. That evening at the Met Life/Pan Am Building, I wasn't there to combat terrorism, but instead, to consider fulfilling another important compliance officer mandate: protecting retail and small business customers—especially the elderly, those in lower income brackets, and those within the safety net of the

US government through deposit insurance. The meeting to discuss the California consumer compliance position went well, but as I was preparing to leave, into the conference room walked Paul,[1] a former colleague who'd been in HR at a prior employer. Small world! Paul and I had previously worked very well together, in part because we both believed in the important partnership between compliance and human resources. Corporate culture, compliance, ethics, and conduct are all about *people*. And executing and sustaining a compliant corporate culture successfully and effectively cannot be achieved without the critical role of HR.

Paul explained that he'd left our previous employer to join this recruiting firm. He added that even if the California banking opportunity didn't work out, he thought that I might actually be a *better* fit for an opportunity at General Electric's Corporate Headquarters, in Fairfield, Connecticut. We talked briefly about the GE position and I immediately opted to interview for that job instead of the California consumer compliance position.

Upon leaving the Pan Am[2] Building and walking home, I couldn't help screaming with joy inside my head: "General Electric!"

Compliance and the GE Meatball

When I joined GE in 2006, it'd been only five years since the legendary Jack Welch, CEO from 1981 to 2001, had left the company. Under Welch's leadership, GE had become a global industrial powerhouse, increasing its market value from $12 billion in 1981 to $410 billion in 2001[3], in part

 by adopting Toyota's (and, later, Motorola's) Six Sigma quality program in late 1995. Not surprisingly, in 1999, *Fortune* magazine named him "Manager of the Century."

---

1   Name changed, facts precise
2   Perhaps coincidentally, Pan Am's logo, which featured a blue-and-white globe known as the "Blue Meatball," was oddly similar to the logo of my next employer, General Electric. GE also referred to its logo as "the meatball".
3   Revenues went from roughly $26.8 billion in 1980 (the year before he started) to nearly $130 billion in 2000 (the year before he retired).

I'd been a fan of GE's history and legacy for a long time. Thanks in part to its logo, the GE Meatball, GE was one of the most recognized brands in the United States, right up there with Coca-Cola and IBM. Plus, the company's founder, Thomas Alva Edison—inventor of the light bulb, phonograph, motion picture camera, and many more things that we take completely for granted—was one of my childhood heroes. But I was especially impressed with GE's Statement of Integrity, which recognized that "culture *meets* strategy *over* breakfast":

> "For more than 125 years, GE has demonstrated an unwavering commitment to performance with integrity. At the same time, we have expanded into new businesses and new regions and built a great record of sustained growth, we have built a worldwide reputation for lawful and ethical conduct. This reputation has never been stronger. In several surveys of CEOs, GE has been named the world's most respected and admired company. We have been ranked first for integrity and governance."[4]

Now *that* was the ideal corporate culture (or so I thought at the time), and I was excited to be a part of it. But what attracted me most of all was that after 25 years leading compliance programs in the financial services industry, I'd have the opportunity to learn compliance in a completely different way—the *industrial* way—because, unlike banks, GE manufactured tangible products.[5]

And aside from bringing "good things to life," GE at the time had 300,000 employees in more than 100 countries and ran a dazzling variety of businesses, including healthcare, aviation, nuclear power, rail and transportation, jet engines, water desalination, entertainment, appliances, lightbulbs, consumer goods, and of course, GE Capital, which was a large

---

4   GE "Spirit and Letter" (Code of Conduct), 2005
5   Yes, the Fed prints money, which is tangible, and banks and broker-dealers process, hold, and trade money. But they do it in such vast quantities that it's essentially intangible.

collection of non-banking financial services. With my hunger to swim beyond the sea of banking, I was very much looking forward to diving into the brand-new ocean called GE. What an ocean indeed!

Two and a Half GE Compliance Jobs

I joined GE in December 2006 to fill what I referred to as "two and a half" jobs, which were:

1. Managing director and global compliance leader over the financing and capital markets activities across GE's industrial businesses, in particular over the sale of their healthcare, energy, power, and rail businesses in emerging countries or regions such as the Middle East, China, East Europe, and Russia.[6]

2. CCO over GE's registered broker-dealer subsidiary.

3. And the half-job: Working together with and enlightening the chief compliance counsel at GE Corporate about bank-regulatory compliance principles and expectations, as if GE were considered a "bank holding company," which the Fed would expect to be a "managerial and financial source of strength" to its financial services subsidiaries.

In addition to wearing two and a half hats, I reported dually to the chief corporate and securities counsel (for job #2), and the head of treasury function within finance (for job #1). Both worked very well together, were very senior, and well positioned with GE's executive management. That is, the chief securities counsel reported directly to GE's general counsel, and the treasury executive reported directly to GE's chief financial officer. This pleased me, because I felt that it gave me the access, authority, and autonomy I needed to make a compliance & ethics difference across GE,

---

6   For example, if a GE client wanted to purchase and have GE build a water desalination plant in the Middle East, GE could also finance the project. Or, if a third-party company had been contracted to design, build, and help manage a hospital network in Russia, including GE medical equipment, GE could help finance the project through loan syndications or raising capital.

and to enable GE to grow while executing the type of risk-based enterprise compliance & ethics program expected by the Fed and US Department of Justice.

In each of my main jobs, I was able to leverage my financial-services experience, since both involved Know Your Customer and Anti-Bribery and Corruption/Foreign Corrupt Practices Act (FCPA) issues. I therefore had a fantastic opportunity to teach GE business and compliance leaders how to execute a financial services-type compliance program of a level expected by the Fed, while simultaneously learning from my GE colleagues about how compliance is executed the "GE way," whether manufacturing (and servicing) power turbines, stovetop ovens, lightbulbs, or jet engines; operating as a government and defense contractor; or meeting Federal Communications Commission rules as the owner of NBC Universal. Dream job!!

Of the two jobs, the more appealing one to me was, of course, the fish-out-of-water job: working with and learning from the industrial businesses. In the financial services compliance world, I was a pioneer and had succeeded in re-engineering compliance & ethics programs to enable growth. But after twenty-five years, my learning curve had flattened. One bank's compliance program was not that different from another bank's. But in the completely different world of industrial compliance, I was in the exciting (and sometimes scary) position of not knowing what I didn't know. It was thrilling to learn new things and to be completely out of my comfort zone, while also teaching GE what I'd pioneered with Chase and CIBC and learned from the Fed.

GE's Prior Experience with Capital Markets Trading

One thing I *did* know for sure, though, was that when it came to GE Capital, waking up GE Capital's broker-dealer after a regulatorily induced coma was going to be a major task. That's because for over a decade, until 2006, GE explicitly stayed away from engaging in corporate securities underwriting and capital markets activities. In 1994, GE had lost $350 million before taxes following a major bond trading/false-profits/accounting scandal involving GE's recently acquired Kidder, Peabody subsidiary. And years later, former GE Chairman, Jack Welch, admitted that he regretted purchasing the Kidder business and wished he'd heeded his board's advice to stay away from these riskier activities because they believed that that *strategy* was not consistent with GE's corporate *culture*.[7]

GE Capital was a collection of credit and leasing entities that served its industrial businesses and also provided consumer credit products through its private label credit card, mortgage lending and other retail business lines. It had been the "800-pound-gorilla" of GE for two decades, producing more than half of GE's total profits. It operated autonomously, without tight oversight by Jack Welch, but was so successful that it could be—and frequently was—spoken of on "the street" in the same sentence as Goldman Sachs and JP Morgan. As authors Thomas Gryta and Ted Mann put it, "The most famous industrial company in America had essentially become one of its largest and most inscrutable 'banks.'"[8] However, shortly after new CEO Jeffrey Immelt arrived in September 2001, he split GE Capital into four separate divisions, each one further broken down into numerous business "bubbles."

By the time I arrived in 2006, the capital markets seemed ready for GE to enter into the high-yield (junk bond) securities business.[9] In fact, that business was so attractive that by early 2007, Immelt and his executives reversed course and re-consolidated GE Capital, with junk bonds as one of its engines. But first, GE needed to bring its nearly dormant broker-dealer into compliance. That meant identifying its businesses and

---

7   Welch, Jack. *"Jack: Straight From The Gut"* (2001)

8   Gryta, Thomas and Mann, Ted - *"Lights Out: Pride, Delusion, and the Fall of General Electric"* (2020)

9   Per SEC *Pub. No. 150*, junk bonds are "a type of corporate bond that offers a higher rate of interest because of its higher risk of default. When companies with a greater estimated default risk issue bonds, they may be unable to obtain an investment-grade bond credit rating. As a result, they typically issue bonds with higher interest rates in order to entice investors and compensate them for this higher risk." SEC.gov. Retrieved August 23, 2020

the individuals involved in securities activities, ensuring that they were properly licensed to engage in investment business, and demonstrating that they reported to "supervisory principals." We also had to execute a robust broker-dealer compliance program that would meet the SEC's and Financial Industry Regulatory Authority's (FINRA's) expectations. This was my primary duty as the broker CCO. Interestingly, this assignment was very similar to what I'd done in London twenty years earlier with Chase (now JP Morgan Chase).

Emerging from the Ocean as a Compliance & Ethics Amphibian

Metaphorically, I needed to become an *amphibian*, which you may remember from high school biology is an animal that can live both in the water and on dry land. So did GE, but in very different ways. I needed to drag myself out of the highly regulated and scrutinized securities ocean of the SEC and FINRA and develop lungs so I could survive on the dry land of the GE continent. GE Capital and its broker-dealer had to do the opposite: effectively growing gills so they could move from the familiar safety of dry land compliance and survive in the financial services ocean.

Ultimately, a kind of race was on, at least in my head. On the one hand, if I couldn't learn to breathe on the land of GE and its industrial business culture, I'd find myself gasping for air and wouldn't survive. On the other hand, teaching an 800-pound gorilla to breathe under the water of the Fed's expectations as a highly regulated "bank" wasn't going to be easy. But if we could accomplish those two goals at the same time, my career would flourish and GE would be able to completely dominate both the land and the sea. Sadly, although I was able to evolve, GE wasn't. If you're wondering why, read *Lights Out: Pride, Delusion and the Fall of General Electric* by Thomas Gryta and Ted Mann.

Lessons Learned

- Go amphibious. If you need to develop lungs or gills to breathe in a different business or regulatory environment, do it. The process may be uncomfortable, but by asking questions, trying not to fear the unknown, and continuously learning, you'll greatly improve your chances of success.

- Don't forget the compliance & ethics officer's *raison d'etre* (reason for being). Combatting terrorist financing; knowing your customers; and preventing bribery, corruption, collusion, and price fixing are the common denominators of a successful enterprise-wide C&E program, regardless of business lines, geography, or clients.

- And don't forget compliance officers' other primary duties: to protect your customers and the communities your company serves, and to prevent and detect market abuse.

The Bermuda Triangle:
Credibility and Culture Within Compliance

The following story is a composite of events, institutions, and individuals with whom I worked and/or encountered over the course of my compliance & ethics career. My goal is to consolidate common issues and challenges facing companies across the globe, particularly as I progressed

Source: WindVector/Shutterstock.com

up the "corporate ladder" where more responsibility also came with more corporate politics. I've changed the names of these composite characters from multiple organizations to ensure confidentiality and anonymity.

"**D**on't forget who hired you and pays your salary," one of my three bosses threatened me, quite pointedly. I worked well with all three (whom I've nicknamed Hurricane, Typhoon, and Squall, for reasons which will soon become apparent). But unlike my seven bosses at UBS who generally got along, these three "storms" hated each other so much that they could barely stand to be in the same room. Therefore, it didn't come as a huge surprise that, after only two minutes of a long-arranged, critically important meeting with all three that I'd painstakingly brokered, Hurricane walked out of the conference room screaming profanities.

Ironically, each of my bosses was well-intentioned and wanted to achieve the same goal: to prevent or remediate control weaknesses that were hindering corporate growth. However, their obsessive, competitive nature to get *sole* credit for control improvements at the expense of each other got in the way of working together productively. It was a less than zero-sum game: if one won, the other two had to lose.

Worse still, the overall corporate culture, especially the tone at the top, was marked by finger-pointing and attempts to avoid blame and accountability when controls went sideways or if anyone received criticism from audit or a regulator. Getting anyone to accept ownership and accountability of internal control, audit, or regulatory issues was as rare as finding life on another planet.

Overall, trying to get Hurricane, Typhoon, and Squall to agree on any key decisions was like sailing through the Bermuda Triangle.[1] Stormy seas, sunken controls, and vanishing accountability. It was as if our corporate priorities, our metaphorical vessels to correct weaknesses and strengthen our overall system of internal controls and compliance had been swallowed up in a vortex of corporate politics and personalities.

Not surprisingly, the toxic corporate and ultra-competitive culture among Hurricane, Typhoon and Squall made it nearly impossible for me, as CCO, to accomplish key regulatory and audit deliverables. The politics was interfering with my primary goal for the firm: re-engineering the compliance & ethics program to enable regulatory health and business growth. This included upgrading the skill sets of the compliance staff; making processes more efficient and effective so that controls actually prevented and detected fraud, bribery, money laundering or illegal payments;

---

1   The Bermuda Triangle is a longstanding myth (or not) that a number of aircraft and ships are said to have disappeared under mysterious circumstances.

and ensuring that we had the appropriate technology in place to enable a stronger monitoring and testing control environment. Such was life in the Bermuda Triangle.

But back to the meeting which I'd convened because we were up against major deadlines, and I needed all three bosses to approve a small but desperately needed increase in budget in order for my team to be able to meet them. Hurricane had left in a huff because at the last minute, Typhoon couldn't attend and had sent a delegate—an excellent, smart, and decisive one at that—in her place. In Hurricane's view, even though Squall (whom he didn't respect anyway) was there, Typhoon's having sent a delegate was insulting, and having only two out of the three storms in attendance was a waste of his time. I felt like I was once again "herding cats" while swimming in the Bermuda Triangle.

Knowing that it would be a long time before I could reschedule the meeting, I decided to conduct it anyway—without Typhoon and Hurricane (hence the latter's threatening "reminder" about who hired me and paid my salary). As it turned out, Typhoon's delegate, plus the Squall, and I accomplished a lot at this meeting. Unfortunately, though, we still needed all three of my bosses' approvals.

Risk vs. Compliance

Hurricane (who oversaw risk management at the firm) and Typhoon (who oversaw compliance) were complete opposites in their priorities, perspectives, and personality. Hurricane was highly analytical with an unnecessarily caustic style; and simply, paranoid when it came to managing risk. Typhoon had deep product knowledge but low empathy for others, like the proverbial "bull in the china shop." Hurricane didn't trust anyone or anything; Typhoon was carefree (resulting in a lot of broken china).

In my view, the risk and compliance functions must work together hand in glove. But that wasn't to be. Hurricane's risk staff and some of my own inherited compliance staff were either burnt out from Hurricane's micro-management style, inflexible from inertia, or simply unfit for purpose because they were junior staff placed in senior roles thanks to many prior budget cuts. That's why I was brought in to re-tool the compliance function and teams.

In contrast, Typhoon understood the objectives of *compliance* but hadn't quite figured out the *ethics* part of the compliance & ethics equation. Thus, corporate culture wasn't on her personal or professional radar. Nor was it part of her management style. However, because Typhoon understood regulatory risks, we understood each other. Meanwhile, Squall was passively resistant to both Hurricane and Typhoon.

Unfortunately, rather than operating as hand in glove as risk and compliance should, the two functions were more like match and gasoline. Better yet, like sand and cement. Nothing moved. This situation wasn't entirely their fault, though: their behavior, management style, and overall level of dysfunction were enabled, supported, and encouraged by the overall culture of the firm, which started from the very top.

The Gladiators

Here's an example. Only a month earlier, there was a global conference call with dozens of senior compliance, risk, business, and audit executives in attendance. The call had been set up by audit, ostensibly to decide whether Hurricane (risk) or Typhoon (compliance) owned—and would therefore be held accountable and responsible for mediating (with no additional budget)—a particularly contentious audit-related issue. Or, as a former colleague and executive at another firm used to say, "*Who takes the bullet?*"

Looking back at this incident, it was clear to me that audit had set up the call not to professionally address a problem and agree on a way forward, but instead to create a fight to the death between two giant gladiators at the Roman Colosseum. And like the audiences at those ancient spectacles, the participants on the call were looking for blood. Worse yet, I was put in the uncomfortable position of deciding on the winner.

Compliance as Cinderella: The Stepchild of Legal or Risk

When Roman gladiators fought, the casualties were limited to the participants in the battle. But when corporate gladiators fight, the casualties include shareholders, the community, taxpayers, the markets, and especially, the *liable board of directors* when they get sued by shareholders and sanctioned by prosecutors for an utter failure of their fiduciary duty of loyalty and duty of care over compliance.

Clearly, having risk and compliance fight each other to the death benefits exactly no one. And regulators know this. The problem is that the priorities of the risk function (traditionally market risk, credit risk, and even operational risk) are not always aligned with those of the compliance function. In summary, market-, credit-, and operational risks are generally quantifiable, while compliance risks, particularly those involving culture, ethics, and behavior, are far more difficult to quantify, measure, monitor, and then report to the board. Because compliance's risks are less-easily quantifiable/tangible, a lot of companies see them as less important and make compliance subservient to legal and or audit and beholden to one or both for their salaries, budgets, and bonuses. When that happens, compliance becomes Cinderella, the neglected stepchild who, unlike the better-loved children of the CEO (Legal and Risk), is stuck at the servants' table and doesn't get invited to the board and C-suite tables.

Indeed, "Cinderella" chief compliance officers (CCOs) have little or no control or authority over their share of the budget pie because either the general counsel or the chief risk officer instinctively rewards their own loyal staff first, not the independently minded compliance & ethics officers. Compliance gets the crumbs, sweeps the floors of their chief risk or chief legal bosses, and the firm ultimately ends up with a less-than-effective, unsustainable compliance program in the eyes of the US Justice Department. Who ultimately suffers the major reputational damage, litigation, and significant monetary penalties if compliance & ethics teams don't get to go to the royal ball (have a direct reporting line to the board)? The company, shareholders, markets, customers, taxpayers, the personally liable directors, and of course, Cinderella herself, the personally liable CCO.

The Fight

Before the big gladiator call, I'd suspected that certain people were trying to fix the fight and had set up Typhoon to take the blame. I called and gave her a heads up. The call began and the VIP crowd paused in a hush as the issues were summarized by the chief auditor. I could practically hear the echo of a ring announcer: "In this corner…"

After the chief auditor's opening summary, she gave an ultimatum and demanded an answer immediately: Unless an ownership decision was made, a scathing audit report would be issued and shared with the regulators, with the Typhoon left holding the bag of horse manure. And of course, the audit report would be issued smack in the middle of budget season and performance evaluation time.

In my capacity as regional CCO reporting to both Hurricane *and* Typhoon, and intimately familiar with the audit issue at hand, I was caught in the middle. But the chief auditor demanded my opinion as to who should own the issue—and be solely responsible for correcting it. I felt as though the whole Coliseum crowd was now screaming at the top of their lungs, anxious for me to decide the fate of the two combatants—and, by extension, that of the company and our directors. Relying on facts, I made my decision, assigning ownership and accountability to Hurricane (who had hired me locally and determined my performance and bonus).

Meanwhile, despite the drama, we were approaching a key deadline and my team (and our company) was facing major staff turnover and was therefore, falling further behind on our major deliverables. And it was all happening because my three supervisors were more interested in stabbing each other in the back than in working together and doing the right thing for the company. And this incredibly unproductive turf war was tremendously destructive for the firm.

Navigating the Turbulent "C's"

Over time, I learned how each of my three bosses operated, and more importantly, reminded myself to keep my compliance & ethics compass focused on the big picture: to remediate corrective actions, continue to run our program without incurring new problems, and transform our program (and by extension, our company) into a more efficient and effective C&E culture and function. Like a skilled ship's captain preparing to navigate the Bermuda Triangle, I taught my team to tack and jib against the stormy winds and turbulent waves of politics whipped up by Hurricane, Typhoon and Squall (and their respective staffs). I reminded my own staff regularly to "stay with me" and "stay as one" (as Russell Crowe said to his fellow Coliseum slaves in the movie, "The Gladiator") as we fought our way through those treacherous waters to safety. Ultimately, I wanted to equip my trusty compliance & ethics officers with the five "C's" they'd need to navigate their own rough seas as future CCOs. These are:

1. Calm
2. Confidence
3. Credibility
4. Clarity (of purpose and mission); and
5. Especially, Courage

My wife has always referred to me as "the dog that wouldn't let go of the bone." I was determined and passionate about meeting our regulatory objectives to re-build and sustain an effective compliance program. We had a mission to accomplish despite the Bermuda Triangle and all the other obstacles I faced.[2]

And I've *always* believed that like first responders and the Marines, CCOs are meant to run into a burning building, chase a tornado, take

---

2   When I took this job, I had no idea that I'd be forced to meet major internal control, regulatory, and audit deadlines within extreme constraints, handcuffs and politics; when I was being recruited, no one told me that, despite the steep regulatory and audit cliffs to climb, I'd be unable to hire new staff or replace leavers, or that temporary staff would have to roll-off once their contracts expired.

the hill; and I grew up knowing that *anything* is possible. At least those CCOs who are courageous and compliance & ethics officers who have a backbone and possess the 5C's. Sadly, I've also encountered or managed other compliance & ethics officers who were spineless, non-independent wafflers who'd blow with the wind and opt for the path of least resistance by acquiescing to the aggressive business and not being independently minded.

The Surge

Ultimately, despite the Bermuda Triangle we achieved our internal control, regulatory and audit objectives within three months. How so? Because I created and proposed a common goal with which the Hurricane, Typhoon and the Squall could each relate and therefore agreed in complete harmony.

It was February, and in the "compliance surge" that I proposed to Hurricane, Typhoon, and Squall, we'd have very specific objectives, timelines (no later than April), action owners, and deliverables. We'd temporarily increase our contractor staff, re-tool some of our existing headcount, closely monitor progress, completely re-engineer the end-to-end process through LEAN Six-Sigma methods, celebrate quick wins, and then reduce our contractors to pre-surge levels. Most importantly, we'd keep our board and executive management laser-focused and continuously apprised and would escalate issues immediately as necessary.

Epilogue

Hurricane, Typhoon, and Squall understood the analogy and approved my surge proposal. More importantly, we achieved and sustained our firm-wide objectives with major success. Our skill sets, processes, and technology were all upgraded. It took major alignment among the three storms, but also the critical support of our executive management, board and business leaders. Our culture also improved dramatically. The compliance surge was simple to understand, clear in scope, and targeted in a way that all stakeholders including our board of directors could claim victory from a budgetary, but especially regulatory and audit perspective.

Lessons Learned

- Stick to the facts. Don't let corporate politics dominate and influence your decisions, even if you end up having to contradict your own boss.

- Every company has corporate politics. I've always said that an effective compliance & ethics officer must be *aware* of the politics but remain *apolitical.* Stay above the fray.

- Like a chess player, the CCO must see the whole board, understand the strategy, be very aware of where each piece is, and anticipate each move well in advance. That requires clear thinking, especially if the gladiators are your own bosses.

- Sadly, the corporate culture and "tone at the top" fuels corporate politics. Even though we were able to navigate through the Bermuda Triangle, the politics was ultimately driven by the culture of the CEO and executive management. In my case, a horrible corporate culture of finger-pointing and siloes ultimately hurt the organization.

- *Directors*: Look for signals of corporate politics and dysfunction dominating decisions (or indecisions). Your liability, governance success, and reputation may depend heavily on it.

- When risk (or legal) and compliance colleagues are not aligned, especially very publicly in the eyes of the business executives, the businesses and others will sit back and watch—or worse: arbitrage the compliance (or risk/legal) team to their advantage (and the company's disadvantage).

- Don't be surprised if auditors and regulators see what's going on either.

- Despite this, think *out of the box* to keep your company within the legal, regulatory, and ethical box. In my case, it was the "surge" (among other key decisions I made over the course of my tenure there), that enabled major compliance and company success.

I eventually moved on to a new adventure, serving as chief compliance officer (CCO) with a new firm and exciting mission, a fantastic opportunity, and a feeling of elation as I flew away from Hurricane, Typhoon, and Squall.

Bricks, Horseshoes, Storytelling, and the Importance of Meaningful Reporting

Source: ISSAH_RUS/Shutterstock.com

The following chapter is a composite of events, institutions, and individuals with whom I worked and/or encountered over the course of my compliance & ethics career. My goal is to consolidate common issues and challenges facing companies across the globe, particularly as I progressed up the corporate ladder, where more responsibility also came with more corporate politics. I've changed names and other identifying details to ensure confidentiality and anonymity.

Within two weeks of joining a multinational firm as their new chief compliance officer, I asked my staff for a copy of the most recent four quarters of the department's compliance report to executive management and board of directors. What I received was stunning, and incredibly disappointing. First, each report was at least 300 pages long and so heavy (and full of densely worded, nearly incomprehensible bullets in seemingly random order) that I called them "bricks." Second, the reports had clearly not been proofread and were riddled with spelling and grammar errors. Third, they were obviously cut-and-paste jobs, cobbled together from individual reports from compliance unit heads throughout our very siloed and dysfunctional compliance department who were falling all over themselves trying to outdo one another by expressing how much they'd done over the quarter. Whoever had assembled these endless "me, me, me" exercises hadn't even bothered to use the same font throughout, which had the effect of making the completed reports look like giant ransom notes, as if the text had been cut out of different magazines and glued together. Aside from being absolutely useless, these bricks were supposed to present the face of the compliance department to the board (and our regulators). Instead, they were an embarrassment. And they were so imposing that I doubt that anyone (especially the board) had read—let alone understood—them. That was a huge problem.

The reports told no cohesive story, raised no red flags, and did nothing to articulate a set of compliance & ethics priorities and actions that warranted executive management's and the board's attention. Yes, those critical bits of information might have been included somewhere in the report, but if so, they were so buried underneath 300 pages of BS that no one could have found them. Unfortunately, as far as regulators are concerned, what's documented and presented to board members—even if no one has read it—is *presumed to be known*. So, had there been an internal (or worse, a regulatory) investigation resulting from a major allegation or violation, the board wouldn't have been able to claim ignorance.

I was in shock—and for good reason: It was quite possible that for months—and perhaps years—before I arrived, our board and executive management had been flying virtually blind through a storm of multiple compliance risks. Who knows, there might've been a dead body (a major, as-yet-unaddressed risk) buried somewhere in that stack of bricks.

So, I assembled my newly inherited staff and asked them to explain to me how those reports came into being. It turns out, I was right: the bricks were, indeed, cut-and-paste jobs, with each section submitted by department heads who were more interested in competing with each other than in helping the overall company. And, typically, a day or two before the deadline for submitting the complete quarterly report to the board, some thankless "volunteer" would get stuck with the job of pulling all the pieces together. It was amazing. All these compliance unit heads looking at each other, shrugging their shoulders, and saying that they hadn't had time to do a better job. "Not on my watch," I thought to myself, and over the next few months many of those direct reports found themselves seeking employment elsewhere.

As mentioned, I'd been brought in to completely re-engineer our end-to-end compliance operational and risk management approach, otherwise known as our enterprise compliance risk management program. But I knew that one of my first deliverables would have to be a better system of reporting. Step number one toward that goal was to create reports to the board and executive management that were simple, thematic stories for this audience to understand for oversight (board) and action (management).

Horseshoes

One day, I came into the office and, instead of a brick, found a brand new "compliance risk dashboard" on my desk. It had been drafted using a template provided by our risk department, and, like the illustration below, it was colorful—covered with green, yellow, and red U-shapes that were supposed to highlight a variety of actual compliance risks measured against board-approved risk appetite levels. Emphasis on "*supposed* to highlight."

A few minutes later, my compliance chief operating officer (COO) walked into my office waving a copy of the same document. We both looked at each other. "Looks like horseshoes," I remarked with a look of confused amusement. "More like horse *shit*," he deadpanned. We both

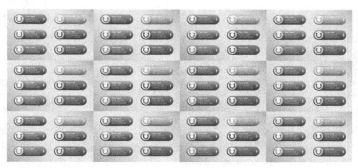

Source: Author

laughed out loud, even though our need to report compliance risks and trends meaningfully to our board of directors was a serious matter. Yes, the new "dashboards" were a lot lighter than the bricks, but the previous problem remained: we had no idea what the horseshoes created by the risk department meant—and if we didn't, the board didn't stand a chance.

In their defense, the risk department had made a serious effort. They were trying to put their own twist on "donut charts," which were all the rage then. The donuts were pie-like charts with a hole in the middle in which there was a very brief explanation (usually a single number, an image, or phrase) of the point to be made.

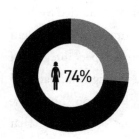

Source: Honza Hruby/
Shutterstock.com

These donuts were themselves a type of "RAG chart," which showed the (R)ed, (A)mber, or (G)reen status of compliance risks. Red indicated that a particular compliance risk policy metric had been breached or that there was an actual violation of law. Amber (yellow) indicated a risk that could be averted, and green indicated areas where no risks (or even risks of risks) were present.

However, unlike donuts, which conveyed important information in an easy-to-understand way, these horseshoes were packed together so tightly on a single page that they looked like hoof prints after a stampede, and conveyed practically no information at all.

Source: David Stearn Photography/Shutterstock.com

I rejected the horseshoe dashboard, explaining that dashboards, like the ones in cars, should be easy to read and understand. Are we operating within the legally allowable limits? Are we low on gas? Do we have enough staff to investigate money laundering or misconduct alerts? Is the car overheating? Are too many employees (including, perhaps, the CEO him/herself) ignoring anti-bribery and corruption training? How could board members understand how fast the firm is going (and how to adjust its speed and direction) if they can't even figure out what the horseshoe is trying to measure?

Source: Lauris A/Shutterstock.com

Avoiding Trash-in, Trash-out: Treating Compliance Risk Reports like Financial Reports

I explained to my team (and the risk department) that we needed to think of our reports to management and the board as the functional equivalent of financial statements. Just as investors and regulators expect integrity of a company's financial information and statements through standardized accounting principles, methodologies, and controls, so too should the output and analytics of compliance risk reports and dashboards. That way, stakeholders such as executive management and the board will know what to expect, will be able to compare like-for-like data from quarter to quarter, and will have confidence that the information they're receiving is the result of a disciplined process of information input, control, and consistent review and sign-off, ultimately resulting in compliance risk data with integrity.

That meant that we'd have to data mine our brick reports for the most meaningful compliance metrics and risks. If we tried to put every single detail—relevant, consistent, complete, verified or not—into the report, we'd wind up with the epitome of the expression, "trash-in, trash-out." In other words, a dashboard summary of a 300-page avalanche of disorganized, unintelligible, meaningless information can only produce a disorganized, unintelligible, meaningless summary that would provide zero strategic value to management, the board, or even to our own team.

Corporate Bodies Are like Animals and Humans

I also explained to the team that a corporate body should be viewed just like an animal's or a human body, or even a car. For example, bodies are comprised of many organs (functions and businesses); muscle and bones (policies and controls); network of nerves, arteries and veins (employees, corporate culture, training, ethics); and an immune system (surveillance, cyber-security, and testing). Like an animal or human body, the corporate body is incredibly complex and intricate and it's therefore necessary to measure and monitor it regularly to keep it operating in the most effective and efficient manner. And just as a physician (or veterinarian) conducts a thorough physical at regular intervals and gives the patient (or its owner) a full report, a corporation's C&E program (consider it the company's heart and soul) must monitor, measure, and report on how well all of the corporation's many parts are operating. In doing so, the compliance & ethics officers can shape the business' behavior, ensuring that it does the right thing for itself, its employees, its customers, and its shareholders. But first, you need a methodology to measure, analyze, and report the right metrics to management, the board, and ourselves. That takes human judgment. And the result is neither a brick nor a horseshoe; it's intelligent data.

The bottom line is that human, animal, and corporate bodies are similar. Each relies on *input* (food, gasoline/electricity, data, investment), which is "digested" internally and produces an output, which is the energy that allows it to survive—and thrive.

Good vs. Bad Input and Output

Good inputs generally lead to good outputs. A horse, well-fed and trained, can plow a field for hours or win a major race. An automobile, running on the right fuel, can take you where you want to go. And with the right inputs (in terms of personnel, intellectual capital, and good management), a company can produce high-quality goods or information responsibly, at a profit.

Another form of output is waste: excrement from the horse, exhaust from the automobile, or way too much (or useless) data from the corporation. The wise owner or manager can reduce waste or channel it into something positive. For example, horse manure can be used as fertilizer to enrich the soil and grow food; one can cut vehicle emissions by getting regular tune-ups or switching to a hybrid or electric vehicle; and boards can use well-constructed corporate compliance risk dashboards to protect customers, markets, and employees of the firm.

Source: decade3d-anatomy online/Shutterstock.com

The challenge, however, is that not all owners or managers are wise. Some will instead mistreat or under-nourish the horse or simply shovel the horse manure away, never tune up their vehicle, or avoid investing in the tools that will allow the company to capture and use data in a way that reduces their risks and enables them to stay competitive—and safe.

Put another way, firms will produce potentially dangerous and meaningless waste if they don't invest in the right care and maintenance of their corporate body. The goal should be to produce the appropriate level of investment in the right people, control and analytical processes, and tools to enable meaningful output in the form of dashboards and risk metrics for the board, management, and compliance itself. With only meaningless waste to operate on, the board and management are driving blind with no awareness of existing or potential risks. As a result, there's a good chance that sooner or later, they'll drive straight into a tree or off a cliff.

Epilogue

It took a few iterations, but eventually, with a more experienced and capable team, we got there. We not only re-engineered a lean-yet-effective process to input consistent C&E data (including corrective actions over audit and regulatory findings), but also created a consistent review and approval governance process that ultimately produced simple, thematic-yet-meaningful compliance risk dashboards for our board to understand.

My presentations to the board were crisp and engaging, and led to plenty of dialogue and probing questions from them. I was quite proud of having transformed our bricks into precious intelligence that enabled our board to fulfil its duty of care over compliance & ethics.

Lessons Learned

- Don't report bricks. Don't throw horseshoes either. Instead, provide management (for action) and your board (for oversight) with simple, thematic dashboards that explain prioritized risks, trends, and required mitigating actions.

- Meaningful compliance & ethics reporting, produced with integrity and consistency will give the board confidence that the company's C&E risks are being properly managed across the whole enterprise.

- The body, whether animal, human, mechanical, or corporate, is made up of multiple moving parts which must work together to be effective and efficient. Effective and efficient compliance & ethics reporting allows the board of directors, executive management, and your own teams to ensure that the many moving parts of the corporate body are operating properly and that there are in place effective controls to protecting the body from harm while continually moving forward.

- The *output* of compliance reporting and analytics (which we'll cover later), but both are only as good as the *input*. If firms don't invest in the right care and maintenance of the corporate body, including investing in the right people, processes and tools to produce high-quality reports and risk metrics for the board, the result will be piles of meaningless waste.

- Not knowing risks or the route to take to avoid them too often leads to driving into trees or off cliffs.

"That Was Then, This is Now, and This is Where We're Heading"

Lucite commemorative sent to me by my BNP Paribas/Bank of the West colleagues, March 2020. Source: author

This book is about how an effective compliance program, together with the right ethical culture is achievable, sustainable, and "critically essential" for a firm's strategic success. As CCO with BNP Paribas, Paris, France (BNP), one of the largest banks in the world and largest in Europe as of 2021, my experience was very stressful—but also quite thrilling, fulfilling, and very productive. I'm proud to have been a member of the BNP family as well as a major contributor with my teams to our compliance & ethics achievements during my tenure (January 2015 through February 2020) as BNP CCO for the United States and the Americas region. This chapter is forward looking and doesn't dive into BNP Paribas' prior compliance challenges before my January 5, 2015 arrival. Such history, occurring before my start date, is publicly available[1,2,3.] It's also why I was hired: to build and transform a sustainable, effective compliance & ethics program.

The Interview

It was the fall of 2014. I was recruited for and interviewing to become CCO of BNP's corporate and institutional banking (CIB) division for North America. The BNP executive across from me spoke softly as if whispering to, rather than interviewing me. His French accent was also heavy, so understanding his already soft voice was a major challenge for me. My recruiter had advised me that this executive would be my most difficult because he was tough and no-nonsense. So, I couldn't afford to lose focus.

The stakes were also extremely high for BNP. They needed to hire an experienced CCO who knew how to remediate, rebuild, and lead an effective, credible, and sustainable compliance & ethics program for the long run. Someone to develop and manage truly independent compliance & ethics officers to work decisively to enlighten business heads, and to measure, monitor, report and escalate compliance exceptions—and solutions—to our directors and regulators as needed.

Twenty minutes into the interview, the BNP executive suddenly began pointing his finger at my left arm. I had no idea what he was getting at, but since he wore a calm, friendly smile, it was clear that it wasn't anything

---

1   For example, Volcker, Paul A., Goldstone, Richard J., and Pieth, Mark. "Manipulation of the Oil-for-Food Programme by the Iraqi Regime: Oil Transactions and Illicit Payments, Humanitarian Goods Transactions and Illicit Payments, The Escrow Bank and the Inspections Companies, Other UN-Related Issues," Independent Inquiry Committee into the United Nations Oil-for-Food Programme, October 27, 2005. https://amlawdaily.typepad.com/amlawdaily/files/paul_volckers_final_oilforfood_report.pdf. Retrieved June 23, 2021

2   For example, New York State Department of Financial Services, "Consent Order Under New York Banking Law § 44 – In the Matter of BNP Paribas, SA, New York Branch," June 30, 2014 - https://www.dfs.ny.gov/system/files/documents/2020/04/ea140630_bnp_paribas.pdf. Retrieved June 13, 2021

3   For example, US Department of Justice Press Release – "BNP Paribas USA Inc. Pleads Guilty to Antitrust Conspiracy," January 28, 2018 - https://www.justice.gov/opa/pr/bnp-paribas-usa-inc-pleads-guilty-antitrust-conspiracy. Retrieved April 27, 2021 (for activities 2007 – 2013).

offensive or embarrassing. "I'm sorry," I said. "I don't understand what you're asking." He leaned forward, cleared his throat, and gestured at the Polar running watch on my left wrist. He paused and spoke slowly. "Are you a marathon runner? I am running in the New York City marathon for the first time." Pleasantly surprised, I congratulated him and replied, "Yes, I ran the Marine Corps[4] marathon in 1991." I proceeded to explain how I'd completely re-learned how to walk and run four years after having shattered my kneecap.[5]

My broken knee had apparently broken the ice. From there I felt the interview went very well and I had a chance to explain how, throughout my career, I'd re-engineered compliance & ethics programs to enable growth. When the executive said he was impressed with my tenacity and ability to overcome major obstacles, I told him that I've always thought of qualified compliance & ethics officers as firefighters running into burning buildings, Marines storming a beachhead, or tornado chasers who brave danger to gather and analyze data that will ultimately save lives. If we're good, we're courageous.

After the interview, we shook hands and the exec quietly said, "You seem so confident." I wasn't sure whether he was calling me arrogant (I wasn't) or was impressed that I wasn't intimidated by him or the huge job ahead that overhauling BNP's compliance program and the overall bank itself would be. I said, "Yes, I'm confident. I've done this work many times before, and I know I can enable BNP to succeed." In hindsight, I should have ended the interview with a phrase that I would end up using often during my five years at BNP: "That was then (BNP's past), this is now, and this is where we're heading."

---

4   The United States Marine Corp embrace the phrase, Semper Fi which means "always faithful" in Latin. The Marine Corps (and our other armed forces), have a credo very important to me because of the esprit de corps it instills, and which is equally important as an independent compliance & ethics officer. Of course, being faithful means being ethically correct for compliance & ethics officers.
5   See chapter 1.16.

My remaining interviews—with BNP executives from New York, Paris, and their consumer bank affiliate Bank of the West in San Francisco—went very well. Our objectives were aligned, and we all agreed that we needed cultural clarity and regulatory success to achieve strategic growth. By December 2014, I got the job.

My scope and authority expanded before I'd even arrived in January 2015. Indeed, US law (since 1956 under the US Bank Holding Company Act[6]) and Fed regulation[7] led BNP to choose between two strategies: (1) a strategy of expansion. In this case, BNP would be compelled to have an integrated "intermediate holding company"[8] (IHC) to serve as a financial and managerial "source of strength" over its US entities, particularly its insured depository institutions Bank of the West and First Hawaiian Bank. And compliance was the path to enable this managerial (i.e., cultural) consistency.

Alternatively, like some other foreign banks, BNP could have chosen option 2: a narrower strategy, shrinking below the required consolidated US asset size threshold to avoid being an intermediate holding company (IHC). BNP chose to expand its US footprint and integrate into a consolidated US IHC. This was a wise move, in my view, as BNP's competitors were reeling from regulatory criticism and/or being challenged strategically and financially. For BNP, to expand was a strategic opportunity. However, to expand meant cultural consistency and compliance & ethical effectiveness. This meant having a more consistent compliance platform and culture across our wholesale (CIB), consumer-oriented businesses (Bank of the West and First Hawaiian Bank) and institutional asset management business.

---

6   Title 12 of the US Code (USC) 1841 – Bank Holding Company Act of 1956 (as amended) - https://www.law.cornell.edu/uscode/text/12/1841 - last retrieved June 27, 2021
7   Title 12 of the Code of Federal Regulations (CFR) 225 – "Regulation Y – Bank Holding Companies and Change in Bank Control" - https://www.law.cornell.edu/cfr/text/12/part-225 - last retrieved June 27, 2021
8   12 CFR § 252.153 – "U.S. intermediate holding company requirement for foreign banking organizations with combined U.S. assets of $100 billion or more and U.S. non-branch assets of $50 billion or more" - https://www.law.cornell.edu/cfr/text/12/252.153 - last retrieved June 27, 2021

As in many organizations, strengthening existing regulatory compliance and internal controls over BNP's people, process, and technology was an immediate priority. However, I had a broader objective—let's call it "Young's Vision."[9] I sought to develop and strengthen a sustainable BNP Americas compliance & ethics program to: 1) maintain our day-to-day activities (to "run BNP") in a way in which we would continue to comply with all *other* laws and regulations, and most importantly, 2) upgrade (transform) our compliance program with the *right* people, process, and essential technology across BNP's multiple businesses, legal entities, and Americas region. I'll discuss Young's Vision more broadly in part 2.

Re-engineering the Culture of Compliance Like Chess

To me, BNP was operating in the US—a highly regulated jurisdiction—with multiple businesses, legal entities, and many regulators, all while in the middle of a remediation and transformation. I therefore approached BNP and

Source: Billion Photos/Shutterstock.com

its Americas and IHC strategy as if it were a massive, global "chessboard" requiring an overall compliance & ethics vision and enterprise strategy.[10] It was the best way to fix, run, and change BNP's compliance culture to achieve regulatory health and strategic growth in a safe and responsible manner.

---

9   I didn't call it *"Young's Vision"* at the time, but that's what it was. This vision converged DoJ Sentencing Guidelines, Fed SR 08-08, and COSO's Integrated Framework for Enterprise Risk Management (among other guidance) while addressing BNP's existing controls. This was also integrated with the global remediation and transformation program of BNP globally. *"Young's Vision"* focuses on the US and Americas program reflecting US regulatory expectations. See chapter 2.8 for further details about Young's Vision.

10   The Federal Reserve expected an enterprise compliance risk management program. See chapter 2.8.

As I would have with any large, complex organization involving multiple moving "chess pieces," I sought to strengthen a compliance & ethics program that could anticipate multiple moves ahead (emerging risks through predictive analytics) with respect to BNP's clients, geographies, third party vendors, or BNP's underlying products and services. But to excel in the chess game of compliance & ethics, I also needed to understand our own employees—that is, the compliance team and our business colleagues—so I could navigate the macro- and micro-cultures at head office in Paris, New York, San Francisco (Bank of the West), Honolulu (First Hawaiian Bank), Sao Paulo (Brazil), and our other locations. Each piece of BNP needed comprehension, appreciation, and deployment in the compliance chessboard to fix, run, and transform the entire organization. To accomplish this would ultimately produce a long-term, effective, and sustainable, enterprise-wide compliance risk management program.

Only Two Very Important Reporting Lines

The moment I entered BNP's New York offices on January 5, 2015, I knew immediately that its corporate and compliance culture felt right. For example, I knew precisely from whom to take direction and to whom I was accountable. That's because I reported to only two people. Period. And if you multiply two clear and simple reporting lines by tens of thousands of employees across BNP globally, that simplicity helped streamline and align the cultural and strategic direction for the bank. Quite a contrast from my seven bosses at one firm, or reporting to three dysfunctional, hate-each-other bosses at another.

As CCO for BNP Americas, I reported directly into the Group Head of Compliance[11] in Paris. He reported directly into the Group CEO. That's direct and real access to the top. And the Group Compliance Head had stature, courage, and the Group CEO's respect. His opinion mattered. His unwavering support of my compliance vision and strategy for BNP

---

11   He's since retired.

Americas enabled me to achieve our compliance & ethics objectives without fear of retribution or political games (a reality everywhere at every company). To this day, I respect him immensely because he possessed the rare, combined qualities of intellect, integrity, gravitas, and genuine compliance independence to enable a robust, effective, and sustainable compliance program. Plus, his well-timed sense of humor was always dry and helped keep all of us loose as BNP transformed globally.

I also reported functionally into the CEO of the Americas CIB region, who was also CEO across all our US retail, wealth, and institutional businesses through our Bank of the West, First Hawaiian, and asset management units. He too, was well respected and worked very closely with the Group CEO. In many ways, the regional CEO treated me as if I were his equal rather than his subordinate. "How can I serve you?" he'd often say to me and others. This of course, required earning his respect to achieve a close and mutual partnership. He often already had a solution in mind when we were discussing an issue, but he still listened to and heard me. I admired that. If convinced, the regional CEO was open to changing his mind. Which he did, thoughtfully, particularly over our regular one-on-one breakfasts to discuss all things compliance, ethics, culture, and strategy.

Both of my bosses worked quite well together, given the daily work at hand to transform the compliance & ethics program globally. I'd walked into BNP with a clear vision (Young's Vision), which was to remediate, transform, and sustain BNP Americas' compliance & ethics organization and culture by integrating the (1) US Department of Justice Organizational Sentencing Guidelines[12] and (2) the Federal Reserve Board's corporate compliance expectations expressed in its Supervision and Regulation (SR)

---

12   US Department of Justice. "Principles of Federal Prosecution of Business Organizations," Title 9-28.000: Corporate Compliance Programs," Title 9-28.800, Justice Manual - https://www. justice.gov/jm/jm-9-28000-principles-federal-prosecution-business-organizations - last retrieved June 17, 2021

letter 2008-08,[13] while also (3) executing BNP's other initiatives. Reporting to these two senior executives enabled me to leverage my then-35 years of CCO experience and skills, to exert my compliance authority where needed, and, most importantly, to execute my vision.

No Longer Cinderella CCO

Unlike many of the Cinderella CCO jobs I held previously, I didn't report to, and therefore wasn't a "stepchild" of the general counsel or chief risk officer or anyone else. Instead, I was their equal, their peer, and a member of the CEO's executive committee or ExCo. This meant that our compliance & ethics function had stature; we sat at the adult table and were therefore a direct, unfettered part of the strategic decision-making process across BNP Americas, with direct access to the independent board of directors over their US consolidated operations.

And as a direct report to the group head of compliance, I was also a member of the Compliance Executive Committee (Comex). This meant that my diverse, non-head office (in my case, non-French) compliance & ethics voice was heard and mattered. My decisions withstood and indeed avoided being continuously overridden or bypassed if a business leader was unhappy with my opinion or position. For a while, I felt like I was in compliance heaven, or like a kid in a candy shop!

All of this demonstrated to me that BNP understood the importance of compliance independence. And with my Asia Pacific CCO counterpart as a fellow member of the Comex, BNP had a meaningfully balanced and diverse, international perspective to reflect and reinforce BNP's compliance & ethics culture. Our skills also made the Comex diverse and balanced.

The group head of compliance embraced and respected our local (Americas and Asia Pacific) regulatory and reputational risks. A red

---

13   Federal Reserve Board, "Compliance Risk Management Programs and Oversight at Large Banking Organizations with Complex Compliance Profiles," Supervision and Regulation ("SR") Letter 2008-08, October 16, 2008 (revised February 26, 2021) - https://www.federalreserve.gov/boarddocs/srletters/2008/sr0808.htm - last retrieved June 14, 2021

flag for many foreign banks (or more broadly, any foreign institution) operating in the US is whether their head office is too dominant and "too head office," meaning that they don't embrace enough of the local traditions and expectations of US markets and in particular, the local federal and state (such as New York State) regulatory and enforcement expectations.

My First BNP Compliance Town Hall

"Change is opportunity." That was the forward-looking message that I delivered on January 5, 2015 at the first compliance town hall[14] with my newly inherited New York-based corporate and institutional banking (CIB) compliance team. To reinforce the importance of this lesson, my regional CEO boss and a Paris-based global BNP compliance executive joined me. We reinforced that we'd succeed together as an institution, as a team, and as individuals.

A message that I'd regularly and thematically communicated at my compliance town halls and elsewhere, was that BNP's historic compliance issues were just that: in the past. As I liked to put it, "That was then, this is now, and this is where we're heading." My goal was to keep the team looking forward. For example, upon meeting my Bank of the West compliance teams in San Ramon, California in January 2016, my stated commitment to them and to the Americas compliance team was that I'd lead BNP Americas to a level we'd all be proud of. To achieve this, I sought their commitment, leadership, assistance, and willingness to believe in and execute our collective vision.

---

14   It's so important to stay connected with your team and town halls are excellent vehicles. I tried to hold them quarterly or semi-annually but wasn't always able to schedule them. We also tried to keep them relatively light, with some executive leaders speaking, guests or panelists who were entertaining, and cross-regional team competitions (whose winners would be honored during town halls). But we also covered very serious topics, in question-and-answer format. Entertainment ultimately, is not substance.

Another Rubik's Cube

With multiple financial products and services and millions of accounts and customers across the Americas and globally, BNP's inherent compliance & ethics risks, like those of other large banks, were quite complex. And with consumer and wealth management offices across the US through BNP's Bank of the West and First Hawaiian Bank subsidiaries, BNP's "Rubik's Cube" of cultural, strategic and compliance issues was incredibly complex.

Young's Vision helped navigate this complexity. For one thing, executing the Fed's SR 08-08 enables large, complex banking organizations such as BNP to successfully manage their "compliance risks that transcend business lines, legal entities, and jurisdictions of operation."[15] Young's Vision was intended to manage BNP Americas' risks to manageable, acceptable, and board of director-approved enterprise-wide levels.[16]

Esprit de Corps

I worked very closely and at times intensely with some of my compliance peers who comprised the Comex. The expectations we placed on the bank and on ourselves warranted it. Some of them became my very good friends because they truly "got it" with integrity. Two in particular come to mind. The head of the New York-based group financial security (GFS)-US team, and the Paris-based global CIB head of compliance. I met them both in 2015, shortly after they were appointed to those roles. To me, they epitomized why I enjoyed my time and succeeded with BNP.

The GFS-US head at the time was incredibly focused, yet like my group head of compliance boss, had an incredible sense of humor. To

---

15   Ibid.
16   These were concepts relatively new to (or at least accepted by) many banks even though the existence and expectation of enterprise-wide compliance has been in place since 1991 with DoJ Organizational Sentencing Guidelines, 1992 with the COSO Integrated Framework of Internal Controls, 2008 with the Fed SR 08-08. Perhaps it's because many banks continue to focus their compliance risk management framework over specific topics, e.g., anti-money laundering, sanctions, broker-dealer investor protection and market abuse, but not holistically on an enterprise-wide basis. Or because leadership at many of these firms believe they can afford to pay for breaches while generating multiples of the fine in profits.

be focused and humorous are tremendously important attributes in an effective CCO because you need both to keep your own teams productive while enjoying it. As we often reminded each other, "Life's too short to be too serious." He led his wonderful and productive GFS-US team with serious intent when it mattered most and was very credible with our regulators, but also kept all of us loose.

Similarly, the global CIB head of compliance was (and is) incredibly smart and was the perfect manifestation of pragmatism and adaptability. She and I worked well together, in part because so many of the CIB businesses crossed multiple jurisdictions and we were compelled to work well together. But we also developed a strong mutual respect, understanding that compliance & ethics officers aren't paid to be popular and sometimes have to "break some eggshells" (as another person I highly respect used to counsel me). She also understood the complexities of the US markets and regulatory expectations and therefore, was always open-minded about our people, process, and technology budget needs in the Americas. At the same time, she challenged us with focused and comprehensive questions about our CIB compliance budget and operating requests, and ultimately agreed with our proposals. She and her chief operating officer (COO) also worked very well with my compliance chief operating officer (COO) because she recognized and understood how operational a complex organization like many compliance's processes really are. And even though the global head of CIB compliance was relatively new to the compliance world, she embraced the concepts and expectations of independence quickly and fully.

Over time, and together with the leadership of my Americas compliance COO[17] and some of my other direct reports across CIB, Bank of

---

17   I applaud my compliance COO because he understood, supported, and helped execute Young's Vision of integrating the US Sentencing Guidelines and Fed SR 08-08 for BNP Americas compliance program. The compliance COO, like the CCO, is an underestimated but critically important function within compliance because they provide the behind-the-scenes project management, budgeting, and data governance integrity skills necessary to move our program forward including to produce the key compliance metrics and analytics for the board to hold management accountable.

the West, First Hawaiian, Canada, and our Latin American locations, we were able to build an Americas compliance & ethics team that was diverse and inclusive in every way. Most importantly, while we didn't always agree with one another, collectively we were a team and a family. One day, the global head of CIB compliance was visiting our New York office and she remarked to me that she noticed how hard the team worked but also saw how collaborative they were with each other. She called it an *esprit de corps* that she didn't always see at other CIB compliance units she'd encountered.

It was a very proud moment for me when she said that because it reminded me of the US Marine Corp's semper fi and esprit de corps credos, but most importantly, because it demonstrated the confidence our team had built in one another to achieve our collective strategy that would enable BNP to execute and sustain an effective compliance program. I applaud so many on my teams across the Americas, compliance colleagues globally, my two executive bosses, my Americas compliance COO, and my BNP business, infrastructure, and control leaders. They embraced our compliance vision, and helped enable a compliance culture and strategy to attain an effective Americas compliance program. I also applaud our human resources, marketing & communications colleagues across BNP—they were genuine, empathetic, and collaborative partners.

DoJ Evaluation of an Effective Compliance Program

The DoJ's June 2020 revisions to its "Evaluation of Corporate Compliance Programs"[18] outlined the way forward for BNP and other companies' compliance & ethics programs. It also points to what success needs to continuously look like to them in three simple and important questions (further detailed by 61 sub-questions) which all institutions are expected to answer in "open-book test" format:

---

18   U.S. Department of Justice - Criminal Division, "Evaluation of Corporate Compliance Programs," Updated June 2020 - https://www.justice.gov/criminal-fraud/page/file/937501/ download - last retrieved June 15, 2021

1. Is the corporation's compliance program well-designed?

2. Is the program being applied earnestly and in good faith? In other words, is the program adequately resourced and empowered to function effectively?

3. Does the corporation's compliance program work in practice?

Not the End

I retired from BNP on February 28, 2020, when I was at the top of my CCO game. The timing was right. To many, BNP Americas and I had achieved a level of sustainable compliance effectiveness after five very challenging yet fulfilling years. We'd also achieved a high level of success in terms of culture and strategy involving BNP's people and processes.[19]

My wife was thrilled that I was retiring and that I was planning to write this book. My BNP day typically would begin as my iPhone alarm would awaken me—it was sometimes still in my hand because I'd fallen asleep after emailing Paris or Asia at 3am. The workday would start from home at 5am or earlier (given the French time zone difference of six hours) and would often end 18 hours later. I'd come home by 7pm, eat dinner, catch up in my emails, and practically fall asleep sometimes by 8pm on the sofa. Wash, rinse, dry, and repeat. Weekends included. That's no way at all, to be a devoted, loving husband.

19 Sun, Mengqi. "BNP Paribas Revamps Compliance After Sanctions Violations Settlement." *The Wall Street Journal*, November 19, 2019. https://www.wsj.com/articles/bnp-paribas-revamps-compliance-after-sanctions-violations-settlement-11574204524. Retrieved June 27, 2021

Lessons Learned

- Go big, think big. If you want to succeed as a CCO, you must be fearless—of the person(s) sitting across from you, of the challenge at hand—no matter how massive, steep, or complex.

- Play chess. It's a great and stimulating game regardless of whether you're a CCO, CEO, or anything else. It teaches you about strategy, but also about life.

- Don't panic. Ever. You were brought in as or promoted to CCO for a reason and if you have the right support and team, they'll go above and beyond to achieve the collective objective: to manage the compliance & ethics risk to a residual level which is within the approved risk appetite of the firm and with a fully aligned corporate and compliance culture.

- Your corporate and compliance & ethics culture will make or break your firm's strategic success because if the culture is dysfunctional, fragmented, or plain rotten, your ethical culture and compliance success will crash and burn. That is *not* a sustainable and effective compliance program.

- Keep it simple with respect to reporting lines. Matrixed organizations and reporting are a reality but the clearer you are about whom you report to, the clearer the accountability.

- Culture and strategy go hand in hand, and to integrate the two, your executives will enable credibility for you (if they support you—and vice versa). Mutual support and respect are essential. That's because the right culture will align your teams (both compliance & ethics and 1st line business leaders) to partner and execute a safe and responsible growth strategy.

- Accountability and responsibility must go hand in hand and therefore must be documented through formal policies, terms of reference and approved by your board of directors and/or executive management, particularly with respect to executing effective compliance & ethics remediation and transformation.

- Compliance & ethics officers must never be complicit in illegal, immoral, and/or unethical acts of the businesses, especially if directed by executive management—even if it's the chief executive officer or chief operating officer. Semper Fi means "always faithful," but you must never be blinded by greed, fear, or misguided loyalty to the business. Otherwise, you're not independent.

- Listen, learn, and never give up. Executing Young's Vision, and, as you'll see, the Compliance Hexagon, can be your vision too (see chapter 2.8).

THIS IS THE END OF PART 1.

PLEASE TURN THE BOOK OVER FOR PART 2.

CPSIA information can be obtained
at www.ICGtesting.com
Printed in the USA
LVHW081214130821
695221LV00012B/1388

9 781737 402800

DECLARATION

★ *of* ★

INDEPENDENCE

How Independent Compliance Officers and Directors Can Hold Management More Accountable

PART 2
Duty of Care and Sustaining Effective Compliance Programs

Eric T. Young

Table of Contents

Introduction to Part 2 .... *1*

2.1 The Impact of Monopolies on Corporate Governance
and Compliance 4

2.2 Bribery, Corruption, Accounting Scandals,
and the Foreign Corrupt Practices Act *12*

2.3 Impact of Deregulation Across Banking
and Commerce over the 1980s *16*

2.4 Deregulation of the Telecom, Technology,
and Banking Industries and the Impact on Board
of Director Governance and Compliance *21*

2.5 The Dark Side of Deregulation, the Board of Directors,
and the Shift in the Compliance Paradigm *27*

2.6 Topical Compliance vs. a "New Hope" for Enterprise
Compliance Risk Management *35*

2.7 The Intersection of Board Governance, Financial Integrity,
and Effective Compliance *44*

2.8 "Young's Vision" for an Effective, *Enterprise*
Compliance Program *49*

2.9 The Accountability and Liability Pyramid (US vs. the World) *74*

2.10 Protecting and Enabling Our Salt-of-the-Earth
Whistleblowers... 87

2.11 Citigroup Case Study, and the 2020 COSO/
Enterprise Compliance Risk Framework 94

2.12 Introduction to the Compliance Hexagon and Honeycomb
and Six Recommendations for a "Clean" Organization,
Industry, and Infrastructure 106

2.13 Recommendation No. 1: Educate and Enlighten the Board 112

2.14 Recommendation No. 2: Hold Management
More Accountable and Culpable 119

2.15 Recommendation No. 3: Declare and Enable
Compliance Independence 125

2.16 Recommendation No. 4: Invest in Compliance Resources,
Including GRC and Artificial Intelligence Tools................. 130

2.17 Recommendation No. 5: Transparency
(Sunlight is the Best Disinfectant) 136

2.18 Recommendation No. 6: Protect and Enable Whistleblowers.... 143

2.19 The Way Forward: Cross Pollenating the Hexagon
into the "Compliance Honeycomb"© 150

Acknowledgements 160

About the Author: Eric T. Young 166

Introduction to Part 2

The thesis of this book is that a company's board of directors must strategically partner with the chief compliance officer (CCO) to hold management accountable and culpable. In part 1, we discussed the *what*—the factors and environment that, over the course of my 40-year career, led me to develop that thesis. In part 2, I'll explain *why*. And I'll use my Compliance Hexagon© to explain exactly *how* to "clean" an organization to sustainable health.

More management accountability is needed because, despite a well-intentioned US Department of Justice (DoJ) and its Organizational Sentencing Guidelines, the corporate C-suite and their businesses' misconduct, fraud, internal control weaknesses, and violations of law and regulation continue unabated, and the frequency, severity, and reputational damage to companies has grown exponentially at the viral speed of a Tweet. At the same time, there's an absence of meaningful penalties and jail time against the CEO and the C-suite. And deferred prosecution agreements (DPAs) that are meant to incentivize firms to comply don't really work. As a result, customers, markets, short-term shareholders, and long-term stakeholders including the environment, society, and employees ultimately suffer.

Worse yet, some firms are so large and so profitable, that violating laws, regulations, and codes of ethics/conduct are once again considered

either a "slap on the wrist" or the "cost of doing business." For some of these firms, a multi-billion-dollar fine isn't even a year's profit. These firms really don't care about being branded as "too big to jail" despite being "too big to manage." I'll provide examples throughout part 2.

In contrast, all board members and the CCO remain personally liable for management's actions or inactions, because the CEO and his or her management team aren't held accountable or considered culpable unless they directly engage in egregious misconduct or illegal activities. However, when something goes horribly wrong, shareholders (or other third parties) often sue the directors to hold them personally liable, and regulators and other government agencies too often sanction the chief compliance officer (CCO), attaching personal liability too.

A Note on Organization

I've organized part 2 into three main sections:

1. A chronological overview of how government-encouraged mo-nopolies and deregulation has slowly "evolved" compliance risk management, even though technology has "revolutionized" society and the way businesses operate.

2. An open question as to why companies and their management continuously fail to effectively prevent and detect fraud and vio-lations of law, regulations, and codes of conduct/ethics.

3. Six recommendations (my Compliance Hexagon©) that will act as an organizational and legislative roadmap to assist you in en-abling a more effective compliance & ethics program across all industries. They will provoke thought and controversy. This is especially important in light of the growing interdependence and cyber-risk interjection of our "essential critical" industries (explained through my broader Compliance Honeycomb©).

As a preview, my Compliance Hexagon comprises the following six recommendations:

1. Educate and enlighten the board of directors

2. Hold management more accountable and culpable

3. Declare and enable compliance independence

4. Invest in compliance resources (including budget, skills, artificial intelligence (AI), and GRC (governance, risk, and compliance)) tools

5. Transparency (Sunlight is the best disinfectant)

6. Shield and enable whistleblowers

Within each recommendation are detailed sub-recommendations that are designed to tangibly protect the board and empower the CCO, while making the CEO and management more accountable and culpable.

I'm confident that you'll find this part 2 both informative and provocative.

The Impact of Monopolies on Corporate Governance and Compliance

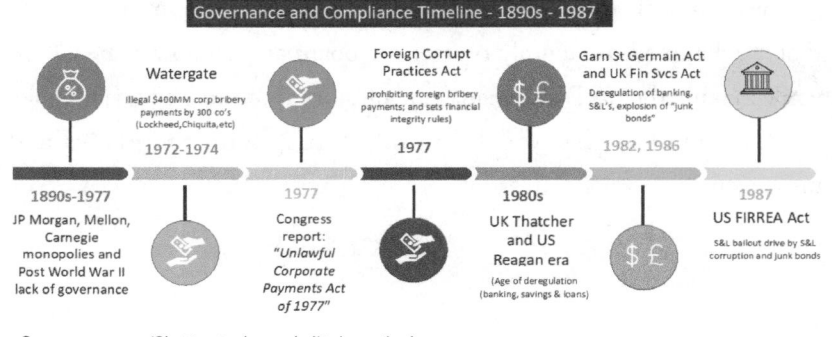

Source: seamuss/Shutterstock.com (edits by author)

> *"Thales... thus [took] an opportunity to secure a monopoly [as] a universal principle of business.... [H]ence even some states have recourse to this plan as a method of raising revenue when short of funds: they introduce a monopoly of marketable goods."*
>
> — A R I S T O T L E [1] *(edits and emphasis mine)*

The following chapters discuss the chronological history and double-edged sword of the partnership between private sector businesses and public sector government. This partnership, to a great extent, depends on the level of market power of very few

---

1   Aristotle, *Politics* (350 BC), Book 1, Section 1259a

institutions and whether enforcement actions deter executives' misconduct or enable them.

Governments protect the national security interests of their country. And in market economies, governments' economic role, broadly speaking, is to: (1) *protect the integrity* of markets, (2) *prevent harm* to consumers of products and services of businesses, and (3) *ensure the safety* of employees and the general public. Government fulfills these objectives through public policy, legislation, regulation, and enforcement. The relationship between government and business has always been delicate and dynamic and depends on the government in power as well as the state of the nation (war, economic prosperity, social unrest, public safety, etc.).

Good Monopolies

How governments regulate business monopolies is a good example of this delicate and dynamic relationship. Sometimes, governments encourage business monopolies to achieve critical mass, economies of scale, and structural efficiencies, such as when the nation is struggling, when an industry or technology is new, or to better compete against other nations/regions. In these situations, because the government's policy goal is to enable price efficiencies and avoid duplication and confusion to the markets and consumers, government-supported monopolies are considered "good monopolies."

The Potential Abuse of Business Monopolies

In other situations, the role of government, self-governance by a business (through its board of directors), and self-regulation (by a cooperative of industry participants as well as a company's CEO and functions such as finance and compliance) must be scrutinized to assess whether the public policy objectives of protecting markets, the public, and consumers are being preserved.

For example, barriers to competitive entry into a particular industry might be too high, or a business (whether in banking or commerce) may be

so dominant that it's able to dictate (abuse) pricing, engage in illegal reciprocity, or influence social thinking by filtering news or other information, to the detriment of markets or the consumer. To paraphrase the old saying, *information is power*.[2] Other examples of abuse by business—particularly monopolistic ones—and even governments themselves, include:

- Restricting supply (to drive prices up)

- Predatory pricing (undercutting competitors with the goal of driving them out of business)

- Price discrimination (where comparable goods or services are sold at different prices by the same company in different markets)

- Refusal to deal (e.g., boycotts) and/or exclusive dealing (vs. competitive bidding)

- Tying (commerce) and product bundling (requiring one service to get another or that groups of products be purchased together)

- Controlling (by withholding or flooding) the public's access to information in an attempt to shape public opinion (e.g., election outcomes, government policies, and in 2020–21, public safety policy over the treatment of and vaccination against the COVID-19 virus)

- Blacklisting individuals within a given industry (e.g., a known whistleblower).

These abuses are especially common during times of economic uncertainty or financial crisis, when companies are under tremendous pressure to achieve business and shareholder objectives to maximize profits and share price. Sometimes, plain greed drives businesses and individuals on behalf of themselves or the businesses they represent, to prioritize financial gain over

---

2   Francis Bacon (1597), later referenced by Thomas Jefferson, the primary author of the Declaration of Independence and third President of the United States, who wrote the phrase, "knowledge is power" in letters written in 1817, 1820, and 1821.

the social good. Economic pressures, greed, and even political viewpoints can all shape and influence the culture of a business and its employees.

Commingling Banking and Commerce

Historically, monopolies can't succeed unless they enjoy both financial (banking) and government support. Thus, it's important to understand the relationship and underlying risks of the role of finance (especially, banks and other financial institutions) vis-à-vis government and commerce.

The first two industrial revolutions (steam and textile production; and electricity and the mass production of steel and automobiles) were initially supported by the US government and resulted in the consolidation of commercial enterprises into industrial giants in the late 19th and early 20th centuries. The net result was the creation of immense monopolies and economic power in the hands of a few individuals. For example, John D. Rockefeller's Standard Oil Company, Andrew Carnegie's Steel Company, Andrew Mellon's Alcoa Aluminum Company, and John Duke's American Tobacco Company. John Pierpont Morgan, Sr. went a step further, owning JP Morgan & Company, which saved the US government financially during the depression of 1897 and panic of 1907, while also controlling major railroads and US Steel.[3]

Concentration of Power and Government's Intent to Promote Competition

The economic, financial, and commercial power held by these individuals and their monopolies ultimately led to populist unrest in the workplace, and, ultimately, to the US Congress enacting the Sherman Anti-Trust Act of 1890, which some believed was too sweeping and many saw as having stunted economic growth. At the same time, the Sherman Act was too

---

3   Luke, Jim. "JP Morgan: Competitive or Monopolistic?" https://econhist.econproph. net/2012/12/j-p-morgan-competitive-or-monopolistic/

vague, and did little to prevent the predatory pricing practices of the major monopolies, which continued to hurt consumers.

The 1914 Clayton Antitrust Act was a major improvement on the Sherman Act and took significant steps toward promoting the public good and protecting consumers by targeting price fixing, mergers and acquisitions, and other granular activities. Even today, the US Congress, the US Department of Justice (DoJ), and the US Federal Trade Commission (FTC) continue to invoke and increasingly enforce the Sherman and Clayton Acts on multiple fronts:

1. Price-fixing scandals by large US and foreign banks operating in the US during and after the financial crisis of 2007–2010 and the Wells Fargo fictitious account sales scandal continue to infuriate legislators and regulators, who (rightfully) questioned why none of the executives were criminally charged, and whether and why the big banks "are too big to jail." We'll discuss this in more detail in later chapters in part 2.

2. Bid rigging, price fixing, and collusion among at least ten executives and employees at major broiler chicken producers for conspiring to fix prices and rig bids from as early as 2012 until as recently as 2019.[4]

3. Some assert that the healthcare and life sciences industry is full of monopolies, ranging from hospital systems and medical equipment manufacturers to insurers and pharmacies.[5]

---

4   US Department of Justice Press Release. "Six Additional Individuals Indicted On Antitrust Charges In Ongoing Broiler Chicken Investigation," October 10, 2020 - https://www.justice.gov/opa/pr/six-additional-individuals-indicted-antitrust-charges-ongoing-broiler-chicken-investigation. Retrieved October 11, 2020
5   Baker, Sam. "The U.S. health care system is full of monopolies." https://www.axios.com/health-care-costs-monopolies-competition-hospitals-9839f396-c95d-4792-b106-663a727ef1f4.html. October 2019. Retrieved October 11, 2020; and Longman, Philip. "Time to Fight Health-Care Monopolization." *Democracy Journal*, Fall 2016. https://democracyjournal.org/magazine/42/time-to-fight-health-care-monopolization.

Big Tech

Continuing US Congressional and European Commission inquiries have challenged whether Big Tech including social media companies, such as Amazon, Google, Microsoft, Apple, Twitter, and Facebook exercise too much market power, as they are very much the beneficiaries and drivers of the third and fourth industrial revolutions (introduction and proliferation of computers, and automation and artificial intelligence, respectively). As the World Economic Forum predicts, "increased automation, artificial intelligence (AI), and continued technological disruption will fundamentally change the way we live, work, and relate to one another."[6] Indeed, yesterday's Morgan, Rockefeller, Carnegie, and Mellon are today's Bezos (Amazon), Zuckerberg (Facebook), Cook (Apple), Gates/Nadella (Microsoft), Dorsey (Twitter), and Schmidt/Pichai (Google). The challenge, however, is how the words of the US DoJ, and FTC and the European Union Competition bureau will translate into anti-trust enforcement.[7]

The Separation of Banking and Commerce (Then, Now, and Going Forward)

Governments have tried to regulate banks and their activities for more than 600 years. For example, back in 1374, "the Venetian senate prohibited bankers from dealing in copper, tin, iron, lead, saffron, and honey... [and] the intent was probably to keep banks from undertaking risky activities and monopolizing the specified commodities... In 1450, banks were restricted in extending credit to purchase silver, presumably to limit their lending for speculative purposes."[8]

---

6   World Economic Forum. "Bend, don't break: how to thrive in the Fourth Industrial Revolution." January 13, 2020. https://www.weforum.org/agenda/2020/01/the-fourth-industrial-revolution-is-changing-all-the-rules. Retrieved October 13, 2020
7   Hirsch, Michael. "Big Talk on Big Tech—but Little Action". https://foreignpolicy.com/2021/04/06/big-tech-regulation-facebook-google-amazon-us-eu/. Retrieved April 6, 2021.
8   Shull, Bernard. (Hunter College of the City University of New York Visiting Professor for the Office of the Comptroller of the Currency). "The Separation of Banking and Commerce in the United States: An Examination of Principal Issues." *Economics Working Paper,* 1999 – 1.

Banking laws in the United States through the 19th and early 20th centuries attempted to separate banking and commerce in order to prevent conflicts of interest and unfair competition. This culminated in the US Bank Holding Company Act of 1956 (and amended in 1970, to close loopholes that allowed many commercial firms to own banks). Unfortunately, many loopholes still remain and political pressure to deregulate banking and commerce have cyclically and progressively chipped away at this separation—and continue to do so today.

English-Speaking vs. Japanese and German Banking and Commerce Models

While the US and British models are comparable in terms of the separation of banking and commerce, Japan (Zaibatsu, then Keiretsu) and Germany (pure "universal banking") have long embraced a closer, interlocking directorate and cross-shareholding relationships, in which giant banks serve as financial hubs for their industrial affiliates.

From a governance and compliance perspective, history has shown that the Japanese and German models, whether legal or informal, represent "loose monopolies" and can compromise both the independent self-governance oversight of a non-executive board of directors, and the self-regulatory compliance & ethics effectiveness of the compliance function, because management is often left unchallenged by a board and less accountable for management's conduct and business decisions.

In the US, we're getting dangerously close to replicating the Japanese and German models. Banking and other regulators are now seeking to enable "fintechs," (companies like Personal Capital and Venmo), Big Tech (like Amazon, Apple, Google, Microsoft), and even social media companies to acquire and/or be licensed as limited chartered "banks." If that happens, then by definition, Amazon, Facebook, Apple, Microsoft, Twitter, and Google could, in the not-too-distant future, also be considered fintech companies and therefore potentially eligible to own a bank. The future is now.

The Post-World War II Business Boom and the Role of the Board of Directors (1945–1973)

With business in the United States booming after World War II, being a corporate board member in the United States and likely, elsewhere in the western world, was a relatively easy, cozy job. CEOs (predominately white and male, who often also served as the chairmen of the board of directors), sought and received approval for their friends, business buddies, or closest clients to join their boards. It was an interlocking directorate, the "good old boys club" we hear so much about and still encounter. Unfortunately, even today, surveys underscore the fact that "diversity, equity, and inclusion" efforts at many publicly traded corporations continue to be an aspirational goal rather than a reality, although some, tangible progress is being made.[9]

Pulling It All Together

Depending on its objectives, governments may either promote or restrict monopolies. A concentration in market power, pricing, and especially information can be abusive, and today's independent boards of directors need to be enlightened about the government's expectations and enforcement risks to the reputation of the company, and therefore, the board's fiduciary duty of loyalty. In addition, the board has a fiduciary "duty of care" to be well informed of—and actively demonstrate that it's carrying out—its control, compliance, and ethical responsibilities, including to effectively challenge the CEO and management. The chief compliance officer can assist and prompt the board in fulfilling these duties if he or she has the authority to educate and inform them regularly (see Recommendation #1).

---

9   Deloitte/*Wall Street Journal* Risk and Compliance Report. "Women and Minorities on Fortune 500 Boards: More Room to Grow." March 12, 2019. https://deloitte.wsj.com/riskandcompliance/2019/03/12/women-and-minorities-on-fortune-500-boards-more-room-to-grow. Retrieved October 24, 2020

Bribery, Corruption, Accounting Scandals, and the Foreign Corrupt Practices Act

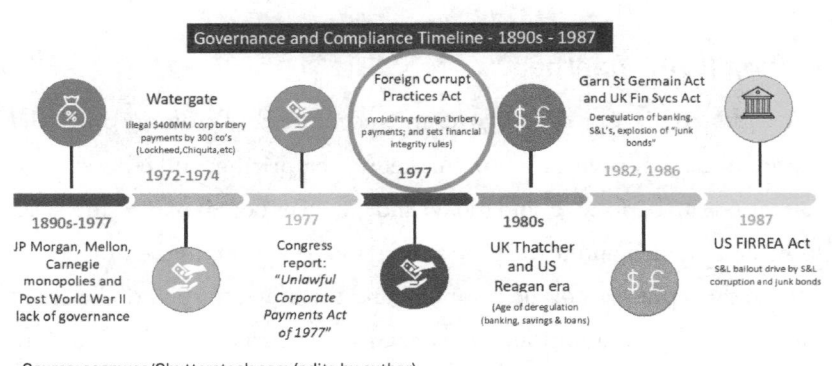

Source: seamuss/Shutterstock.com (edits by author)

Corporate Bribery and Corruption in the 1960s and 1970s

The phrase "corporate governance" didn't enter the business vocabulary until 1976 and 1977, when the Watergate Special Prosecution Force revealed to the US Securities and Exchange Commission (SEC) "th(at)… some companies… falsified entries in their own books and records."[1] This devastating investigation also noted that more than 400 U.S. companies admitted to making questionable or illegal

---

1   Baruch, Hurd. "The Foreign Corrupt Practices Act." *Harvard Business Review*, January 1979. https://hbr.org/1979/01/the-foreign-corrupt-practices-act. Retrieved October 24, 2020

payments in excess of $300 million to foreign government officials, politicians, and political parties.[2]

It was a true Oh My God moment for the SEC and the general public. Or was it? The Vietnam War and the Watergate scandal in the 1960s and 1970s jaded the American population about government and big business. Lockheed Corporation, Chiquita Brands, and others illegally paid off foreign government officials. For example, Lockheed bribed officials of friendly governments to guarantee contracts for military aircraft,[3] and hundreds of other companies hid similar payments by manipulating their accounting books and records. Illegal financial and accounting misconduct by management and boards was designed to increase shareholder return and to produce personal gain. Eventually, Lockheed's board and other corporate boards were sued by the US SEC for inadequately disclosing their past payment practices to investors and therefore not exercising their fiduciary duty of loyalty to their shareholders. Ultimately, these bribery, foreign corruption, and accounting scandals led to the landmark US Foreign Corrupt Practices Act (FCPA). They also led to multiple resignations of senior government officials in Japan, the Netherlands, and Italy, and charges filed against others.

US Foreign Corrupt Practices Act (FCPA)

In its 1977 report to the US Senate, the SEC requested[4] that the auditing profession, the New York Stock Exchange, and others study and

---

2   House of Representatives Conference Report. "Unlawful Corporate Payments Act of 1977" to amend HR 3815 to amend the Securities Exchange Act of 1934. September 28, 1977. https://www.justice.gov/sites/default/files/criminal-fraud/legacy/2010/04/11/houseprt-95-640.pdf. Retrieved October 24, 2020

3   Jones, William and Berry, John. "Lockheed Paid $38 Million in Bribes Abroad." *Washington Post*, May 27, 1977. https://www.washingtonpost.com/archive/business/1977/05/27/lockheed-paid-38-million-in-bribes-abroad/800c355c-ddc2-4145-b430-0ae24afd6648. Retrieved November 1, 2020

4   Committee on Banking, Housing and Urban Affairs, United States Senate. "Report of the Securities and Exchange Commission on Questionable and Illegal Corporate Payments and Practices." May 14, 1976. https://www.sec.gov/spotlight/fcpa/sec-report-questionable-illegal-corporate-payments-practices-1976.pdf. Retrieved October 24, 2020

recommend ways to "strengthen the ability and resolve of the boards of directors of our major corporations to act independently of operating management... to restore the integrity of the disclosure system, and to make corporate officials *more fully accountable to their boards of directors and shareholders.*"[5] (emphasis mine)

Signed into law by President Jimmy Carter in December 1977, the FCPA: (1) prohibits U.S. citizens and entities from bribing foreign government officials to benefit their business interests, and (2) requires all companies with securities listed on exchanges in the U.S. to meet certain accounting provisions, such as ensuring accurate and transparent financial records and maintaining internal accounting controls. This is just another way of saying that companies must have robust policies and procedures, training, awareness, and a set of accounting and other internal controls to monitor against illegal payments and a lack of financial and accounting integrity.

Since the entire concept (not to mention the actual role) of regulatory compliance was barely known in the corporate world of the mid 1970s, the FCPA was one of the first attempts to force management to ask itself:

- "Are we complying?" and

- "How can our board of directors and (the person to eventually be called the chief compliance officer) strategically partner to challenge and hold the CEO and management more accountable?"

Sadly, just two years after the FCPA became law, management experts still viewed the role of the board as minimal. As William Wommack put it in a 1979 article in *Harvard Business Review,* "[T]he board of directors' most important function is to approve or send back for amendment management's recommendations about the future direction of the corporation... *This function usually receives minimal attention.*"[6] (emphasis mine)

---

5   Ibid, Introduction, pages b and c.
6   Wommack, William. "The Board's Most Important Function." *Harvard Business Review*, September, 1979

Unfortunately, as you'll read in the following chapters, companies around the world still bribe foreign government officials, act corruptly, and manipulate their financial records. Towards the end of this part of the book, I'll present six recommendations that are designed to correct inadequacies and inefficiencies in the system.

Impact of Deregulation Across Banking and Commerce over the 1980s

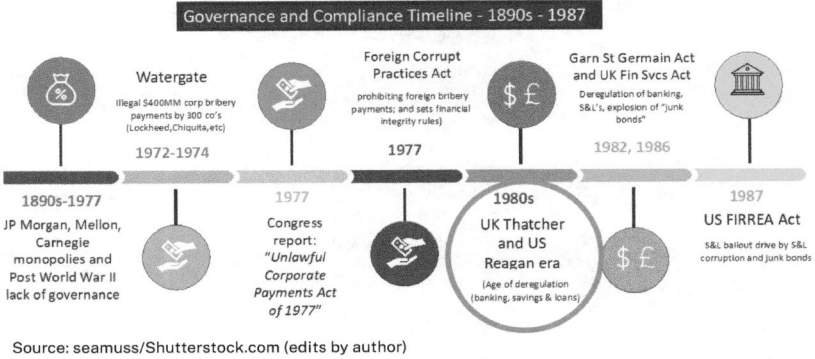

Source: seamuss/Shutterstock.com (edits by author)

I n the previous chapter, I highlighted the Foreign Corrupt Practices Act (FCPA), which prohibits illegal payments to facilitate non-US bribery and corruption *and* requires companies to demonstrate reasonable assurance that their system of internal accounting controls produced financial-statement integrity.

In this chapter, I'll explore: 1) why accounting scandals, typically intended to mask fraud, misconduct, and violations of law and regulation, continue despite the FCPA's financial integrity requirements; (2) how deregulation fostered an increase in competition laced with "occupational fraud"; and (3) why and how an effective enterprise compliance

risk-management program can help protect the board of directors through the monitoring, prevention, and detection of fraudulent behavior, legal and regulatory violations, and reputational damage to the company and you, as a board member or compliance & ethics officer.

Limitations of the FCPA's Accounting Provisions

The FCPA's accounting provisions remain effective in successfully prosecuting US and foreign corporations and individuals. However, major accounting scandals continue to plague us even today. Will they continue to prevail going forward, unless dramatic legislative and industry action is taken? (Yes.)

Macroeconomic Reasons

The 1970s were marked by global hyperinflation, driven mainly by the major oil price hikes of the Organization of the Petroleum Exporting Countries (OPEC). Despite the political risk, President Carter and Federal Reserve Chairman Paul Volcker drove a draconian Fed monetary policy that significantly raised interest rates, resulting in a deep economic recession that lasted through late 1982. This put tremendous pressure on businesses to meet financial earnings and share price projections, let alone survive. With the COVID-19 pandemic and global financial consequences over 2020 and 2021, financial earnings and mere survival again have put tremendous pressure on businesses of all sizes.

Political and Deregulatory Reasons (1980s–early 2000s)

In 1980, President Carter lost the presidency to conservative Republican Ronald Reagan, who ushered in a wave of deregulatory, market-driven economic policies (Reaganomics) that were designed to jump-start business recovery nationally and internationally. The UK's Margaret Thatcher was Reagan's key counterpart economically, and in 1979, began executing her own deregulatory, monetarist, and privatization policies. The two leaders

enabled a number of deregulatory and economic success stories, including the following:

- The US's Depository Institutions Deregulation and Monetary Control Act of 1980 and the Garn-St. Germain Depository Institutions Act of 1982 loosened restrictions on bank interest rates and raised limits on commercial lending to allow savings and loan institutions to engage in banking activities.

- The UK's Financial Services Act of 1986 deregulated financial services broadly, empowering a wider range of entities to provide investment businesses, as long as those entities were licensed as "fit and proper."

- On the commercial side, energy, transportation, communications, aviation, shipping, and many other industries thrived through the 1980s and 1990s, enjoying less regulation or streamlined regulatory costs and burdens.

Regional Competition Reasons

The European Union was born as a result of multiple treaties, including the Treaty of Rome (1957–1992) and the Maastricht Treaty (1992–2007), culminating in lower pan-European trade and business-entry barriers, and, in 2002, a common European currency (the Euro).[1]

The Downside of Deregulation in the 1980s

The previously mentioned Garn-St. Germain Act deregulated savings and loans institutions, (aka thrifts or S&Ls), which allowed them to take taxpayer funded (FDIC-insured) deposits and make more commercial and real estate loans. While technically banks, S&Ls enjoyed much less regulatory scrutiny. As a result, they grew very aggressively, made speculative real estate loans, and competed fiercely to generate tremendous profits.

1   https://europa.eu/european-union/about-eu/history_en

Deregulation also spawned a market for high-yield corporate (junk) bonds that were peddled by overly-willing-to-underwrite-and-sell investment banks such as Drexel Burnham Lambert.[2] Those same junk bonds enabled S&Ls to fuel their growth by overleveraging themselves. Without close government scrutiny or adequate self-governance, a number of S&L CEOs were ultimately caught in scandals involving political corruption, embezzlement, and/or fraud.[3]

Nearly a third of the 3,000+ S&L institutions failed, in large part because of deregulation. The net result was the enactment in 1989 of the Financial Institutions Reform, Recovery, and Enforcement Act (FIRREA), which re-regulated thrift institutions and imposed strict requirements on real estate appraisals (appraisers were found to have been party to many of the thrifts' frauds). Since then, junk bonds have been major contributors to two other financial crises: the dotcom bubble of the early 2000s, and the 2008 financial crisis.[4]

Control Fraud as a Weapon to Commit Fraud

Former bank regulator William Black coined the term "control fraud,"[5] to describe a situation where a business or national executive uses the entity he or she controls as a weapon to commit fraud. Black cited deregulation "as (a) control fraud (which) can occur in waves created by poorly designed deregulation that creates a criminogenic environment."[6]

---

2   Drexel itself ultimately went bankrupt due to multiple illegal acts, including insider trading and stock manipulation, as well as the threat of being charged under the powerful Racketeer Influenced and Corrupt Organizations (RICO) Act. Drexel was potentially liable under the doctrine of *respondeat superior*, which holds that companies are responsible for employee's crimes. See *The Predators' Ball: The Inside Story of Drexel Burnham and the Rise of the Junk Bond Raiders*, by Connie Bruck.
3   See for example, the "Keating 5" scandal.
4   Jark, Daniel. "The History of High-Yield Bond Meltdowns," *Investopedia*, July 6, 2016. https://www.investopedia.com/articles/investing/022616/history-high-yield-bond-meltdowns.asp. Retrieved October 26, 2020
5   Black, William K. (2005). *The Best Way to Rob a Bank Is to Own One*. University of Texas Press.
6   Ibid.

Pulling It All Together

The 1980s witnessed a period of market deregulation and decreased government intervention, in which self-governance and self-regulation prevailed once again. But without effective checks and balances over management's conduct, abuse of power, personal greed, and the junk-bond-fueled over-leveraging of balance sheets by savings and loan institutions, the result was multiple business failures, fraud, and misconduct. A more effective corporate board of directors and an empowered C&E department would have helped place checks and balances against management misconduct and "control fraud."

As we'll see in the next chapter, the excesses of the 1980s that led to fraud and malfeasance also brought a return to regulation (including landmark steps by the US Department of Justice to require new enterprise-wide compliance and internal control standards) and court cases that defined the fiduciary duty of loyalty expectations of a board of directors. We'll also see that, despite stiffer monetary penalties for violation of laws and regulations, deregulation came back with a vengeance in the 1990s and led to another spate of accounting scandals and corporate fraud in the 2000s.

Deregulation of the Telecom, Technology, and Banking Industries and the Impact on Board of Director Governance and Compliance

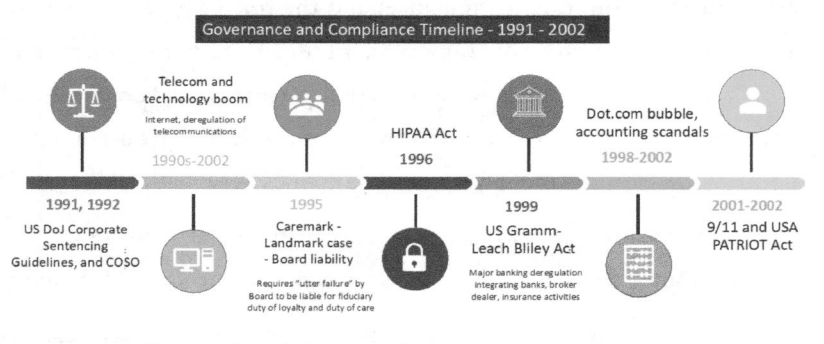

Source: seamuss/Shutterstock.com (edits by author)

I n the previous chapter, we discussed how the deregulation of the US savings and loan (S&L) industry and other industries fueled by high-yield junk bonds and personal and corporate greed through the 1980s led to corporate fraud, S&L failures, and massive government bailouts. Unfortunately, corporate management and board members didn't learn much from the mistakes of deregulation. In this chapter, we'll explore how even more deregulation in the 1990s led to accounting scandals and corporate fraud in the early 2000s, despite:

- The accounting provisions of the US Foreign Corrupt Practices Act of 1977

- Enactment of tougher penalties against banks due to the Financial Institutions Reform, Recovery and Enforcement Act of 1987 and other US banking laws, including the FDIC Improvement Act of 1991 (FDICIA).

FDIC Improvement Act: Convergence of Financial Accounting, Compliance, and Board of Director Audit Committee Governance

The US FDIC Improvement Act of 1991 (FDICIA) was one of the first acknowledgments that the government considered that internal controls over financial accounting, compliance, and the role of board of director audit committees were interconnected. FDICIA required greater (and tougher) supervision of foreign banks operating in the United States, as well as mandated certifications by all insured banks' CEO, chief accountant, and in some cases, the independent accountant, of:

- Early identification of problems in financial management at insured depository institutions through annual independent audits

- Assessments of the effectiveness of internal control over financial reporting

- Compliance with designated laws and regulations

- Requirements for audit committees at these insured depository institutions.[1]

---

1   US Congress. FDIC Improvement Act, PUBLIC LAW 102-242—DEC. 19, 1991 105 STAT. 2243. https://www.govinfo.gov/content/pkg/STATUTE-105/pdf/STATUTE-105-Pg2236.pdf; and Federal Deposit Insurance Corporation, "Independent Audits and Reporting Requirements," Amendments to Title 12, Code of Federal Regulations, Part 363, Final Rule, as amended November 8, 2005. Retrieved November 1, 2020.

I'll discuss FDICIA in greater detail later. But for now, let's take a look at how the birth of the internet, the growing monopolistic power of Big Tech, and the role of investment banks fueled the deregulatory environment of the 1990s.

Structural and Technological Deregulation in the United States

The US Telecommunications Act of 1996 (Telecom Act) deregulated the telephone industry by breaking up the "Ma Bell" telephone monopoly, with the goal of inviting competition and driving down customer pricing. The Telecom Act also fueled fierce competition among cable; media; and new telecom companies such as WorldCom, Global Crossing, America Online, and others; while eBay, Amazon, Microsoft, Google, Apple were also competing to pave, build, and drive fast along the information highway. Thus, we moved from the third industrial revolution (computers) to the fourth (the internet, artificial intelligence, and the continued technological disruption on how we live, work, and relate to one another). Perhaps the best example of this is Apple's iPhone, with its open apps platform that completely disrupted the telephone industry and revolutionized how and why people live through apps and the 'net).[2]

The Role of the Investment Bankers and the Dotcom Bubble

The Telecom Act, together with capital gains tax relief in 1997, fueled a boom in dotcom start-ups. With the information age taking off like a rocket, investment banks were enthusiastically ready to launch initial public offerings (IPOs) and were once again underwriting junk bonds to fuel those start-ups.

With the exception of the original Ma Bell, the US Federal Communications Commission (FCC) took a light-touch approach to auditing

---

2   Peccarelli, Brian. "Bend, don't break: how to thrive in the Fourth Industrial Revolution," World Economic Forum, January 13, 2020.- https://www.weforum.org/agenda/2020/01/the-fourth-industrial-revolution-is-changing-all-the-rules. Retrieved October 24, 2020

and enforcing the Telecom Act, leaving the start-ups and their equally ambitious competitors to self-regulate with little or no board-of-director (or compliance) oversight. Ultimately, many investment banks were found to have violated conflict of interest rules because their research analysts were promoting IPO and other stocks led by their M&A and equity underwriting capital markets bankers.[3]

Banks Unleashed: The Gramm-Leach-Bliley Act of 1999

As I described in part 1, back in the 1980s, when I was starting my career as a supervisory analyst with the Fed, Citibank and its parent bank holding company, Citicorp, were pushing the regulatory envelope to achieve their strategic business expansion objectives. That same attitude was alive and well nearly 20 years later, when, in 1998, Citicorp merged with a giant insurance company, The Travelers Group, even though existing banking law actually prohibited the joint ownership of a commercial bank (Citibank) with an investment bank/broker-dealer (Smith Barney, which Travelers owned), and/or an insurance company. The newly combined Citigroup was granted a one-year waiver from the prohibited separation expressed in the Glass-Steagall Act of 1934 which had been in place for over 50 years. Both Citi and Travelers gambled that the deregulatory environment would prompt legislative and regulatory changes to eliminate the Glass-Steagall separation.

And that's precisely what happened a year later, when the US Congress enacted the Gramm-Leach-Bliley Act (GLBA), otherwise known as the Financial Services Modernization Act. This Act also allowed officers and directors to "interlock" previously prohibited affiliated banking, broker-dealer, and insurance companies to form financial "supermarkets" or "universal banks" comparable to their counterparts in Germany (e.g., Deutsche Bank), Japan (e.g., Dai Ichi Kangyo Bank), Switzerland (UBS), or the United Kingdom (HSBC).

---

3   See for example, SEC vs. Credit Suisse First Boston LLC fka Credit Suisse First Boston Corporation, April 28, 2003. https://www.sec.gov/litigation/complaints/comp18110.htm. Retrieved October 25, 2020

The "Irrational Exuberance" of the 1990s

"Irrational exuberance is the psychological basis of a speculative bubble... [It's defined] as a situation in which news of price increases spurs investor enthusiasm... [then] spreads by psychological contagion... [and] amplifying stories that might justify the price increases... [attracts more] investors who, despite doubts about the real value of an investment, are drawn to it partly by envy of others' successes and partly through a gambler's excitement."[4] Or, as then-Federal Reserve Chairman Alan Greenspan put it, "... do we know when irrational exuberance has unduly escalated asset values..."?[5]

Lemmings, anyone?

Pulling It All Together

The deregulatory environment of the 1970s, '80s, and '90s paved the way for greater competition spurred by the US government in the US transportation, energy, telecommunications, technology, and financial services industries. It also opened the door to new entrants and new products, which fueled market enthusiasm and "irrational exuberance." Along the way, competition became more fierce, dark clouds were gathering around corporate culture as accounting irregularities created false profits, and there was little or no challenge by boards of directors and/or compliance to the behavior, activity, or accountability of CEOs' or CFOs' actions.

Chief Financial Officers: Transforming from "Bean Counters" to Profit Makers

The role of the CFO evolved between the 1980s and 1990s. Previously viewed as "bean counters," chief accountants or corporate controllers traditionally maintained a company's accounting books and records. However,

---

4   Wikipedia: "Irrational Exuberance," citing Schiller, Robert J. *Irrational Exuberance*. Princeton University Press. (2000).
5   Remarks by Greenspan, Alan at the Annual Dinner and Francis Boyer Lecture of The American Enterprise Institute for Public Policy Research, Washington, D.C., December 5, 1996. https://www.federalreserve.gov/boarddocs/speeches/1996/19961205.htm. Retrieved October 25, 2020

as businesses sought to expand aggressively during these deregulatory times, these controllers morphed into CFOs, and positioned themselves to CEOs as more strategically focused, creative, and value-added business partners. No longer a second line of defense and no longer fulfilling a control function as gatekeepers of financial integrity, some CFOs instead became the first line of aggressive accounting practices, despite the FCPA's accounting provisions, generally accepted accounting principles, and securities law disclosure rules. We'll take a closer look at this CFO evolution in our next chapter.

A Similar (or Vestigial) Path for Chief Compliance Officers?

Today, some compliance & ethics officers have sought to transform themselves in much the same way as the short-term-profit-maximizing CFOs did, seeking to become more "creative and value-added business partners." Sadly, we've seen a trend of compliance & ethics officers either compromising their ethical integrity or being weakened through significant budget cuts (often at the hands of aggressive CFOs), which effectively have made compliance & ethics officers (and the whole C&E function) vestigial.

The Dark Side of Deregulation, the Board of Directors, and the Shift in the Compliance Paradigm

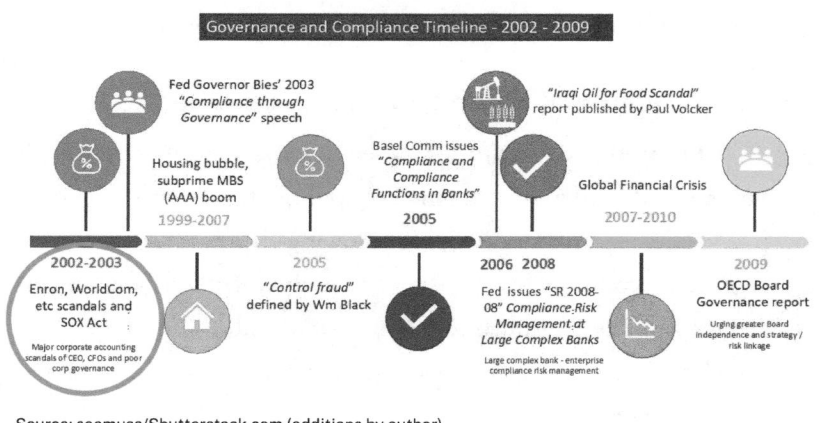

Source: seamuss/Shutterstock.com (additions by author)

Deregulation Done Right... and Wrong

Done right, deregulation provides tremendous strategic and economic value: it sparks innovation, greater competition (in the short run), lowers prices (until monopolies emerge), and enables technological disruption. All of these things can benefit consumers—and society at large—by creating new and better ways of living and working. That's the good news.

The bad news is that deregulation also puts new pressure on companies to produce and to perform in ways that may blur (or obliterate) the line between good behavior and bad. Whenever there's competition, there'll be winners—and losers. Deregulation magnifies and intensifies competition, at least initially until, eventually, those that succeed swallow up those that fail. Big fish eats small fish, then gets eaten by an even bigger fish, and so on… And desperation in these smaller (or even big but unprofitable) fish breeds desperate acts.

And remember, deregulation also means less (if any) government oversight and regulatory scrutiny, both of which are supposed to keep companies on the straight and narrow. Instead, the government allows companies to self-govern and self-regulate. That approach, as we've seen (and will discuss more below) doesn't always work out well.

Personal Liability of Enron and WorldCom Directors

"The Enron Board of Directors failed to safeguard Enron share-holders and contributed to the collapse of the seventh largest public company in the (US), by allowing Enron to engage in high-risk accounting [and]… extensive undisclosed off-the-books activities…. The Board witnessed numerous indications of ques-tionable practices by Enron management over… years but chose to ignore them."[1]

The intersection of individuals giving in to the dark side of corporate and human behavior, and the government's light touch to supervision and enforcement is precisely where board members and compliance & ethics (C&E) officers may become vulnerable or exposed to personal liability based on others' (most notably, management's) actions or inactions. For

---

1   Permanent Subcommittee on Investigations of the Committee on Governmental Affairs; United States Senate. "The Role of the Board of Directors in Enron's Collapse." July 8, 2002. https://www.govinfo.gov/content/pkg/CPRT-107SPRT80393/pdf/CPRT-107SPRT80393.pdf. Retrieved October 24, 2020

example, here's how the *Los Angeles Times* described the spectacular crash and burn of Enron and WorldCom—and their directors:

> "Ten former Enron Corp. directors will pony up *$13 million out of their own pockets* to help settle a shareholder lawsuit... The $168-million deal by the former Enron directors was announced two days after 10 former board members of WorldCom Inc. (now MCI Inc.) agreed to *personally pay $18 million* to settle an investor lawsuit triggered by (WorldCom's) collapse... [T]he settlements put corporate directors on notice that they had '*an affirmative obligation to investigate*' when allegations of corporate misdeeds are brought to their attention... The settlement also sends a signal to corporate directors that they cannot just accept the privilege and benefits of being on a board without also accepting the responsibilities."[2] (emphasis mine)

WorldCom: A Dark Storm (1990s–2002)

WorldCom, through multiple acquisitions in the 1990s, had taken the telecom industry by storm. Recognizing that telecom profits were thinly margined, CEO Bernie Ebbers led WorldCom into internet and data communications, where it soon was handling 50 percent of all United States internet traffic and 50 percent of all e-mails worldwide. By 2001, WorldCom owned a third of all data cables in the United States, and from 1998 to 2002, they were the second-largest long-distance carrier.[3]

---

2   Lifsher, Marc. "10 Enron Ex-Directors to Pay $13 Million to Settle Suit by UC and Other Investors." *Los Angeles Times*, January 8, 2005. https://www.latimes.com/archives/la-xpm-2005-jan-08-fi-enron8-story.html. Retrieved October 25, 2020
3   Background based on Leann Obringer's "*How Cooking the Books Works,*" https://money. howstuffworks.com/cooking-books9.htm. Retrieved October 25, 2020

The Bubble Bursts

A series of events led to the internet bubble bursting and left telecom and internet companies scrambling. Fed Chairman Alan Greenspan announced in February 2000 an intent to aggressively raise interest rates. That immediately created major equity-market volatility, particularly in tech stocks, which were highly leveraged. At the same time, the Japanese economy was re-entering a major recession; Yahoo! and eBay abandoned a planned merger, which sent markets reeling further; and Microsoft[4] was found to have violated the Sherman anti-trust laws as a monopoly because it had been "tying" its Internet Explorer browser to its Windows operating system, thus making it extremely difficult for Windows purchasers to use any other browser.

In the meantime, companies (including WorldCom) scrambled to survive by allegedly cooking their books:

> "In 1999, revenue growth slowed and the stock price began falling. WorldCom's expenses as a percentage of its total revenue increased because the growth rate of its earnings dropped... In 2000, WorldCom began *classifying operating expenses as long-term capital investments. Hiding these expenses* in this way gave them another $3.85 billion. These newly classified assets were expenses that WorldCom paid to lease phone network lines from other companies to access their networks. They also added a journal entry for $500 million in computer expenses but *supporting documents for the expenses were never found.* These changes *turned WorldCom's losses into profits* to the tune of $1.38 billion in 2001. It also made WorldCom's assets appear more valuable."[5] (emphasis mine)

---

4   One of the first (of likely, many), anti-trust cases against the Big Tech companies going forward in the Unites States and Europe.
5   op cit, Leann Obringer.

Meanwhile, Back at Enron… The Perfect Storm: An Uninformed Board and the Absence of Enterprise Compliance Risk Management

Plain and simple, the meteoric rise and fall of Enron, from small utility to major energy markets and trading firm, was the result of a series of complex derivatives transactions (special-purpose vehicles meant to hide losses, mask expenses, and enable personal gain) and fraudulent activities by a number of executives, including the CFO. It truly was a perfect storm, because, despite accounting rules:

- Financial entries are based on generally accepted accounting principles, rather than prescriptive law or regulation.

- US generally accepted accounting principles at the time were flawed, thus enabling the CFO and his team to manipulate undefined, gray areas of accounting, which, in turn justified entries that had no economic purpose or were opaque in complexity. This enabled the CFO to mislead shareholders and the company's uninformed board of directors.

- The vast network of Enron's legal entities and complex transactions masked the enterprise-wide risks, including reputational and compliance risks.

- Many banks, including Citibank, JP Morgan, Merrill Lynch, and Canadian bank CIBC, were prosecuted for allegedly aiding and abetting (and not just enabling) Enron's fraud.

- CIBC, in particular, paid a very high price. Despite extensive efforts to build an effective risk and compliance infrastructure, [6, 7] the bank's reputation suffered and its global litigation settlement with plaintiffs of $2.4 billion (on top of the previous year's

6   Baily, Jeff. "CIBC pays to Settle Enron Case." *New York Times,* August 8, 2005. https://www.nytimes.com/2005/08/03/business/worldbusiness/cibc-pays-to-settle-enron-case.html.
7   Bagnell, Paul. "Why History Hasn't been Kind to CIBC." *BNN Bloomberg*, June 29, 2016. https://www.bnnbloomberg.ca/why-history-hasn-t-been-kind-to-cibc-s-forays-in-the-u-s-1.517734.

$80 million regulatory fine) was at the time one of the largest ever for a financial institution. By comparison, the University of California reported that Citi and JP Morgan paid about $2.2 billion each. However, comparatively speaking, Citi's and JP Morgan's capital (and therefore, financial cushion) were multiples of CIBC's.

The WorldCom and Enron Whistleblowers

The most troubling things about the WorldCom and Enron cases (and many others since then) were (and still are) the absence of proactive corporate governance and risk oversight by the board of directors, and the tremendous influence of WorldCom's and Enron's chief financial officers. More broadly, directors and others should have been asking pointed questions about the influence that CFOs had (and continue to have) over the CEOs and the audit committees they're supposed to serve.

As Sherron Watkins, Enron's former VP of Development put it during her Congressional testimony about her blowing the whistle on Enron, "I do believe that they mis-served Mr. Lay, the board, Enron, and its shareholders."[8] Ms. Watkins also testified that she had directly informed Mr. Lay of her concerns and had urged him to disclose the company's losses. Ultimately, little was done to disclose Enron's financial wrongdoings in a timely manner.

In the case of WorldCom, Cynthia Cooper and her internal audit team were simply doing their jobs when they discovered and investigated accounting irregularities. Cooper escalated her concerns to the chair of WorldCom's audit committee, who advised Cooper to inform WorldCom's external auditor, which she did. Unfortunately, the chair chose to delay

---

8   Stout, David with Day, Sherri, "*Enron Official Says She Warned Lay About Financial Irregularities.*" *The New York Times*, February 14, 2002.- https://www.nytimes.com/2002/02/14/business/enron-official-says-she-warned-lay-about-financial-irregularities.html. Retrieved December 8, 2020

informing the full audit committee and WorldCom's board of directors until later in the year.[9]

Pulling It All Together

Over my forty-year career in the compliance & ethics field, I've experienced the cyclical (and admittedly, cynical) nature of deregulation. As companies thrive and innovate under less-burdensome regulation and government supervision, they feel (and become) freer to self-regulate their activities. Too often, that freedom leads some CEOs, CFOs, and others to commit fraud, cook the books, or engage in other types of illegal or unethical misconduct. The natural and inevitable result is a return to legislation that re-regulates with even more government scrutiny.

I strongly believe that, sadly, people are (or can become) flawed and that many will commit illegal and unethical acts to enrich themselves and/or do desperate things when confronting perceived or real, desperate circumstances. But I also believe that major scandals like Enron and WorldCom, and hundreds if not thousands of known (and not-yet-known) financial scandals that have happened since then could have been avoided—and could be avoided in the future, if:

- Boards of directors were educated and enlightened about, among other things, the US Department of Justice Corporate Sentencing Guidelines and the importance of an enterprise-wide compliance risk management program (see Recommendation #1).

- Board members and the CCO had the knowledge, authority, and skill sets necessary to strategically partner and hold CEOs and their C-suite and management teams accountable and culpable for their misconduct and unethical behavior (see Recommendation #2).

---

9   Cooper, Cynthia (April 15, 2009). *Extraordinary Circumstances: The Journey of a Corporate Whistleblower.* Hoboken, New Jersey: John Wiley & Sons. ISBN 978-0-470-12429-1.

- The chief compliance officer (CCO) reported directly to the board's audit, risk, or compliance committee so that compliance (and the board itself) could "declare independence" from an unaccountable CEO and management team (see Recommendation #3).

- Whistleblowers were empowered to raise integrity issues without fear of retaliation, and in partnership with the compliance & ethics function and the board of directors (see Recommendation #6). Unfortunately, as we'll see in chapter 2.8, that is far from reality.

Topical Compliance vs. a "New Hope" for Enterprise Compliance Risk Management

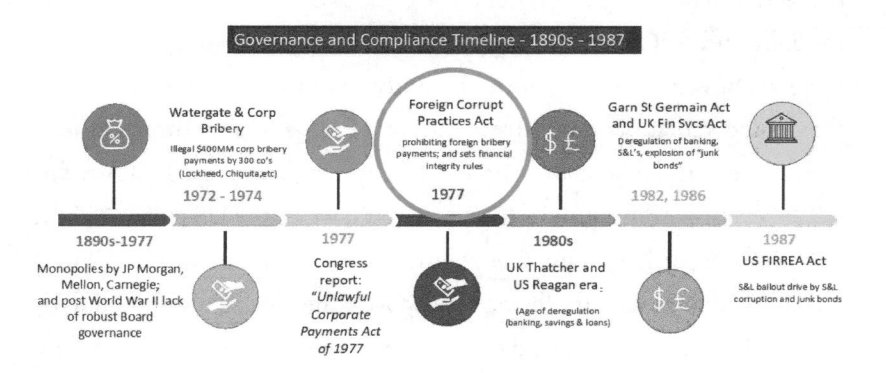

Governance and Compliance Timeline - 1890s - 1987

Watergate & Corp Bribery
Illegal $400MM corp bribery payments by 300 co's (Lockheed, Chiquita,etc)
1972 - 1974

Foreign Corrupt Practices Act
prohibiting foreign bribery payments; and sets financial integrity rules
1977

Garn St Germain Act and UK Fin Svcs Act
Deregulation of banking, S&L's, explosion of "junk bonds"
1982, 1986

1890s-1977
Monopolies by JP Morgan, Mellon, Carnegie; and post World War II lack of robust Board governance

1977
Congress report: "Unlawful Corporate Payments Act of 1977"

1980s
UK Thatcher and US Reagan era.
(Age of deregulation (banking, savings & loans)

1987
US FIRREA Act
S&L bailout drive by S&L corruption and junk bonds

Source: seamuss/Shutterstock.com (edits by author)

A New Hope: The FCPA (1977) and the 1997 OECD Global Prohibitions against Bribery and Corruption

The very first *Star Wars* movie was released in May 1977, and was subtitled: *Episode IV: A New Hope*. Just a few months later, in December 1977, the Foreign Corrupt Practices Act (FCPA) was enacted and, like *Star Wars*, promised hope against the "dark side" of corporate misconduct, unethical behavior, financial smoke and mirrors, and corruption. The FCPA prohibited direct or indirect payments by

US companies to corrupt foreign government officials, especially if done through the manipulation of the company's financial books and records. See timeline, above.

Unfortunately, many US executives feared that the FCPA would also place US companies at a competitive disadvantage vis-à-vis their foreign competitors who weren't subject to the Act. In effect, non-US companies could continue to bribe while their US counterparts could not, at least on paper.

The OECD Prohibits Bribery and Corruption Globally (1997)

Throughout the US presidential administrations of Reagan, George H.W. Bush, and Bill Clinton of the 1980s and 1990s, the FCPA was largely ineffective in deterring bribery and corruption. Critics questioned whether the DoJ and SEC were taking a light-touch approach to enforcement, thereby allowing US companies to continue to bribe foreign officials so they could remain competitive with their foreign competitors. In fact, enforcement to prevent bribery and corruption under the FCPA didn't produce more meaningful results until 1997, when the US persuaded the Organization of Economic Cooperation and Development (OECD) to publish global guidelines for non-US governments that would similarly criminalize illegal bribery and corruption payments. See timeline, below.

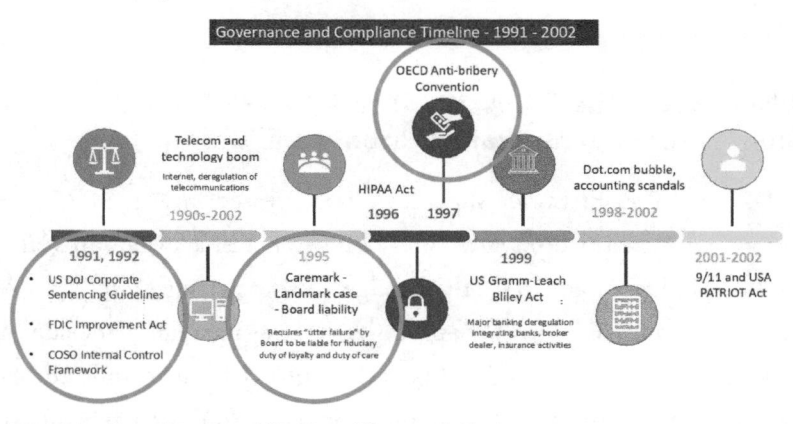

Enterprise Compliance and the Board/Caremark Test

The Flaws of Siloed, "Topical" Compliance and the Birth of the DoJ Organizational (Corporate) Sentencing Guidelines

Another reason why companies, (regardless of industry) were ineffective to stem the flow of bribes, corruption, money laundering, fraud, and other financial crimes from 1970 through the early 1990s was that they didn't take an *enterprise-wide* approach to managing their risks (nor were they required to do so at the time—or sanctioned for the absence if they didn't). Managing compliance risks on a topic-by-topic basis (what I call "topical compliance") is inefficient and ultimately ineffective because it reactively addresses only specific laws rather than proactively addresses the entire enterprise.

For example, a company may be a leader in managing its bribery and corruption or anti-money laundering risks in one region (say Latin America or the Middle East) but may have numerous blind spots in another region. That leaves them vulnerable to a corrupt government or client with tentacles embedded within the company's affiliates and agents located across the globe. It's a classic case of the right hand (one division or business or manager) not knowing what the left hand (a different division or business or manager) is doing–particularly if the right hand is competing against the left for finite budget and resources. This often happens because many firms silo their divisions or regions, decentralizing their budgets and reporting lines and have no sense of cohesive compliance & ethics independence or a firm-wide corporate culture.

Firms that manage compliance topically may also have major blind spots in their ability to address other compliance risks beyond their silo, including privacy, employee safety, and vendor risk management. These compliance risks remain inherently and likely, residually high today. I'll address this in more detail in later chapters and highlight enterprise-wide compliance risk management programs and the increased expansion of behavioral ethics and compliance programs.

Too often, local regions, divisions, and their management don't want their local dirty laundry aired out to the corporate headquarters by local

compliance officers (or others, such as whistleblowers, who raise integrity issues). This is called local, regional, or divisional arbitrage and suppression of the head office corporate compliance & ethics program. And when things go horribly wrong, organizations behave like the famous chicken without its head.

Think of Corporate (Enterprise) Compliance as a General Ledger

The corporate head office, or corporate compliance function's objective is to coordinate the overall firm's compliance & ethics program on a coordinated and consistent basis. That's no different than a business or local subsidiary's financial statement "sub-ledger" rolling up to and consolidating with the parent company's consolidated financial statements, consistent with generally accepted accounting principles and securities laws.

Sadly, too many local compliance & ethics officers and their CCOs are too loyal and/or too afraid to stand up to their local business or regional heads who, too often, are ignorant of or ignore directives from the Head Office CCO. This culture of fear (or cowardice) enables local businesses to act locally and autonomously and adopt local behaviors that are counter to the ethical culture of the organization as a whole. Consequently, without an independent "check and challenge" and oversight by Head Office, local employees, particularly large-revenue producers, are incentivized to act illegally and/or engage in misconduct for personal financial gain at the expense of customers, employers, and shareholders.

Limitations of *Respondeat Superior*

There's a longstanding legal concept called *respondeat superior*, which holds an employer (and by extension its CEO and management team) responsible for an employee's fraud. However, the judicial and regulatory history of actually holding companies liable under *respondeat superior* has been limited at best.

US companies, let alone companies outside the United States, weren't even prosecuted for the criminal activities of their employees until 1991, when the US Department of Justice issued its Organizational Guidelines of the US Sentencing Commission (US DoJ Corporate Sentencing Guidelines).

Planting the Seeds of Effective Enterprise Compliance Risk Management Programs

Recognizing that corporate abuse continued despite the FCPA and other criminal laws, Congress began to enact laws to empower the US DoJ, banking regulators, and others to issue "guidance" designed to promote and enable "effective, enterprise-wide compliance risk management programs." These included independent compliance officers' access to boards of directors, providing more effective corporate governance from above, compliance education, and challenging authority from below in order to hold management accountable. Disappointingly, even today, the CEO and his or her management teams remain largely unaccountable because whistleblowers are suppressed and/or retaliated against when they try to raise integrity concerns, and because the CCO is unable to escalate issues freely and directly to the board of directors. And unless management's actions are egregious, company directors are still subject to personal liability and reputational damage caused by management's misconduct and unethical behavior.

The Seven Elements of an Effective Compliance Program, per the DoJ Organizational Sentencing Guidelines

The US DoJ first issued its Corporate Sentencing Guidelines[1] so that companies (like individuals) could be found guilty of criminal conduct, and

---

1   Chapter 8 of the US Sentencing Commission's Federal Sentencing Guidelines. https://www.ussc. gov/guidelines/2018-guidelines-manual/2018-chapter-8. Retrieved March 21, 2021. Known formally as the Organizational Sentencing Guidelines, I prefer to reference them as the Corporate Sentencing Guidelines to emphasize the relationship between the corporate board of directors, management and the chief compliance officer.

the measure of their punishment for felonies and Class A misdemeanors would depend on whether a Federal judge determined that mitigating circumstances could reduce the maximum fine. The Guidelines simultaneously brought *respondeat superior* to life, while also providing a set of potentially mitigating considerations that might be used in a corporate defense, particularly in cases of criminal actions by employees.

The Corporate Sentencing Guidelines sent a strong message to the corporate world, offering them an incentive to implement and sustain an effective compliance program. The message was simple: you are liable for your employees' criminal activities, and you (as a corporation) will suffer less as long as you meet the following seven elements:

1. Compliance standards and procedures must be established to deter crime.

2. High-level personnel (now called the chief compliance & ethics officer or CCO) must be involved in oversight.

3. Substantial discretionary authority must be carefully delegated.

4. Compliance standards and procedures must be communicated to employees.

5. Steps must be taken to achieve compliance by establishing monitoring and auditing systems and of reporting systems with protective safeguards.

6. Standards must be consistently enforced.

7. Any violations require appropriate responses, which may include modification of compliance standards and procedures and other preventive measures.

The Seven Elements Become Enterprise-Wide and Are Embraced by Regulators

The architect of the Sentencing Guidelines described them as a: "[n]ovel sentencing approach," adding that: "[T]hey not only encourage corporations to exemplify 'good corporate citizenship,' but also provide a means to 'rehabilitate' corporations that have engaged in criminal conduct by requiring them, as a term of probation, to institute and maintain effective compliance programs. The organizational guidelines provide that '[t]he hallmark of an effective program to prevent and detect violations of law is that the organization exercised due diligence in seeking to prevent and detect criminal conduct by its employees and other agents.'"[2]

The Guidelines' author is not mistaken in concluding that, "[t]he Federal Sentencing Guidelines for organizations represent a milestone both in federal criminal law and in *organizational behavior*. Their impact has been wide ranging. They are a real success story for the United States Sentencing Commission in its work to deter crime and encourage compliance with the law"[3] (emphasis mine). The question is whether the Sentencing Guidelines are sufficient. (Answer: not enough today.)

Leveraging the Sentencing Guidelines for Civil Violations

Nonetheless, the Sentencing Guidelines influenced policy statements and guidance for criminal violations beyond the DoJ. For example, industries ranging from energy and healthcare to banking have each adopted variations of the seven elements of the Corporate Sentencing Guidelines for civil, regulatory violations. In addition, accounting firms (for internal controls and risk management) and bank regulators[4] have leveraged the

---

2   Murphy, Diana, E. "The Federal Sentencing Guidelines for Organizations: A Decade of Promoting Compliance and Ethics." *Iowa Law Review*, January 31, 2002. https://www.ussc.gov/sites/default/files/pdf/training/organizational-guidelines/selected-articles/Murphy1.pdf. Retrieved November 4, 2020
3   Ibid, p 219 (Conclusion)
4   Supplementing this was the requirement that CEOs and chief accountants certify that they comply with laws and regulations as well as having their independent accountants attest to the integrity of a bank's financial statements. See chapter 2.4.

seven elements to fit their own expectations of compliance & ethics programs for civil violations.

But the Sentencing Guidelines are only as good as their effectiveness in deterring criminal activities and employee misconduct. And by the time the DoJ gets involved and the Sentencing Guidelines are considered, it's too late. As I describe in Recommendation #1, educating and enlightening the board of directors by the CCO is one of the cornerstones of a strong strategic partnership between the board and compliance to hold the CEO and management more accountable—*before* criminal activities and employee misconduct occur.

The COSO Integrated System of Internal Controls and Enterprise Risk Management

In 1992, a year after the Corporate Sentencing Guidelines were issued, the Committee of Sponsoring Organizations of the Treadway Commission (COSO) together with Coopers & Lybrand (now PWC) issued an "Internal Control framework" designed to combat corporate fraud and transnational bribery. Specifically, the COSO framework was a "[p]rinciples-based guidance for designing and implementing effective 'internal controls.' COSO developed the framework in response to senior executives' need for effective ways to better control their *'enterprises'* and to help ensure that organizational objectives related to operations, *reporting, and compliance* are achieved. This framework has become the most widely used internal control framework in the U.S. and has been adapted or adopted by numerous countries and businesses around the world"[5] (emphasis mine).

What's noteworthy about the COSO framework is that it:

- Leveraged the same guidelines as the internal accounting control framework envisioned by the books and records provisions of the FCPA Act of 1977

---

5   Committee of Sponsoring Organizations of the Treadway Commission (COSO). "Guidance on Internal Control." 1992. https://www.coso.org/Pages/ic.aspx. Retrieved November 4, 2020

- Recognized the concept of an enterprise being comprised of multiple divisions, legal entities, businesses, products, corporate cultures, and in particular a triad of three important integrated control components:
  - □ People
  - □ Process
  - □ Technology/systems

Many countries including Japan, China, and South Korea have modeled some financial reporting legislation and other enterprise risk management frameworks related to internal control using concepts in the 1992, 2004, and 2013 versions of the COSO framework.

Pulling It All Together

Unfortunately, the laws, regulations, and guidelines that led to the creation of the FCPA and the OECD Principles on Bribery and Corruption have not been successful in enabling the establishment of enterprise-wide compliance risk management programs. Neither have the DoJ's Corporate Sentencing Guidelines and similar international efforts been sufficient to effectively deter misconduct, bribery, corruption, and other crimes. And, as we've seen, topical compliance is too reactive and siloed to be effective. Even after the significant increase in enforcement after the Financial Crisis of 2007–2010, ensuring management accountability remains elusive. As a result, management has little or no incentive to rein in or change their behavior.

The Intersection of Board Governance, Financial Integrity, and Effective Compliance

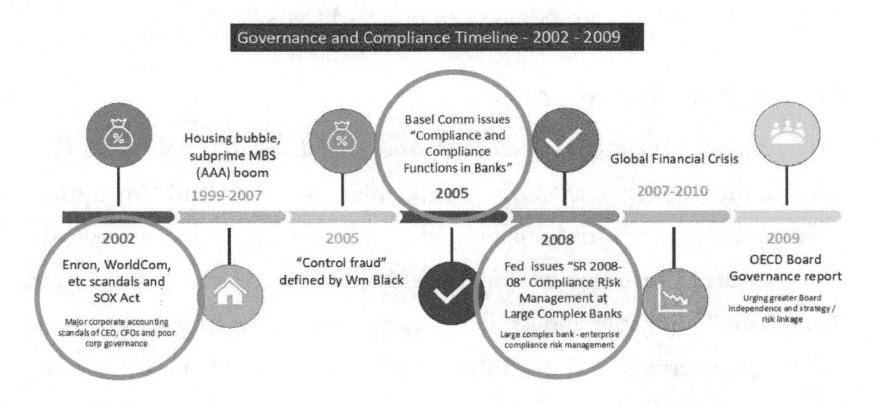

CEO/CFO certifications under SOX and enterprise-wide compliance

The following two chapters introduce how the: (1) US Sarbanes-Oxley Act of 2002 (SOX), (2) international Basel Committee Principles of Compliance at Banks (2005), (3) Federal Reserve's written "compliance risk management" expectations (2008) over large, complex banks, and (4) US Sentencing Guidelines (collectively, "Young's Vision")—can be executed as a *combined, comprehensive program,* which can benefit all companies across all industries, globally.

This chapter will cover SOX. I'll cover the Basel and Fed compliance risk management expectations, and Young's Vision in the next chapter.

US Sarbanes-Oxley Act of 2002[1] (SOX)

In response to the Enron, WorldCom, and other major accounting scandals, SOX created strict new rules—including more stringent record-keeping requirements—for accountants, auditors, corporate officers, and directors. SOX also added new criminal penalties for violating securities laws and empowered employees to raise integrity issues without fear of retaliation while also incenting such whistleblowers with significant monetary rewards.

I'll focus on three of the eleven SOX sections, in particular, Sections 302, 404, and the board audit committee requirements of Section 301.

These three sections require rigorous process mapping, testing, and certification, and compel companies to document and understand the end-to-end interaction of people, processes, and controls over financial reporting, accounting, and fraud risk management. The benefit of this rigorous exercise of mapping, identifying, and certifying the existence of controls is that it compels individuals to take accountability for these controls so that audit committees of the board of directors can more clearly oversee and hold management accountable. At least that's the theory.

SOX Section 302

Section 302 requires disclosure of controls and procedures, plus certification (and personal accountability) of the CEO and CFO to attest that the company's financial information is accurate and reliable. These attestations are included within the quarterly and annual reports filed with the SEC and apply to the implementation and maintenance of internal controls and procedures, as well as the reporting of deficiencies or changes related to internal controls.

---

1   There is no shortage of literature describing SOX. Wikipedia (Sarbanes-Oxley Act of 2002) and Investopaedia are good starts.

SOX Section 404

Section 404 requires that companies annually assess/test and report on their internal control structure, including the design and operating effectiveness of financial reporting. The results of the testing must be reviewed by management, and all identified control testing failures must be categorized as either a "deficiency," "significant deficiency," or "material weakness." Deficiencies and significant deficiencies must also be reported to the audit committee and the full board, and material weaknesses must be publicly disclosed.

SOX also mandates that public companies have an independent external auditor inspect their internal control practices and include the audit report within the company's financial report. While SOX 302 involves a survey and review of related reporting before the CEO and CFO certify financial reporting, financial controls and fraud activity, SOX 404 includes much more rigorous processes and procedures for setup as well as risk management through monitoring and measuring to control risks associated with financial reporting.[2]

Section 301

SOX sets independence and accountability expectations on the board directors who serve on the audit committee. Specifically, they must:

- Be *independent* directors and not affiliated with the company other than in their capacity as directors.

- Be directly responsible for the appointment, compensation, and oversight of the work of the auditors.

- Have free reign to interview and question auditors without the company's executive officers being present.

---

2   This summary is based on an excellent overview by Shanna Nasiri, "The Differences Between SOX 302 and 404 Requirements," Reciprocitylabs.com, December 5, 2019 - https://reciprocitylabs.com/the-differences-between-sox-302-and-404-requirements/ - retrieved November 7, 2020

- Develop procedures for addressing complaints regarding the audit process.

- Include at least one competent financial person.

- Be barred from accepting consulting fees from the company.[3]

Since the 2002 enactment of SOX, the New York Stock Exchange and others have imposed additional corporate governance requirements on boards, including the creation of a fully independent governance and nominating committee and a compensation committee.

International Adoption of SOX

Widely criticized within and beyond the United States, SOX 404 imposes a tremendous regulatory and operational burden on publicly traded companies to demonstrate that their system of internal controls over financial reporting including fraud risk management are effective. However, as described in a very thorough 2006 report by the SEC, many aspects of SOX have been universally adopted internationally.[4]

Leveraging SOX to Address Compliance Risk Management

Leveraging the process mapping, certification, and board oversight expectations in Sections 301, 302, and 404 can provide a template to manage compliance risks too. For example, the certification requirements of the "Volcker Rule" under the 2010 Dodd-Frank Act and the New York State Department of Financial Services (DFS) Rules 500 (cybersecurity) and 504 (anti-money laundering and sanctions compliance), can each help management map out and document a company's risks and control processes and hold management more accountable.

---

3   HGExperts.com (website for expert witnesses) - "Corporate Governance Under the Sarbanes-Oxley Act" – https://www.hgexperts.com/expert-witness-articles/corporate-governance-under-the-sarbanes-oxley-act-24966 - retrieved October 25, 2020

4   Tafara, Ethiopus, Director, Office of International Affairs - U.S. Securities and Exchange Commission, International Financial Law Review, *"Statement by SEC Staff: A Race to the Top: International Regulatory Reform Post Sarbanes-Oxley,"* September 2006 - https://www.sec.gov/news/speech/2006/spch091106et.htm - retrieved November 7, 2020

The DFS rules are especially rigorous and tremendously helpful in compelling processes to be mapped, controls to be understood with attestations, and most importantly, for data to have governance so that compliance exceptions and reporting will have integrity and actionable steps designed to remediate to acceptable residual levels. Although the DFS rules don't apply to the universe of corporations, they can be utilized as a helpful benchmark to measure your processes, controls, and integrity of your data.

As I'll discuss in the next chapter, the board of directors' role over self-governance and the compliance function's role over self-regulation are interdependent, just as the SOX requirements under Section 301 vis-à-vis the board audit committee and the internal audit and external audit functions.

"Young's Vision" for an Effective, *Enterprise* Compliance Program

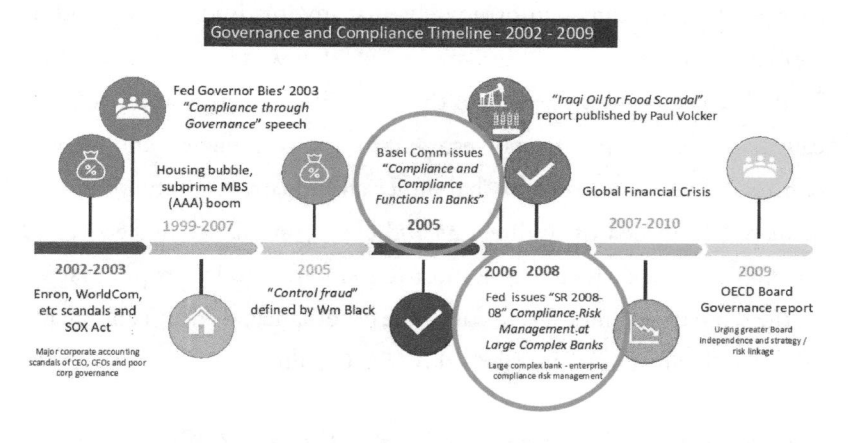

Source: seamuss/Shutterstock.com (edits by author)

This chapter compares the Fed's enterprise-wide compliance expectations (SR 08-08) with the US Sentencing Guidelines. I believe that executing the Sentencing Guidelines alone (as many firms do) is not sufficient to *sustain* an effective compliance program. Implementing the Fed's SR 08-08 alone (as many banks try) is also insufficient. However, integrating the two models together will achieve and sustain the compliance program needed to satisfy both the DoJ and the Fed. I refer to this integrated model as Young's Vision.

First, I'll discuss why continuing a short-term profit maximization strategy continuously repeats compliance, cultural, and internal control blow-ups, and why it's so critical that compliance & ethics officers be independent. I'll then discuss how Young's Vision of combining the Fed and DoJ expectations helps all firms beyond banks, achieve an effective compliance program.

Myopia

As in Plato's cave (which we discussed in the Introduction to this book), the CEO and CFO use shadows to create a type of corporate myopia, focused on short-term financial gain and shareholder return rather than on operating ethically. Unfortunately, that myopia leads to misconduct, regulatory violations, and fundamental breakdowns in internal controls. That's because history has shown that a profit-at-all costs approach typically involves cuts in critical investment in risk, compliance, and financial controls. These are problems that afflict all industries. Without effective challenge from boards of directors and chief compliance officers, CEOs and CFOs will keep focusing on short-term revenue and share price targets. At the same time, longer-term corporate governance, risk, and compliance efforts will continue to be blocked by the C-suite.

Recent Cultural and Strategic Headlines (2020, 2021)

Wirecard, Wells Fargo (continued[1]), Luckin Coffee, Deutsche Bank, and Pacific Gas & Electric[2] are recent examples of major ethics and compliance violations of 2020. And Citigroup (see chapter 2.11) and JP Morgan in October and December 2020, respectively, were finally penalized and

---

1   Clark, Simon, "Wells Fargo Acted Like a 'Mafia' to Suppress Internal Critics, Former Executive Said." *The Wall Street Journal.* July 1, 2021. https://www.wsj.com/articles/wells-fargo-acted-like-a-mafia-to-suppress-internal-critics-former-executive-said-11625169200?mod=djemRisk Compliance. Retrieved July 3, 2021
2   Jaeger, Jaclyn. "Top ethics and compliance failures of 2020." *Compliance Week*, December 8, 2020. https://www.complianceweek.com/opinion/top-ethics-and-compliance-failures-of-2020/29797. Retrieved June 26, 2021

publicly cited by regulators for years of recidivist internal control, compliance & ethical weaknesses.

In 2021, Credit Suisse (CS) melted down because of poor risk management and oversight of its Greensill Capital and Archegos Capital Management exposures. Foolishly, CS's chair and CEO both believed that they could place "anyone clever into a job and they will be a success, even if they had *no experience*... [O]ther (CS) executives pushed for risk and compliance to be combined to *save money*, and *'more commercial' and 'aligned'* with the front office traders and dealmakers... *Risk lost its independence"* [3] (Emphasis mine).

How often have we heard these short-term goals and consequences before? CS's chief risk officer, a career businessperson, reportedly wasn't qualified to be a chief risk or chief compliance officer (let alone both). Worse, she reportedly pushed the combined risk and compliance function to compromise its independence in order to maximize profits. Now, CS is paying a major reputational price. Not surprisingly, CS profits from Archegos will turn out to be a very small fraction of what it will be paying in remediation expenses and lost reputation.

Siloed Compliance vs. the Twin Pillars of the DoJ and Fed Guidance

The DoJ US Sentencing Guidelines and Fed's Supervision and Regulation (SR) Letter 2008-08 are twin pillars of an effective, enterprise-wide compliance program. Together, both address what siloed or topical[4] compliance programs can't or won't: an enterprise-wide risk-based compliance program that identifies and addresses all activities and their underlying risks, including behavioral or conduct risks. Like siloed moons suspended

---

3   Glazer, Emily, Farrell, Maureen and Patrick, Margot. "Inside Credit Suisse's $5.5 Billion Breakdown." *The Wall Street Journal.* https://www.wsj.com/articles/inside-credit-suisses-5-5-billion-breakdown-archegos-11623072713. Retrieved June 26, 2021

4   For example, anti-bribery and corruption, anti-money laundering, privacy, lawyer-centric broker-dealer programs, each of which are critically important to manage. The challenge is that organizations often have to manage each of these and so much more every day.

and isolated by the gravitational push and pull of the Department of Justice, topical or siloed compliance programs are not enough to achieve an effective compliance program.[5]

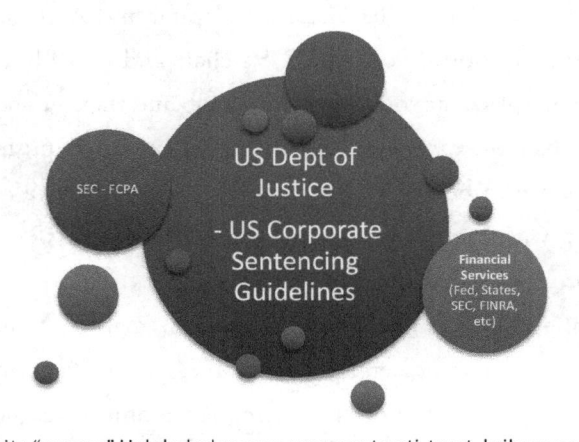

The DoJ and its "moons." Unlabeled moons represent anti-trust, bribery and corruption, money laundering, sanctions, third-party risk, privacy, and other topical compliance programs. Source: author

The Fed's SR 08-08

"A firmwide compliance function that plays a key role in managing and overseeing compliance risk while promoting a strong culture of compliance across the organization is particularly important for large, complex organizations that have a number of separate business lines and legal entities that must comply with a wide range of applicable rules and standards."[6]

Fed Governor Susan Bies' speech in 2003[7] discussed the need to link culture across a large organization's complexities to harmonize compliance

5   See chapter 2.6 for a more detailed analysis of siloed compliance programs.
6   Federal Reserve Board. "Compliance Risk Management Programs and Oversight at Large Banking Organizations with Complex Compliance Profiles," Supervision and Regulation (SR) Letter 2008 – 08, October 16, 2008. https://www.federalreserve.gov/boarddocs/srletters/2008/sr0808.htm. Retrieved June 13, 2021
7   Bies, Susan, Governor. "Strengthening Compliance through Effective Corporate Governance." American Bankers Association, Annual Regulatory Compliance Conference, Washington, DC, June 11, 2003.

& ethics consistently. The Fed speech also recognized the important link between the board of directors and compliance, citing the Enron and WorldCom accounting scandals fueled by the technology bubble bursting in the early 2000s. In October 2008, the Fed ultimately released Supervision and Regulation (SR) letter 2008-08, entitled, "Compliance Risk Management Programs and Oversight at Large Banking Organizations with Complex Compliance Profiles."

Managing compliance & ethics risk on an enterprise-wide basis is even more important today. Technology dominates our society culturally and economically today. Behind this domination are Big Tech, fintech, cryptocurrencies, and social media blurring (disrupting) the lines between banking and commercial industries—which in turn is muddying the inherent risks across industries and sectors. Consequently, firms are even more exposed to cyber-attacks and compliance breakdowns because technological disruption and industries blurring have made the process of identifying emerging and unknown risks even more difficult. The Fed's SR 08-08 helps address these enterprise compliance risks.

Below is a simplified visual of the Fed's SR 08-08, which, not surprisingly, shares similar elements as the seven elements of the DoJ Sentencing Guidelines. The visual also incorporates what it would take for a strong CCO to execute SR 08-08 (and the Sentencing Guidelines).

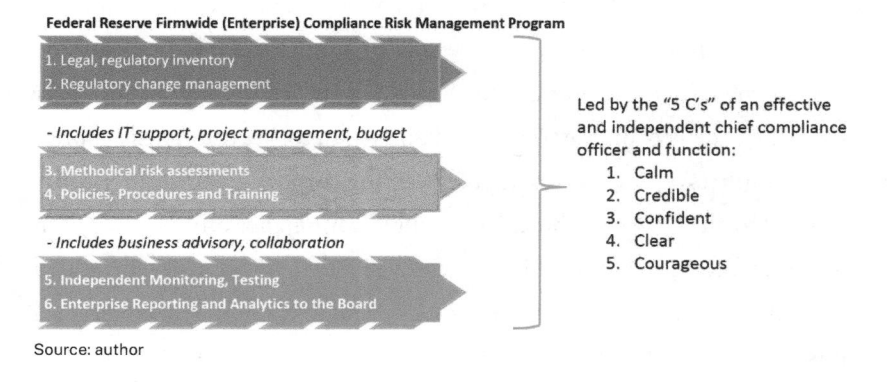

Federal Reserve Firmwide (Enterprise) Compliance Risk Management Program

1. Legal, regulatory inventory
2. Regulatory change management

- *Includes IT support, project management, budget*

3. Methodical risk assessments
4. Policies, Procedures and Training

- *Includes business advisory, collaboration*

5. Independent Monitoring, Testing
6. Enterprise Reporting and Analytics to the Board

Led by the "5 C's" of an effective and independent chief compliance officer and function:
1. Calm
2. Credible
3. Confident
4. Clear
5. Courageous

Source: author

Young's Vision

Put simply, Young's Vision combines the Fed's SR 08-08 and the DoJ's Sentencing Guidelines to enable all companies to achieve four objectives:

1. Become and remain independent

2. Align corporate culture and strategy

3. Keep business focused on long-term stakeholder metrics

4. Demand adequate resources (especially quality skills and predictive and analytical technology)

1. Become and Remain Independent

Both the DoJ and Fed expect compliance & ethics programs to operate independently from the businesses. Too often, businesses seek to override the C&E function's authority or decisions over proposed transactions or new account openings when issues are raised. Having an independent function with truly independent compliance & ethics officers is therefore paramount to the DoJ, Fed, and other regulators' expectations. More importantly, it's critical for the ethical and cultural alignment that leads to strategic success.

Local, business-embedded compliance & ethics officers whose compensation is overly influenced by the business heads create ethical and regulatory red flags. That's because issues of non-compliance, misconduct and/or unethical behavior can too easily be suppressed (swept under the rug) by the local office without the head office (or central leadership) ever knowing. The Fed and international bank regulators continuously express these conflicts of interest/loyalty between the corporate compliance function led by the CCO and business-captured compliance officers. To whom is the local compliance & ethics officer loyal? Are these business-embedded compliance & ethics officers courageous enough to stand up to their local business leaders? Typically, not. They often say, "I have to work with them every day!" It's hard to be ethical when a businessperson is unethical!

Indeed, the Fed's SR 08-08 asserts that if a compliance & ethics officer reports dually into a business head and the chief compliance officer at the corporate head office, the compliance officer should be accountable to the CCO to remain independent. Similarly, if the CCO reports into the CEO, CFO, GC, or other executive who prioritizes short-term profit and maximum share price over effective controls, the CCO's independence is compromised.

Having encountered these conflicts too many times, I've consistently moved to centralize the compliance & ethics function. Young's Vision expects all compliance & ethics officers to be accountable centrally to the chief compliance officer, with all compliance resource decisions (budget, hiring, bonuses, firings) resting directly or indirectly with the CCO. This breaks the perception of conflicted compliance officers. Achieving and sustaining this independence is a daily challenge for all CCOs.

2. Align Corporate Culture and Strategy

Meet frequently with your CEO, over breakfast or coffee (or by video), if possible. This enables the two of you to speak informally, regularly, and candidly about your compliance & ethics culture and growth strategy. My discussions with various CEOs helped me articulate Young's Vision and transform my employers' corporate culture. Of course, we'd discuss immediate and day-to-day issues and priorities too.

Implementing Young's Vision in your company will help you develop a longer-term strategic outlook that will protect your customers and preserve the integrity of local and global markets. For any institution, identifying and remediating compliance & ethics issues is an important objective, but it should be viewed as just the first step toward achieving and sustaining long-term cultural and strategic success.

3. Keep Business Focused on Long-Term Stakeholder Metrics

No longer will maximizing profit and share price—at any/all costs in the shortest timeline be tolerated reputationally by society nor by our future Gen Z and millennial leaders. No longer could or should the financial services industry (or any other industry) embrace the "greed-is-good" culture epitomized by the movie *Wall Street*. Instead, Young's Vision adopts a "change-is-opportunity" strategy to embrace a longer-term, stakeholder-focused culture with a growth—and ethical—strategy that benefits the greater good.

Industry needs to operate profitably to "do good" for our overall environment (broadly defined), society, the communities in which we operate, and especially for our employees who have endured and adapted in a COVID-19 (and variant) pandemic world.

4. Demand Adequate Resources (Especially Quality Skills and Predictive and Analytical Technology)

One fundamental expectation of regulators is for firms to have "adequate resources" to execute an effective compliance & ethics program. This foundational principle exists in virtually all regulatory guidance globally. Young's Vision equips a critical mass of compliance & ethics officers and technologies essential to fix, run, and transform compliance paradigms. Inadequate resources rely too heavily on the same high performers, ultimately running the risk of burning them out.

Young's Vision means a skilled operational team *within* the compliance & ethics function is needed. CEOs and the C-suite don't realize that the compliance & ethics function is very operational with processes requiring precise execution from start to finish. Like an assembly line. A gear falls off and the assembly shuts down. A well-oiled machine or company needs to run and manage compliance & ethics like an operational process and project management machine to track deadlines and parachute in "special ops" support whenever compliance & ethics units are short-handed (in

either quantity or quality). For example, to review suspicious activity alerts, investigate unusual trading or sales activities, and ultimately determine whether a violation has or will happen. If so, the next step is to self-disclose these suspicious (or actual violations) to the authorities.

4a. The Compliance Surge

To realize Young's Vision, I was able to justify a significant increase in headcount, budget, and technology resources without instantly losing credibility or getting an automatic rejection from my executive management. I did so by introducing and proposing the "compliance resource surge."[8] *So can you.*

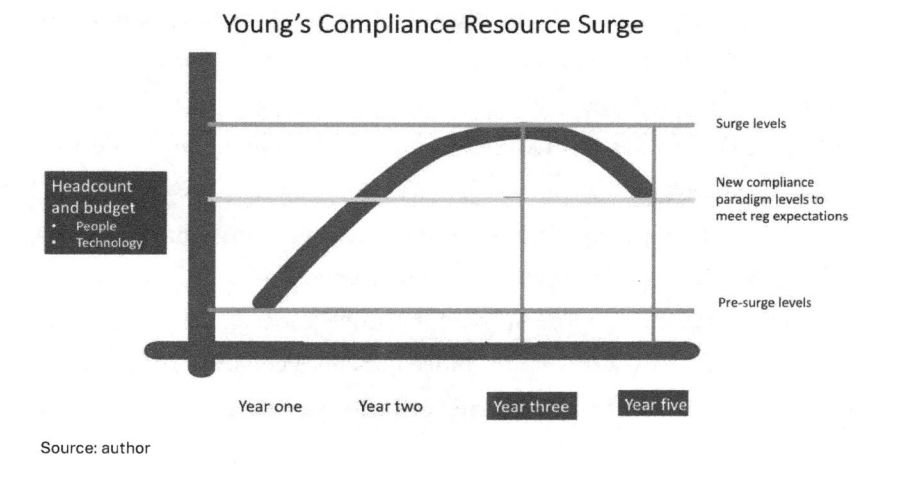

Young's Compliance Resource Surge

Source: author

As shown in the illustration above, you should request a temporary (not permanent) budget proposed increase for compliance specialists, project management, and technology support to fix, run, and transform your company's infrastructure and controls. This approach often succeeds because by year three of the surge, you'll have stabilized your compliance

---

8   Once again, invoking General David Petraeus' successful Iraq War counterinsurgency strategy in 2007 in which he proposed a temporary surge in US troops in Iraq to re-take control of Iraq.

risk management platform and compliance & ethics risk levels to an acceptable level (as defined and approved by your board of directors). Then, between years three and five, you'll be able to reduce your head-count and budget with the right mix of quality compliance skill sets (not just quantity), creating a new paradigm that will enable you to meet the continuously rising regulatory expectations. Of course, your management and CFO will need to support your surge to obtain the funding needed, however temporary.

4b. What if You Don't Apply the Surge?

Not approving the budget increase and surge could cause significant regulatory and reputational damage, since companies are torn between spending millions in remediation (which is compulsory) and continuing to focus on cost reductions. Not approving the budget increase also means that Young's Vision won't be realized, meaning that your company won't be able to meet the Fed's and DoJ's expectations of maintaining an effective compliance program in a sustainable manner.

On paper, proposing, approving, and executing a surge may look easy. Believe me, it wasn't. It takes persistent, courageous, and collaborative compliance officers who "get it," and executive leadership (locally and at your head office) to partner with. Indeed, there's a concept called "pareto optimality," which pinpoints where both effectiveness and efficiency can be achieved.[9]

4c. Compliance Information Technology

Adequate resources are not just about the size of the headcount. It's about the *quality* of the compliance staff as well as their technology skills. More importantly, it's about having the budget to build and/or buy and customize robust compliance technology tools to onboard

---

9   Young, Eric. "Achieving the Right Balance: Optimizing AML Compliance." *ACAMS Today*, June-August 2009. ACAMS.org/issue-8-3/. Retrieved July 5, 2021

clients effectively and efficiently; monitor and surveil electronic communications, trading activities, and anti-money laundering, payments; and multiple other compliance responsibilities. I've sought to build and implement compliance technology tools throughout my career, and too often I encountered a lack of understanding of the need (from management, and sometimes even compliance or legal), lack of adequate budget, or at times, arguments that a compliance technology tool is better integrated into a broader audit, risk, and compliance tool (one with multiple stakeholders, objectives, and budgets). Sadly, too often, the end result is that no tool is built or one is retrofitted from an existing tool which is, in most cases, not fit for purpose.

Artificial intelligence (AI); machine learning; and governance, risk, and compliance (GRC) tools with data integrity are essential technology tools and processes, which all firms (not just financial institutions) should already have in place to enable robust analytics, predictive risk assessments, and meaningful compliance reporting to the board, CEO, and compliance management. They're not "silver bullets" that solve all problems, but neither is a hammer or a saw. They are but one important tool among many in a toolbox of important means to collect data from multiple sources in order to compile, analyze, learn, and report meaningfully to the board, CEO, and the compliance team itself. How else can a second line of defense function effectively measure, monitor, and report compliance risks and minimize them to acceptable levels?[10]

---

10   I applaud the New York State Department of Financial Services (DFS) in particular for recognizing the important relationship between culture, compliance & ethics, and data integrity (see for example, DFS Banking Law §§37(3)(4); Financial Services Law §302): "Banking Division Transaction Monitoring and Filtering Program Requirements and Certifications." https://casetext.com/regulation/new-york-codes-rules-and-regulations/title-3-banking/chapter-iii-superintendents-regulations/subchapter-c-general-regulations-banking-and-non-banking-organizations/part-504-banking-division-transaction-monitoring-and-filtering-program-requirements-and-certifications. Retrieved July 5, 2021

Young's Vision Provides a New Paradigm for Your Organization

Young's Vision foresees the future of your company's compliance & ethics function under a new paradigm. The phrase "new normal" is too cliché, too linear. "New paradigm" means "an important change that happens when the usual way of thinking about or doing something is replaced by a new and different way."[11] Compliance & ethics must be thought of and executed creatively to keep our business leaders, C-suite, and management accountable while toeing the legal, regulatory, and ethical line.

Deconstructing Young's Vision

Below is a comprehensive illustration that integrates the Fed's and DoJ's compliance framework. It looks complex, but don't forget that companies can be incredibly complex. This includes their culture. Your culture.

Corporate culture is a collection of individual personalities, hopefully aligned to execute a focused strategy and compliance risk management program. In the sections that follow, I'll break this complex illustration (and the process) down into manageable chunks so you can see both the enormity of the task of creating a path to compliance & ethical success—and, at the same time, the feasibility of implementing it.

---

11 Merriam-Webster Dictionary: "Paradigm Shift"

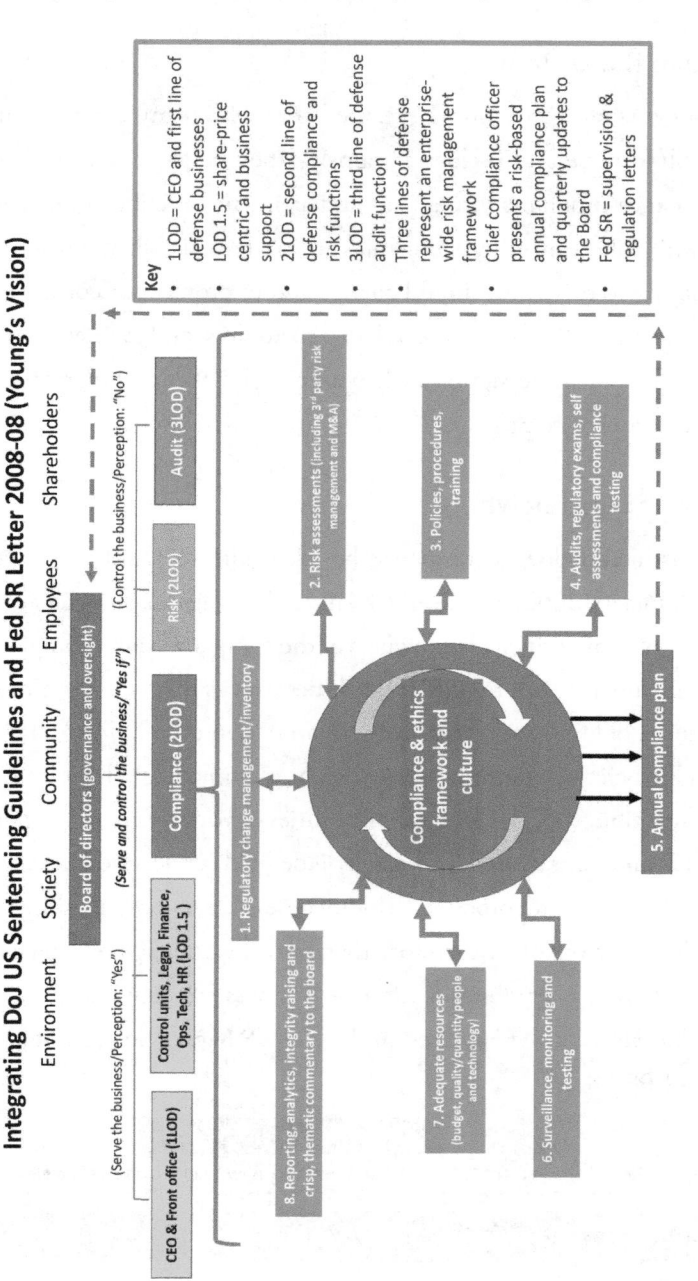

Young's Vision: A visual interpretation of Fed SR 08-08 converged with DoJ Organizational Sentencing Guidelines. Source: author

What's the Outcome?

With every reorganization I executed throughout my career, I built incredibly diverse and inclusive teams.[12] They helped me transform our compliance programs into a truly independent function, some (but not all) with sole control over our budget. We had visibility, authority, and credibility to drive meaningful change and to protect our company's reputation and its directors, shareholders, customers, and markets. I'm proud of how we partnered significantly with our global counterparts to build a global compliance program.

From the Top Down

As illustrated below, a company's board of directors and CEO typically have fiduciary duties of care and loyalty as both agents on behalf of shareholders who are principals as owners of the company. Maximizing profits is traditionally the path to fulfil these duties. But as I'll discuss in a moment, the duties of loyalty and care must extend to non-shareholder stakeholders as well (society, community, markets, and employees). To reinforce this prioritization, the roles and responsibilities of your business, support, and control functions should be formally redefined, understood, and codified through policies and processes. This includes a clear and formally approved role for your board of directors that provides independent governance and oversight over the execution of business strategy and its controls. This has always been expected under the US Sentencing Guidelines and Fed SR 08-08.

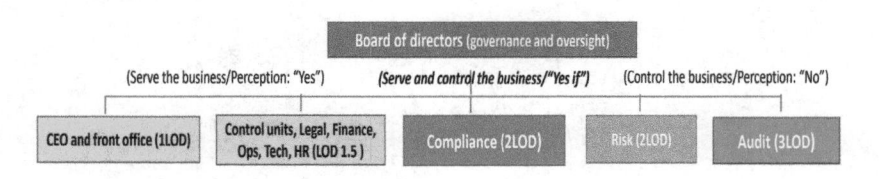

---

12   By way of race, gender, religion and beliefs, skill sets, career experience, and so many other open-minded approaches to consider great compliance & ethics officers.

The Three Lines of Defense[13]

The first-line businesses and support functions: Saying "Yes"

The revenue-generating businesses (see the yellow boxes) represent the first line of defense (1LOD) because the Fed expects the businesses to *manage* their credit, market, liquidity, financial, and other operational risks. Some units, such as human resources, operations, technology, legal and finance[14] support the business. That support enables the 1LOD businesses to execute, process, and settle their activities. Supporting the business means serving it, having a propensity to say "yes" to the businesses. This tends to be either because they're paid by the businesses or because the business' budgets are influenced heavily by the 1LOD. For this purpose, I unofficially consider these support functions to be "line of defense 1.5" (LOD 1.5). Are they independent? No.

The third-line auditors: Saying "No" to the businesses

In contrast, the internal audit and its chief auditor are considered purely independent from the 1LOD businesses. They're known as the third line of defense (3LOD) since internal auditors are charged with testing the effectiveness of both the first-line businesses and second-line independent compliance and risk functions (which we'll discuss below). Audit (shown as the red box on the right side of the chart) tests the business, risk, and compliance programs and reports exceptions to the efficacy of the company's internal control structure to its board of directors. By definition and charter, auditors typically must be independent, and therefore have a propensity to say No to the business. If regulators or prosecutors like the DoJ question the integrity and independence of the 3LOD auditors, it's game over. Nothing else matters.

---

13   The Institute of Internal Auditors, "The Lines of Defense in Effective Risk Management." January 2013. https://na.theiia.org/standards-guidance/Public%20Documents/PP%20The%20 Three%20Lines%20of%20Defense%20in%20Effective%20Risk%20Management%20and%20 Control.pdf. Retrieved June 24, 2021

14   The roles and independence of finance and the CFO are debatable. Are they independent enough to price securities objectively for a daily profit/loss of the firm, or are they still vulnerable to manipulating the books and records to inflate profits or hide losses?

The second line: Saying "Yes if" by serving and controlling the businesses
Finally, the second line of defense (2LOD) includes the independent compliance & ethics function, and the risk management function (the blue box in the middle of the chart). Smaller, less complex firms sometimes combine both compliance and risk, but as a firm matures and becomes larger and more complex, case studies have demonstrated that risk and compliance should be separate. As we discussed earlier, Credit Suisse is the latest example of how trying to be efficient by combining the units leads to being ineffective.

The goal of the 2LOD is to adopt a compliance philosophy of "yes-if" with the businesses. That is, to serve (advise) *and control* (make decisions) the businesses simultaneously with a goal of getting to yes. But this is a delicate balance, because if they're too service- rather than control-oriented, the compliance & ethics officer is no longer independent.

Effective compliance & ethics functions must have the capacity and critical mass to meet the different elements or components articulated and expected by the Fed, DoJ, and New York State Department of Financial Services (DFS) since compliance & ethics should be viewed as an operational cycle or continuum. My teams conducted compliance risk assessments, issued and updated compliance policies and procedures, provided compliance awareness and training, and most importantly, monitored, surveilled, and tested our 1LOD businesses independently.

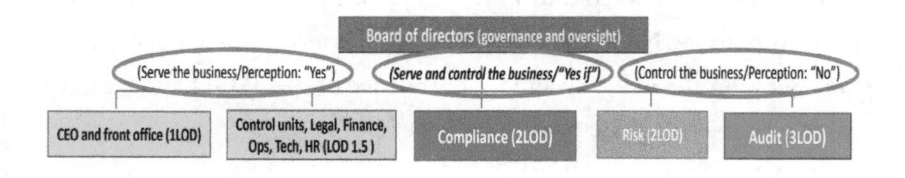

Taken together, the collective board of directors, CEO, and businesses (1LOD), support functions (LOD 1.5), compliance and risk management (2LOD), and internal audit (3LOD) represent an "enterprise-wide risk management framework," with each player having clear roles and responsibilities.[15] The clarity of roles with respect to "complying" is essential. Further, having an independent 2LOD reporting process and line directly to the board enables a direct dialogue with directors whether the 1LOD defenses are indeed complying.

---

15   As described earlier in part 2, the three lines of defense model is evolving, with the Institute of Internal Auditors (IIA) issuing revised guidance in 2020 which posits that there be only two lines (the first and third). I don't agree with this view, because it would render compliance & ethics extinct, which would be disastrous both ethically and culturally for firms. Since then, the IIA has emphasized that is guidance only, as most banking regulators continue to insist on the prior three lines of defense model, which includes an independent compliance function that reports directly to the board.

Compliance (2LOD) – and the CCO

Compliance & ethics framework and culture

1. Regulatory change management/inventory

2. Risk assessments (including 3rd party risk management and M&A)

3. Policies, procedures, training

4. Audits, regulatory exams, self assessments and compliance testing

5. Annual compliance plan

6. Surveillance, monitoring and testing

7. Adequate resources (budget, quality/quantity people and technology)

8. Reporting, analytics, integrity raising and crisp, thematic commentary to the board
- Includes key risk and performance indicators, emerging risks, red flags/actions, and whistleblowing analytics/root cause

Building the Compliance (and Ethics) Program and Culture

You can design, re-engineer, and maintain each of the eight compliance elements listed in 1–8, above. They are key compliance components of the Fed's SR 08-08 and seven DoJ Sentencing Guidelines elements. These are enumerated in the illustration above around the large circle. Importantly, these component elements aren't (and never should be) mutually exclusive and in fact, are mutually *dependent* upon one another. For example, compliance element 2 (executing a robust, methodical *compliance risk assessment*) produces inherent and residual risk ratings that ultimately produce priorities for compliance to prioritize revised or new policies and procedures and training (process 3). Those risk assessments also drive focused *surveillance, monitoring and testing* of key business and other elements (processes 4 and 6).

As noted earlier, having *adequate resources* (process 7) is paramount to executing—and sustaining—an effective compliance program. This not only includes having resources to continuously assess and enable a sufficient level of qualified staffing, but also the critical technology budgets to invest in compliance know-your-customer (KYC) onboarding, trading, electronic communications, and anti-financial criminal compliance surveillance tools, which over time need to include AI capabilities that enable predictive analytics. Tools to monitor conflicts of interest, gifts, and entertainment are also essential. And as described below, the resources to build and implement GRC tools are ultimately the most important when it comes to serving as an automated Fed SR 08-08 repository across each compliance process, so that the input illustrated in the chart below, can produce meaningful compliance analytics to report key, residual compliance risk metrics to the board of directors.

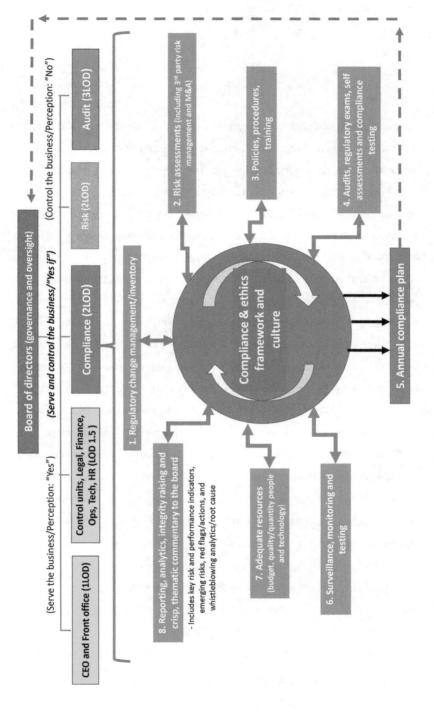

The Annual Compliance Plan and Board Reporting

Your compliance team and more broadly, your company can achieve a sustainable level of compliance program effectiveness because, among other reasons, your compliance processes should produce meaningful and formally approved, annual compliance plans (ACPs). These ACPs are formal documents that are presented to and approved by your legal entity, business line, and divisional executives, and in turn should be approved by your CEO and you as CCO. They're then presented to and approved by your board of directors. Articulate a "state of the compliance program" for your region, divisional, and legal entities that highlights your key compliance risks by topic, transversal laws, and regulations, as well as emerging compliance risks. This ACP provides directors with a forum to discuss, challenge, and question you as CCO, and will help your board members address whether your organization is meeting the DoJ's Sentencing Guideline's seven elements of an effective compliance program, illustrated in simplified form below.

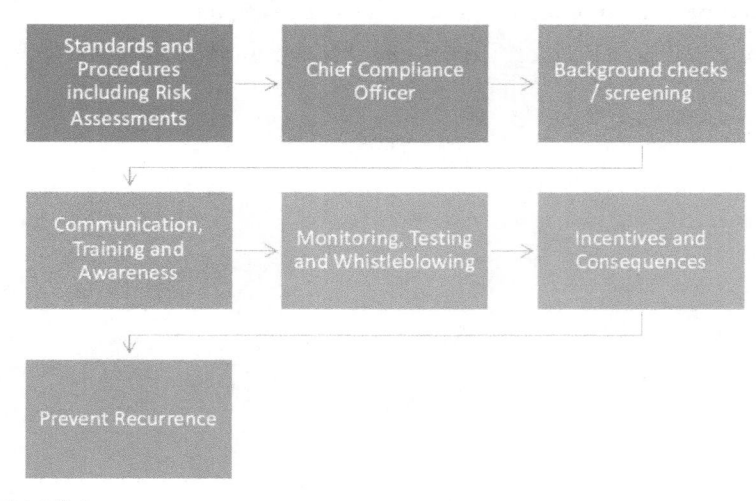

Source: author

The ACP (with quarterly updates) can also be used to address the DoJ's "Evaluation of Corporate Compliance Programs"[16] and answer whether your program is well designed, applied earnestly, and actually working in practice.

Board Reporting, Particularly Whistleblowing Metrics

Among other metrics, inherent and residual compliance risks should be identified and updated on a quarterly basis, supported by key risk indicators exceeding or falling below acceptable compliance risk appetite statements (quantifiable risk metrics such as backlog of surveillance alerts, incomplete compliance training, or reviews of electronic communications, cancelled trades). Most importantly, whistleblowing statistics would be reported on a quarterly basis to disclose material and less material issues raised by integrity-raising employees. Over my career, over 60 percent of whistleblowing cases related to human resources/employment issues (e.g., workplace harassment, sexual harassment, and fears of retaliation). Others highlighted more serious issues, such as fraud (or worse). The board often would be quite interested in these whistleblowing reports since they had been raised (as with most large firms) through third-party hotlines.

---

16   U.S. Department of Justice, Criminal Division. "Evaluation of Corporate Compliance Programs," Updated June 2020. https://www.justice.gov/criminal-fraud/page/file/937501/download. Retrieved June 15, 2021

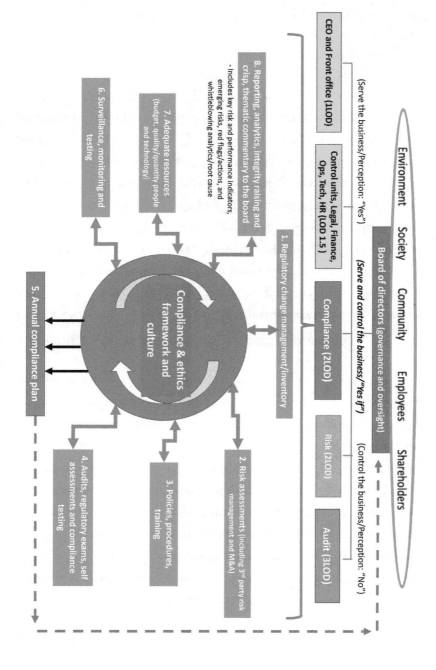

Breaking the Short-term Myopia of the CEO and CFO to Achieve Long-term Success

To be safely and responsibly profitable, your company must focus their corporate strategy around corporate and social responsibility (CSR) wisely. More broadly, they must embrace environment (E), society (S) and governance (G), or ESG. Green investing and green financing have become financial institutions' core business strategies. They enable your operations to focus not only on the company's short-term objectives to maximize profits, but also to address non-shareholder concerns over the climate, broader environment, social class, and broader concerns of society including the communities in which they operate, as well as to strengthen the overall governance, risk, and compliance infrastructure necessary to sustain an effective compliance & ethics program.

The Longer-Term Stakeholder Expectations and (E)ESG[17]

Retired Delaware Supreme Court Chief Justice Leo E. Strine, Jr. wisely adds another E to the ESG we discussed above: the employee. Chief Strine and his co-authors remind us all that employees are critical stakeholders in our future, long-term success. Without employees, companies cannot operate sustainably. This common-sense but often forgotten principle was obvious when the COVID-19 pandemic exposed just how vulnerable employees are to employee safety. Then, many companies faced acute employee shortages in 2020 and 2021 when COVID-induced legislation enabled many unemployed employees to be paid to stay home rather than actually work (nor pay their rent without eviction in many cities).

---

17   Strine, Leo. Kirby Smith, and Reilly Steel. "Caremark and ESG, Perfect Together: A Practical Approach to Implementing an Integrated, Efficient, and Effective Caremark and EESG Strategy." July 30, 2020. *Iowa Law Review*, Forthcoming, U of Penn, Inst for Law & Econ Research Paper No. 20-45. Retrieved June 26, 2021

Transforming the Culture

Executing Young's Vision can result in a cultural sea change that can help meet the expectations of our US and other regulators. More broadly, it can help you meet your stakeholders' expectations, including those of your employees, communities, clients, the environment which your firm operates, as well as society at large. Your long-term strategy will flourish too. However, if your corporate culture remains short-term and myopic, then your program will ultimately fail if the CEO and CFO will fall prey to short-term cost cutting to maximize profits and share price.

The next two chapters underscore why Young's Vision will enable you to achieve an effective compliance program. However, they are both stark reminders of why it's not enough. Chapter 2.10 reminds us why employees who raise integrity issues (i.e., whistleblowers) are essential to maintaining an effective compliance & ethics program and strengthening the corporate culture. And chapter 2.11 is a case study in recidivist behavior and culture.

Achieving an effective program is the first step, one that will ensure day-to-day success. However, you also need to make permanent changes. And that's why I've provided the six provocative recommendations in chapters 2.12–2.18. I refer to these six recommendations as the "Compliance Hexagon," which, together with Young's Vision, will enable your compliance & ethics program, culture, and strategy will be effective, successful, safe, and responsible for the long run.

The Accountability and Liability Pyramid (US vs. the World)

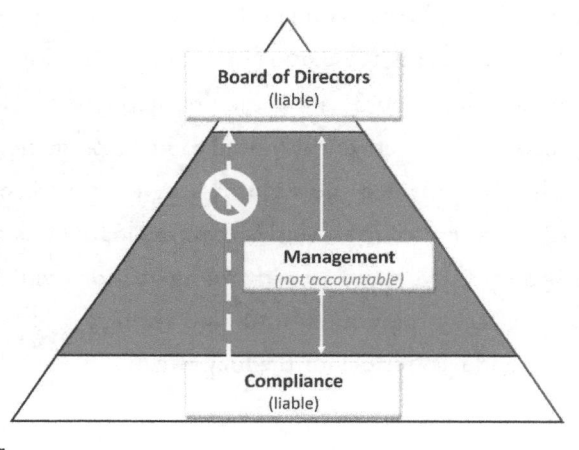

Source: author

A company's board of directors and chief compliance officer (CCO) must have an ongoing, important, and strategic partnership to hold management accountable and culpable. This is especially true for US-based companies.

Both board members and the CCO are personally liable for management's actions or inactions. At the same time, the CEO and his or

her executive management team are *not* accountable or culpable unless they engage in egregious misconduct or illegal activities directly. When something goes wrong, often the shareholders (or other third parties) sue the directors, who are held personally liable; regulators and others often sanction the CCO personally.

Lack of Board and Compliance Interaction

Furthermore, and as illustrated above, in most US-based companies, the dialog between the board and compliance (if it exists at all) is neither regular enough nor substantive enough. This point was underscored in a recent Deloitte study, which found that despite the long-standing US DoJ Corporate Sentencing Guidelines and Corporate Compliance guidance, some boards may not fully understand or appreciate the importance of their fiduciary obligations with respect to compliance & ethics.[1] In the 11th edition of the *Board Practices Report*, a collaborative effort between Deloitte LLP's Center for Board Effectiveness and the Society for Corporate Governance revealed that:

- Almost 40% of the public company boards surveyed reported that their company's chief compliance officer does not regularly attend audit committee meetings.

- 70% reported that the chief compliance officer does not regularly attend board meetings.

- Only 17% of those surveyed reported that the chief compliance officer is responsible for managing culture risk (*most assign this to Human Resources*).

- Only 50% reported that their board training includes content on ethics and compliance.

---

1   Biskup, Robert, Parsons, Krista and Lamm, Robert of Deloitte LLP, *"Board Oversight of Corporate Compliance: Is it Time for a Refresh?"*, Harvard Law School Forum on Corporate Governance, October 15, 2019. https://corpgov.law.harvard.edu/2019/10/15/board-oversight-of-corporate-compliance-is-it-time-for-a-refresh/. Retrieved November 14, 2020

- Only 14% of full boards of directors cover ethics & compliance topics.

- Only 3% of those surveyed have compliance committees, of which none are financial institutions and 4% are non-financial institutions.[2]

The CEO "Didn't Know"

In the United States, CEOs and the rest of the C-suite whose employees commit misconduct or other crimes are typically found not guilty because they're viewed as (or claim to be) "too far removed" from the day-to-day decision making of those employees. In other words, they "didn't know."

It's this lack of accountability and culpability by management—in particular the executive suite, which leads directly to continuous corporate prosecutions, class action litigation, share prices plummeting, and ultimately, Congressional wrath, and reputational ruin. Meanwhile, the CEO's and C-suite's behavior and corporate culture remain unchanged.

The Board's Fiduciary Duties and Liability

We've learned that the board (as agent) has fiduciary duties of loyalty and care to protect the interests of the shareholders (as principal). Under the "business judgment rule," the board delegates day-to-day decision making and management of the company to the CEO and his or her management team to maximize profits and/or execute the strategy of the company. Shareholders can file derivative litigation against directors for failing to fulfill these fiduciary duties, typically citing the high standards of the 1996 Caremark case described below, as the litmus test.

---

2 Deloitte LLP and Society for Corporate Governance, "Board Practices Report Common Threads across Boardrooms," 11th Edition as of Q4 2018. https://www2.deloitte.com/content/dam/Deloitte/us/Documents/center-for-board-effectiveness/2018-board-practices-report.pdf. Retrieved November 14, 2020

Blue Bell and Clovis Cases Have Made Directors More Vulnerable

As summarized in chapter 1.16 (with more detail below), in the derivative class action Caremark case,[3] the Delaware State Chancery Court defined a high "utter failure" standard and multi-factor test designed to determine when directors' fiduciary duty of care is breached. To show that directors breached their oversight duty, plaintiffs had to show that, "The directors knew *or* should have known that violations of the law were occurring, and in either event:

- The directors took no steps in a good faith effort to prevent or remedy the situation, and

- Such failure proximately resulted in the losses complained of (though this last element may be thought to constitute an affirmative defense)."[4]

Two major cases lowered the Caremark threshold for determining whether the board of directors "utterly failed" its fiduciary duties of loyalty and care: Marchand v. Barnhill[5] (the Blue Bell Ice Cream case described in chapter 1.16) and Clovis Oncology.[6] Blue Bell highlighted the failure of its board because it received no reports regarding Blue Bell's food safety (among other failings). And in Clovis Oncology, the Court found that the company's board ignored red flags that revealed a "mission-critical" failure to comply with drug protocols and associated US Food and Drug Administration (FDA) regulations. The court noted that a board's oversight

3   In re Caremark International Inc. Derivative Litigation, September 25, 1996, 698 A.2d 959 (Del. Ch. 1996) - https://law.justia.com/cases/delaware/court-of-chancery/1996/13670-3.html - last retrieved June 30, 2021
4   Ibid.
5   Marchand v. Barnhill - 212 A.3d 805 (Del. 2019). https://courts.delaware.gov/Opinions/Download.aspx?id=291200. Retrieved June 30, 2021
6   In re Clovis Oncology, Inc. Derivative Litigation, C.A. No. 2017-0222-JRS (Del. Ch. Oct. 1, 2019). https://courts.delaware.gov/Opinions/Download.aspx?id=295870. Retrieved June 30, 2021

obligations are enhanced with respect to mission-critical products while operating in a heavily regulated industry.[7]

"Mission Critical" Operations and Compliance's Strategic Value to the Board

Plaintiffs are increasingly using the Blue Bell and Clovis cases as a path to holding directors liable. The results have been mixed so far, but nonetheless underscore why the full board of directors and the CCO need to dialogue and partner more strategically. As articulated clearly by two attorneys at law firm, Simpson, Thacher & Bartlett:

> "It is clear that, as Marchand signaled, Delaware courts will more readily permit a Caremark claim to proceed when the company conducts its 'essential and mission critical' operations under obligations imposed by external regulation or law, yet fails to implement compliance systems, or fails to monitor existing compliance systems, and compliance lapses result in regulatory or legal violations with attendant monetary loss."[8]

The board is therefore at risk of being personally liable for the actions or inactions of the CEO and his or her team.[9]

---

7   Stark, Lisa R. and Kirkpatrick, Sara M., "Another "Well-Pled" Caremark Claim Survives a Motion to Dismiss." American Bar Association, January 13, 2020. https://www.americanbar.org/groups/business_law/publications/blt/2020/01/caremark-claim/#:~:text=In%20Clovis%2C%20the%20Court%20of,the%20same%20board's%20oversight%20of. Retrieved November 15, 2020

8   McLaughlin, Joseph M. and McGovern, Shannon K. *"Director Oversight Duty Claims." New York Law Journal*, October 7, 2020. https://www.law.com/newyorklawjournal/2020/10/07/director-oversight-duty-claims/. Retrieved February 27, 2021

9   Directors & Officers liability insurance is available, but only up to a point.

Chief Compliance & Ethics Officer Liability, Particularly in the Financial Sector[10]

It's abundantly clear—and often explicit—that CCOs are personally liable for corporate violations of laws and regulations, globally. The personal liability has had a chilling effect on the market for highly skilled CCOs because of their growing hesitancy to allow themselves to be targeted and liable. Some initiatives seek to remedy this, but they don't go far enough.

How accountable is management outside the US? And even if they're legislatively or otherwise more accountable, how potentially liable are the CCOs? Below is a sample of countries that target CCOs, particularly those in the financial services industry:

United States

The DoJ, US Securities and Exchange Commission (SEC), Financial Industry Regulatory Authority (FINRA), New York State Department of Financial Services (DFS), US Treasury Office of the Comptroller of the Currency (OCC), and other government bodies have increasingly prosecuted CCOs, especially over weaknesses in financial crime compliance programs, anti-money laundering (AML) and Office of Foreign Asset Control (OFAC) sanctions compliance. In some instances, the authority is explicit. In other instances, the prosecution proceeds even if implicit. Many enforcement actions by the DoJ and the SEC over the US FCPA have also targeted CCOs. Unlike CEOs and their management teams, CCOs are viewed as accountable and liable because they "should have known."

10   Special thanks to Corporate Counsel and its publication Law.com and its authors: Ann Sultan, Shula de Jersey, Daniel Travers, Robin Lööf, Ariane Fleuriot, Ario Dehghani, Maarten 't Sas, and Georgianna Verhage for their very helpful two-part article: "Criminal Liability Risks for Compliance Officers: a Multi-Jurisdictional Perspective—Parts 1 and 2." July 14, 2020 and August 11, 2020, respectively at: https://www.law.com/corpcounsel/2020/07/14/criminal-liability-risks-for-compliance-officers-a-multi-jurisdictional-perspective-part-i/ and https://www.law.com/corpcounsel/2020/08/11/criminal-liability-risks-for-compliance-officers-a-multi-jurisdictional-perspective-part-ii/. Retrieved November 13, 2020

Most, but not all, prosecutions involve the heads of financial crimes (better known as the money laundering reporting officers or MLROs) because they're directly accountable for managing a program to detect and prevent money laundering, terrorist financing, and other financial crimes; and for reporting unusual or suspicious activities to the US Treasury Financial Crimes Enforcement Network (FinCen). Many enforcement actions have cited violations of the US FCPA, in which the SEC's director of enforcement set forth three criteria explicitly to be considered against CCOs:

- When a chief compliance officer is "*affirmatively involved* in misconduct unrelated to their compliance function"

- When a chief compliance officer "engage[s] in efforts to *obstruct or mislead* the [SEC] staff"

- When the chief compliance officer has "*exhibited a wholesale failure* to carry out his or her responsibilities." The question for this third prong is whether the CCO is fully at fault for a lack of budget, ability to escalate candidly, and for the front-line sales activities of the businesses which prompted the misconduct.

United Kingdom

The UK's Financial Conduct Authority (FCA) sets forth for all FCA-regulated firms the Senior Managers and Certification Regime (SMCR). This regime focuses on the individual accountability of senior managers of regulated businesses (including compliance officers) who have a statutory duty of responsibility. In the event of a breach, the senior manager responsible for that area could be held personally liable in regulatory proceedings if he or she did not take reasonable steps to prevent the breach.

The FCA has a history of taking regulatory enforcement action against compliance officers for, among other reasons, failing to implement or monitor systems. With the SMCR's focus on individual accountability,

there is likely to be an increase in such proceedings. And at least the CEO and business heads are included in this scope of accountability.

France

French law, as enforced by the French anti-corruption agency (l'Agence Française Anticorruption, or AFA), doesn't explicitly hold compliance officers criminally liable for offenses committed on their watch. However, they can still be investigated and prosecuted for failing to stop offenses of which they were aware and had the power (and responsibility) to prevent. It's not unthinkable that senior compliance officers could be prosecuted on this basis, although no such case has yet been brought. As a result, compliance officers in France remain exposed.

Germany

Under German criminal law, a compliance officer can be held personally criminally liable for offenses committed by (other) company employees, provided that the compliance officer at least suspected that a crime was ongoing and *deliberately looked the other way*. More frequent, however, are cases where the compliance & ethics officer has *no knowledge* of an ongoing crime within the organization. In such cases, German prosecutors accuse the compliance officer "only" of a *breach of supervisory duties*—a regulatory offense that carries a personal fine of up to 1 million euros.

Unlike the US Corporate Sentencing Guidelines, German law does not yet hold corporations criminally liable. Prosecutors searching for evidence against a high-ranking manager, sometimes take a close look at the chief compliance officer, in an attempt to base a corporate fine on an alleged breach of supervisory duties. Thus, in criminal proceedings, the prosecutor will investigate the actual crime (such as a corruption offense) and then initiate regulatory fine proceedings against management—specifically the CCO (who is often also the anti-money laundering officer) for having breached his or her supervisory duties in failing to prevent the

crime. Investigators are increasingly targeting the compliance and legal departments directly during searches to find out how suspected employee misconduct was handled internally. The result is often a regulatory fine on the company, in some cases in the hundreds of millions of euros.

The Netherlands

In 2019, a legislative amendment was announced that would introduce judicial oversight of major (multimillion-euro) settlements. In response, the Dutch Public Prosecutors Service declared that settlements will in principle be offered only to companies and not to natural persons against whom a prosecution will be launched or a penalty order issued in case of sufficient proof of misconduct.

As a result, it seems unlikely that members of a Dutch company's management board or individuals employed by a company will be able to settle charges against them. Compliance officers operating in the Netherlands will therefore likely be even more exposed to prosecution or receiving a penalty order for their alleged involvement in corporate misconduct and will not have the opportunity to settle.

Hong Kong[11]

Similar to the UK's Senior Manager and Certification Regime, the Hong Kong Securities and Futures Commission (SFC) has a "responsible officer" regime, which includes the following four key areas:

- The SFC is willing to act against individuals. Many have targeted responsible officers, particularly AML officers.

- Neither the SFC nor a court needs to demonstrate that actual money laundering has occurred. The mere fact that controls

---

11   McCormack, Urszula. "SFC imposes personal liability for AML/CTF failures: 5 lessons for senior managers." *King and Wood Mallesons*, March 13, 2017 - https://www.kwm.com/en/hk/knowledge/insights/sfc-imposes-personal-liability-for-aml-ctf-failures-20170313. Retrieved November 13, 2020

were not implemented or followed is sufficient to impose fines, reprimands, and other penalties.

- Senior managers will be held accountable to a broad compliance mandate. The SFC equates a broad scope of responsibility with a broad scope of accountability.

- The SFC and other regulators are actively investigating AML/ Counter Terrorist Financing (CTF) control failures.

Japan[12]

Under Japanese criminal law, "dual criminality" allows for sanctioning both an individual and a corporation. Many regulatory laws, such as the Pharmaceutical and Medical Devices Act, provide administrative penalties, where the government may issue cease-and-desist orders and ban specific actions. In addition, the court may order confiscatory measures against corporations. There are no independent monitors, as there are in the United States, and no "model" compliance programs per se.

Liability exists over directors or managers for not having adopted (intentionally or negligently) measures to prevent crimes. According to a Supreme Court Decision on March 26, 1965, representative directors may be held liable under a dual liability clause, unless it's proven that the business operator paid necessary attention to selecting or supervising its agents or employees in order to prevent unlawful activities committed by them.

Australia

The Australian Transaction Reports and Analysis Centre (AUSTRAC) has been quite actively prosecuting violations of financial crimes against Australian financial institutions, including multi-billion-dollar penalties

12   Kengo Nishigaki and Yoshiaki Muto. "Corporate Liability in Japan." Baker McKenzie Japan, *Global Compliance News*. https://globalcompliancenews.com/white-collar-crime/corporate-liability-japan/. Retrieved November 13, 2020

against WestPac, Commonwealth Bank, and other Australian Depository Institutions (ADIs). Similar to the UK Senior Managers and Certification Regime (SMCR), the Australian Treasury has proposed rules in which "accountable persons" including the CEO, compliance head, and other executives are liable for up to A$1.05 million.

China

The People's Republic of China has a corporate liability program over criminal activity that focuses on public safety, undermining China's economy, financial crimes, infringing upon citizens' personal or property rights, trafficking, risks to national security, and accepting and offering bribes. Liability is predominantly monetary under Section II of the People's Republic of China Criminal Law, which states that:

> "[T}he only sanction applicable to a company is monetary fines. However, under administrative regulations, the authorities can publicly disclose the company's behavior, suspend the company from some business operations, ban the company from participating in public procurement or disqualify the company for government-funded incentive programs."[13]

Recently, Lai Xiaomin, the former chairman of state-owned Huarong Asset Management, was found guilty by a court in the coastal city of Tianjin of corruption, bigamy, and having received some $277 million in bribes between 2008 and 2018. The government will confiscate his personal assets. Lai Xiaomin might consider himself lucky, as perhaps the most notable sanction for individuals is the death penalty.[14] Although the

---

13   Hu, Vivian and Hui, Simon. "Corporate Liability in China," Baker, McKenzie, Global Compliance News - https://globalcompliancenews.com/white-collar-crime/corporate-liability-in-china/. Retrieved February 21, 2021
14   Stevenson, Alexandra. "China Sentences Former Bank Chief to Death in Rare Move." *The New York Times*, January 5, 2021. https://www.nytimes.com/2021/01/05/business/china-huarong-death-penalty.html. Retrieved February 27, 2021.

number of executions has declined since 2009 after public outcry within and beyond the country, executions are carried out.

Overall Trends Against CCOs and Financial Crime Compliance Heads

Policymakers are seeking to tackle misconduct through personal accountability and a renewed consideration of incentives and remuneration. Although the UK is probably leading the way with its SMCR, it is by no means alone, with Australia, Hong Kong, and others refining their approach to senior individual accountability. During a Thomson Reuters webinar on regulatory risk in Asia in 2017, an audience poll found that 70% saw a need for a senior management liability equivalent regime in Asia.[15]

This has led—in the US and abroad—to an environment of fear and exposure among CCOs and financial crime compliance officers, and a departure of skilled compliance officers who fear being targeted and held personally liable for the misconduct and wrongful actions of their CEO and/or business colleagues.[16] Indeed, as reported in *The Wall Street Journal*, I personally recommend two tangible steps. I'll describe these in the Recommendations section in chapters 2.13–2.18.[17]

---

15   Hammond, Susannah. "Ten things compliance officers need to do in 2018." *Thomson Reuters Regulatory Intelligence.* https://legal.thomsonreuters.com/en/insights/articles/10-things-compliance-officers-need-do-in-2018. Retrieved November 13, 2020

16   For an excellent overview of the SEC's empathy and recommendations to CCO's, please refer to Jonathan T Marks' article, "Chief Compliance Officers (CCOs) and Personal Liability," Board and Fraud, Baker Tilley, which was adapted from Robin Burton's article in the *Anti-Corruption Report*, November 11, 2020 - https://boardandfraud.com/2020/11/11/chief-compliance-officers-ccos-and-personal-liability/. Retrieved November 13, 2020

17   Sung, Mengqi. "Guidance on Charging Compliance Chiefs Could Bring Clarity, but Some Seek More Protections." *The Wall Street Journal,* June 17, 2021 - https://www.wsj.com/articles/guidance-on-charging-compliance-chiefs-could-bring-clarity-but-some-seek-more-protections-11623963411?st=0o5klahzawd1mj8&reflink=desktopwebshare_linkedin. Retrieved June 30, 2021

The Opportunity for Boards of Directors and CCOs to Strategically Partner to Hold Management Accountable

Although the United Kingdom, Australia, Hong Kong, and other countries do hold CEOs and other "accountable persons" personally liable in addition to the CCO, the United States does not. Even with accountable person liability in these other countries, questions arise whether these powers trigger prosecutions sufficiently or forcefully enough. For sure, not enough is done to support the needs and resources to enable a culture of compliance & ethics on a continuous and sustainable basis.

Protecting and Enabling Our
Salt-of-the-Earth Whistleblowers

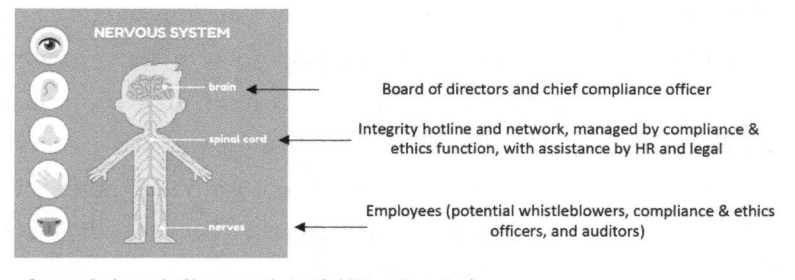

Source: Sudowoodo/Shutterstock.com (additions by author)

"You are the salt of the earth. But if the salt loses its saltiness, how can it be made salty again? It is no longer good for anything, except to be thrown out and trampled underfoot."

— MATTHEW 5:13[1]

Whistleblowers are indeed the "salt of the earth," a phrase that usually refers to people who are "representative of the best or noblest elements of society"[2] or "considered to be of great worth and reliability."[3] In a perfect world, everyone you work with (or for)

---

1   The Bible. Matthew 5:13 ("Sermon on the Mount")

2   Dictionary.com. https://www.dictionary.com/browse/salt-of-the-earth. Retrieved March 13, 2021

3   Phrases.org.uk. https://www.phrases.org.uk/meanings/salt-of-the-earth.html. Retrieved March 13, 2021

would be "salt of the earth." But, sadly, we don't live in a perfect world. As we've discussed throughout this book, there's a crucial link and delicate balance between corporate culture, employee conduct, and compliance & ethics officers. And whistleblowers—the folks who do the right thing by raising concerns about integrity issues or illegalities in their workplace (business or government)—are that link. Supporting and encouraging whistleblowers is an essential part of an effective compliance & ethics program, which, as you've learned, helps meet long-term stakeholders' expectations, protects the board of directors from personal liability, and helps preserve the reputation of the firm.

The Organizational Body

As I've often mentioned, a corporate body is like the human body. Both are the sum of many moving parts, and both involve key circulatory, hormonal, nervous, and other systems and networks. To keep the body and soul healthy, these systems and networks must work harmoniously and symbiotically. The system I want to focus on in this chapter is the nervous system, which is divided into two parts. The first is the *central nervous system*, which is comprised of the brain (the board of directors and the CCO) and the spinal cord (internal or external[4] hotlines and other whistleblowing channels that are managed by compliance & ethics officers with support from others, including HR, employee relations, and legal).

Second is the *peripheral nervous system*, the network of nerves that connect the spinal cord and brain to the rest of the body. In humans, nerve endings throughout the body transmit chemical, electronic, or verbal messages to the brain, which sends back instructions on how to respond to a variety of situations (such as heat, fear, fever, disease, and love). In the corporate body, employees (or "sensors"[5]) alert compliance of problems. The CCO, in turn, compiles those messages and presents

---

4   For example, independent third parties provide integrity hotlines on an anonymous basis, such as Clearview (Toronto, Canada), NavexGlobal (Oregon), or ComplianceLine (North Carolina).

5   Credit for this analogy goes to Nick Gallo, Chief Servant and Co-CEO of ComplianceLine.

a summary to the board. That summary must include whistleblowing metrics and analytics (How many incidents were reported? How was each one resolved?) so that the board may effectively govern, oversee, and hold management accountable.

Healthy Nervous System = Healthy Whistleblowing System = Healthy Ethical Culture

In addition to collecting whistleblowing metrics, companies must also ensure that no attempts are being made to suppress the peripheral nerve endings. In other words, all employees, no matter where they're located, must be free to report misconduct without fear of retaliation. If, as is the case in many organizations, despite laws specifically designed to protect them, whistleblowers are penalized, fired, and/or blacklisted (which may keep them from finding employment in the future), the company will eventually lose not only its way, but also its customers and its profits.

The corporate body's nervous system (and corporate conduct) is healthy when there's continuous dialogue between the board, the CCO, and whistleblowers. An enlightened board understands its existing and emerging risks, listens to and heeds the advice of the CCO (including integrity issues raised by whistleblowers), and understands its employees' overall well-being as well as the dynamically changing environment among its competitors, industry, and global ecosystem.

Seeing and treating whistleblowers as the "salt of the earth" ensures that integrity issues will be raised in a timely, complete, and thorough manner and investigated to closure.

A healthy corporate culture identifies, roots out, and disciplines wrong-doers and/or wrongful or harmful activities—whether workplace or sexual harassment, unsafe working conditions or worse, danger to employees and/or markets, or fraud. A healthy culture also remediates the problems and puts controls in place to prevent and avoid recurrence.

A Poor, Retaliatory Culture Leads to Reputational Damage and Worse

Unfortunately, more often than not, a company's overall culture or sub-culture within specific business divisions isn't healthy, particularly with respect to its treatment of whistleblowers. One of the most infamous cases of whistleblowing retaliation in recent history was Wells Fargo Bank's fake account scandal.[6] Other notable examples include Sherry Hunt and Richard Bowen at Citigroup,[7] who raised concerns about Citi's substandard mortgage loan processes—and were then retaliated against; Volkswagen's fake diesel emissions program (2015),[8] which resulted in millions of automobile recalls and hundreds of billions of dollars in penalties; and a series of briberies, cover-ups, and other scandals involving Walmart.[9,10,11,12]

Sadly, whistleblowing—and retaliation against whistleblowers—has been going on for more than 500 years. In 1564, a brave nobleman exposed the horrors of Czar Ivan the Terrible's regime; in 1777 two US continental naval officers blew the whistle over the torture of British prisoners; in 1971, Daniel Ellsberg leaked the famous "Pentagon Papers"; in 1974, Karen

6   Raymond, Adam K. "Former Wells Fargo Employees Say They Were Fired for Whistle-blowing," September 21, 2016. https://nymag.com/intelligencer/2016/09/wells-fargo-employees-were-fired-for-whistle-blowing.html. Retrieved March 13, 2021

7   Lanyon, Charley. "Sherry Hunt Took on One of the World's Biggest Banks and Won;" *New York Magazine.* November 16, 2016. https://nymag.com/vindicated/2016/11/sherry-hunt-took-on-one-of-the-worlds-biggest-banks-and-won.html. Retrieved March 14, 2021

8   Kelton, Erika. "14.7 Billion Reasons Why Volkswagen Should Have Welcomed Whistleblowers," *Forbes,* June 19, 2016. https://www.forbes.com/sites/erikakelton/2016/06/29/14-7-billion-reasons-why-volkswagen-should-have-welcomed-whistleblowers/?sh=29ce80ad7500. Retrieved March 13, 2021

9   Heineman, Ben, Jr. "Who's Responsible for the Walmart Mexico Scandal?" *Harvard Business Review,* May 15, 2014. https://hbr.org/2014/05/whos-responsible-for-the-walmart-mexico-scandal. Retrieved March 13, 2021

10   De Haldevang, Max. "Walmart Dodged US Tax on $2 Billion by Routing Cash through Multiple Countries, Whistleblower Says," *Quartz,* November 29, 2019. https://www.yahoo.com/now/walmart-dodged-us-tax-2-120039434.html. Retrieved March 14, 2021

11   US Department of Justice. "Department of Justice Files Nationwide Lawsuit Against Walmart Inc. for Controlled Substances Act Violations." December 20, 2020. https://www.justice.gov/opa/pr/department-justice-files-nationwide-lawsuit-against-walmart-inc-controlled-substances-act. Retrieved March 14, 2021

12   Aegis Law. "Walmart Whistle blower to Receive $31.2 Mil Settlement for Wrongful Termination," July 14, 2019. https://www.aegislawfirm.com/blog/2019/july/walmart-whistle-blower-to-receive-31-2-mil-settl. Retrieved March 14, 2021

Silkwood exposed safety concerns at Kerr-McKee's nuclear power plant; in 2002, an anonymous whistleblower leaked the "Panama Papers." Most never recovered. Others died.

Too Much Salt Is Bad, But Zero Salt Is Worse

Here's another salt-as-whistleblower example. While we definitely want to encourage whistleblowers to come forward, we don't want to create a system in which everyone is turning everyone else in for insignificant offenses—most issues can be resolved quickly and easily without making a formal complaint to compliance and the board. But just as salt in the body acts as an important electrolyte, maintaining proper fluid balance, muscle function, and nerve transmission,[13] whistleblowers keep the corporate body from shutting down. And just as no-salt diets can harm the human body by raising triglyceride and LDL blood levels and can lead to insulin imbalance, heart disease and/or diabetes,[14] the absence of whistleblowers reinforces poor—and often illegal—corporate conduct, which aside from resulting in huge fines and significant loss of revenue and reputation, can actually kill people (as we saw in the Blue Bell Ice Cream listeria scandal).

Sadly, with increasing frequency, whistleblowers are treated horribly. In the U.S., rates of retaliation against whistleblowers have more than tripled since 2013. And globally, they've almost doubled since 2019, according to the Ethics & Compliance Institute (ECI).[15] Far too often, whistleblowers are seen as "snitches," "bitter," "troublemakers," or not being team players. But the truth is that people who raise legitimate issues in good faith (as opposed to being motivated by financial or other benefits, such as reduced jail time) are demonstrating a high degree of integrity and courage. Nevertheless, many of them suffer financial or personal ruin

---

13   Palsdottir, Hrefna MS. "Salt: Good or Bad?" *HealthLine*, June 18, 2017. https://www.
healthline.com/nutrition/salt-good-or-bad#TOC_TITLE_HDR_3. Retrieved March 14, 2021
14   Ibid.
15   Ethics & Compliance Institute (ECI). "2021 Global Business Ethics Survey® Report—The State of Ethics & Compliance in the Workplace: A Look at Global Trends," March 2021. https://
www.ethics.org/just-released-2021-global-business-ethics-survey-report. Retrieved March 14, 2021

despite, as mentioned earlier, local, regional, state, federal, and even global laws that prohibit retaliation.

And even in cases where a financial reward is offered to encourage whistleblowers to come forward, many are prevented from receiving their reward (or even being recognized for their braveness) by a stressful, labyrinth of processes and time-critical statute-of-limitations deadlines. As a result, too much bad and illegal behavior goes unreported by good people who understandably decide that the risks of becoming a whistleblower are too great.

The Need to Link and Balance the Board, 1LOD Businesses, Independent Compliance, and Whistleblowers

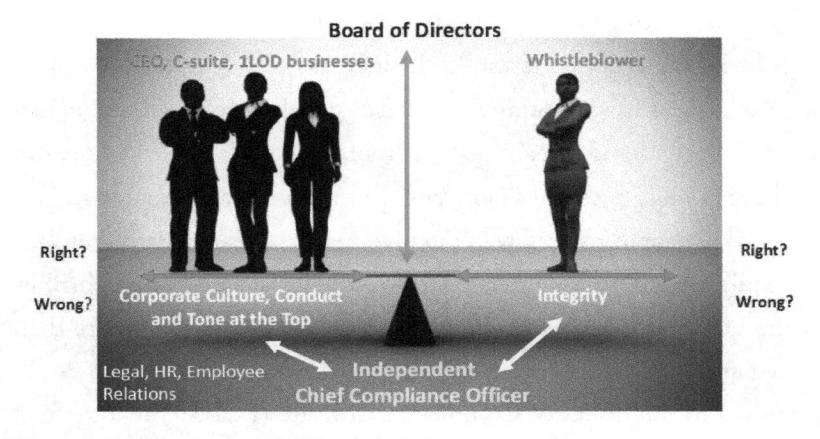

Source: emerge/Shutterstock.com (additions by author)

Salt Can Make Slippery Slopes Less Slippery

An effective compliance & ethics program that supports and encourages whistleblowing can spread the "salt" of integrity across—and against—the slippery slope of misguided, selfish and/or desperate executives and local managers. An empowered and independent CCO can protect employees who raise integrity issues in good faith and can provide traction for the organization by escalating integrity issues to the non-executive board

members without the presence of management. To do so would allow the board to hold management accountable.

Salting those potentially slippery paths will also reduce or prevent personal and professional liability for those harmed by slick, fraudulent, or otherwise unethical leaders, business heads, staff, and overall corporate cultures. That said, compliance & ethics officers alone cannot achieve the delicate balance necessary to monitor ethics hotlines and investigate hundreds—and for some firms, thousands—of whistleblowing allegations. They need the help and support of equally courageous employees in human resources, legal, and employee relations who will demonstrate the same integrity as the CCO and most importantly, those brave whistleblowers.

It's therefore incumbent upon boards of directors to support CCOs and to partner directly and continuously not only to protect whistleblowers from the fear of and actual retaliation, but also to prevent management from discouraging and/or punishing whistleblowers.

However, if the CCO remains toothless in authority because he or she is subordinate to the general counsel, CFO, or chief risk officer at the direction of the CEO, then whistleblowers (and employees who otherwise might consider being whistleblowers) will continue to be "trampled underfoot."

Chapter 2.11

Citigroup Case Study, and the 2020 COSO/ Enterprise Compliance Risk Framework

Source: Lane V. Erickson/Shutterstock.com

The Case of Citigroup, Inc. (Citi)

I've chosen Citigroup as a case study because they've epitomized the linkage between aggressive strategic expansion and corporate culture for decades. As I noted in part 1, Citi was the most aggressive bank strategically with respect to its regulatory applications seeking Fed approvals to expand its activities and products. Citi's international footprint was also much more expansive than others'. They (and the lemmings that followed) utilized legal and regulatory loopholes to engage in activities that weren't explicitly prohibited ("Show us where it says we can't do this," they'd often dare). This culture wasn't just *an* issue, it was the *central* issue.

Citi's aggressive strategies epitomized their culture then, and perhaps even today. Citi is by no means the only banking or nonbanking firm with an aggressive corporate culture. Every day stories break that cause reputational damage—most recently about Credit Suisse (Greensill Capital, Archegos, and its culture towards risk and compliance; see chapter 2.8). Most of the time, the company in question has been trying to make as

much money as quickly as possible, while spending as little as tolerable on compliance and internal controls.

* * *

The Fed and the Comptroller of the Currency's "Cease and Desist"

On October 7, 2020, the Federal Reserve and US Comptroller of the Currency issued individual cease-and-desist orders against Citigroup and its primary consumer banking subsidiary, Citibank, N.A. for longstanding deficiencies in data governance and enterprise risk management, including compliance risk management and internal controls. Citi was fined $400 million (a very insignificant sum compared to Citigroup's earnings). But what's especially noteworthy was the decision by the US and other governments to call out Citi publicly, for decades of remedial actions promised but not met.

Below is a brief history in which the quotes are self-explanatory. But before we get to that, let me point out something both obvious and critical: Deferred prosecution agreements (DPAs) *do not* work. DPAs are promises by board of director resolutions and/or corporate executive management ("we won't do this again") in exchange for avoiding criminal prosecution of individuals, culpability of executives, and no significant demands that the corporations institute real cultural change and meaningfully invest in compliance processes. The sad fact is that DPAs, instead, spawn serial violators and embolden the wrong culture rather than instill a sense of control responsibility.

For a longer, more detailed list of Citibank, legacy Citicorp, and Citigroup violations, including its treatment of New York City and its employees in the 1970s,[1] please refer to the publicly available "Violation

---

1   Mattera, Phillip – "*Citigroup – Corporate Rap Sheet,*" Corporate Research Project - http://www.corp-research.org/citigroup - retrieved November 16, 2020

Tracker" under Citigroup.[2] In the meantime, as the opening of one of my favorite TV shows used to say, "these are their stories."[3]

1. Citibank and Enron (July 2003)

"The Securities and Exchange Commission today instituted and settled enforcement proceedings against two major financial institutions, J.P. Morgan Chase & Co. and Citigroup, Inc., for their roles in Enron Corp.'s manipulation of its financial statements. Each institution helped Enron mislead its investors by characterizing what were essentially loan proceeds as cash from operating activities... without admitting or denying the Commission's allegations."[4]

"As a result of the settlements, the financial institutions will expend financial and human capital to redesign their internal controls. Under Citigroup's and J.P. Morgan's settlements with the Federal Reserve Board, each have agreed to increase risk management controls[5] and provide the regulatory agencies with a new set of standard(s), where senior executives will review complex transactions, such as transactions involving special purpose entities (or "SPEs"). Internal controls will be augmented in three key areas: 1) credit risk management, 2) legal and reputational risk management, and 3) approval and progress reports."[6]

---

2   Good Jobs First – "*Violation Tracker Parent Company Summary: Citigroup*" - https:// violationtracker.goodjobsfirst.org/parent/citigroup - retrieved November 16, 2020
3   "Law and Order."
4   US Securities and Exchange Commission – "*Citigroup Agrees to Pay $120 Million to Settle SEC Allegations that It Helped Enron and Dynegy Commit Fraud,*" July 28, 2003, Press Release - https://www.sec.gov/news/press/2003-87.htm, and Order - https://www.sec.gov/litigation/ admin/34-48230.htm - retrieved November 16, 2020
5   Fast forward to October 7, 2020 Federal Reserve and US Comptroller of the Currency cease and desist orders for the same promises being made by Citigroup and Citibank, NA, respectively.
6   Reynolds, Vaughn, "*The Citigroup and J.P. Morgan Chase Enron Settlements: The Impact on the Financial Industry,*" North Carolina Banking Institute, University of North Carolina School of Law, Volume 8, Issue 1, Article 12, 2004 - https://scholarship.law.unc.edu/cgi/viewcontent. cgi?referer=https://www.google.com/&httpsredir=1&article=1143&context=ncbi. Retrieved November 16, 2020

2. Citibank Japan (2001–2004)

In 2001, the Japanese Financial Services Agency (FSA) issued an "unsatisfactory" rating against Citi. Citi's own internal auditors (who are required to operate independently of business units and are supposed to be a purely independent third line of defense) disagreed. According to a detailed, *Wall Street Journal* investigative article, aptly subtitled, "Obsession with Bottom Line,"[7] four months after the unfavorable FSA report, Citi's auditors had the Japanese private bank rated "satisfactory."

Japanese regulators weren't fooled (in fact, they later stated that they were disrespected), and three years later, the FSA ordered Citigroup to close its private banking business in Japan after finding that Citi's bankers misled clients about investment risks, sold products that they weren't permitted to sell, and, most seriously, failed to take proper precautions to prevent money laundering and other illicit transactions.

Citi's response was a publicly humiliating bow that ended up on the front page of major Japanese papers and a statement from Citi's CEO that while he was sorry for the problems in Japan, Japan was an isolated case. "We had a breakdown in our compliance and governance standards here in private banking... I do not believe we have similar breakdowns elsewhere."[8]

For a while, Citi's CEO continued to "talk the talk," saying all the right things to the right people. For example:

> "It's our fault because all we talk about is delivering the numbers. We've done this forever... But employees must recognize they cannot 'chew up the franchise' in pursuit of short-term profits... The game is a long-term game."[9]

---

7   Pacelle, Mitchell, Fackler, Martin and Morse, Andrew – "For Citigroup, Scandal in Japan Shows Dangers of Global Sprawl - Obsession with Bottom Line," *The Wall Street Journal*, December 22, 2004 - https://www.wsj.com/articles/SB110366226796306310. Retrieved November 16, 2020

8   Famous last words? Morse, Andrew, "Citigroup Extends Apology to Japan," The Wall Street Journal, October 26, 2004 - https://www.wsj.com/articles/SB109868567660354489 - retrieved November 16, 2020

9   Pacelle at supra.

And this:

> "Our job is to set a tone at the top to incent people to do the right thing and to set up safety nets to catch people who make mistakes or do the wrong thing and correct those as quickly as possible. And it is working. It is working."[10]

But talk is cheap. The real proof is what Citi actually did. Read on.

3. Rejection of Mortgaged Backed Securities Settlement by Judge Rakoff (2007–2011)

Apparently, Citigroup's management and businesses didn't heed the lessons learned in Japan.

The SEC and Citigroup agreed to a settlement over a Citigroup $1 billion mortgage fund that it sold to investors in 2007 with securities that it believed would fail—so that it could bet against its own customers and profit when values declined. The fraud, according to the SEC, was in Citigroup's falsely telling investors that an independent party was choosing the portfolio's investments. Citigroup made $160 million from the deal and investors lost $700 million.

Because Citigroup neither admitted nor denied guilt in this settlement, in 2011, Judge Jed S. Rakoff of the United States District Court in Manhattan rejected the proposed $285 million settlement between Citigroup and the SEC, citing that the amount was "pocket change" for Citigroup. (Just a few years earlier, Judge Rakoff rejected a similar settlement between the SEC and Bank of America, stating that the proposed settlement came at the "expense, not only of the shareholders, but also of the truth."[11])

---

10   Opening quote in Arthur E. Wilmarth, Jr., Citigroup: A Case Study in Managerial and Regulatory Failures, 47 IND. L. REV. pp. 69-137, citing a New York Times article: Eric Dash & Julie Creswell, Citigroup Pays for a Rush to Risk, N.Y. TIMES, Nov. 23, 2008, at A1 (quoting a statement by Mr. Prince in 2006): https://scholarship.law.gwu.edu/cgi/viewcontent.cgi?article=2234&context=faculty_publications – retrieved November 16, 2020
11   Henning, Peter J. "Behind Rakoff's Rejection of Citigroup Settlement." *The New York Times,* November 28, 2011 - https://dealbook.nytimes.com/2011/11/28/behind-judge-rakoffs-rejection-of-s-e-c-citigroup-settlement/. Retrieved November 16, 2020

A US Federal Appeals Court overturned Judge Rakoff's rejection. However, Judge Rakoff's criticism of the SEC approach with violators of law made the SEC in 2014 reverse "its longstanding yet unofficial policy of allowing companies to neither admit nor deny wrongdoing, signaling that it would force admissions in particularly egregious cases."[12]

Some argue that the Federal Appeals Court overturned Judge Rakoff because the benefit of settlements is that they extract cooperation, avoid costly trials, and are more pragmatic. The questions, however, are whether overturning Judge Rakoff pursues the truth, and whether settlements really hold executives at the top accountable to set the right culture. For Citigroup and Citibank, NA, the answer to both questions is no: Their culture didn't change and their executives have not yet been held accountable.

4. Citigroup, LIBOR,[13] and Foreign Exchange Misconduct (2007–2012)

> "Citigroup Inc. and J.P. Morgan Chase pleaded guilty and agreed to pay more than $1 billion each to resolve allegations that they tried for years to manipulate the foreign-currency (FX) market, the biggest fines wrung from a group of six banks by regulators in the U.S., U.K. and Switzerland."[14]

> "Citigroup affiliates were also charged with false reporting in connection with ISDAFIX benchmark rates and with false reporting

---

12   Protess, Ben and Goldstein, Matthew. "Overruled, Judge Still Left a Mark on S.E.C. Agenda," *The New York Times*, June 4, 2014 - https://dealbook.nytimes.com/2014/06/04/appeals-court-overturns-decision-to-reject-s-e-c-citigroup-settlement/. Retrieved November 16, 2020

13   A comprehensive summary of the London Interbank Rate Offered Rate (LIBOR) can be found in Wikipedia.com - https://en.wikipedia.org/wiki/Libor_scandal#Fines_for_manipulation. Retrieved November 16, 2020. Some of the cases are still pending.

14   Albanese, Chiara, Enrich, David and Martin, Katie. "Citigroup, J.P. Morgan Take Brunt of Currencies Settlement: Six Lenders to Pay a Total of $4.3 Billion to Resolve Allegations of Foreign-Exchange Manipulation." *The Wall Street Journal*, November 12, 2014 - https://www.wsj.com/articles/banks-reach-settlement-in-foreign-exchange-rigging-probe-1415772504. Retrieved November 16, 2020

of US dollar Libor rates during the financial crisis to protect its reputation, the CFTC said on Wednesday, adding that the various actions occurred between 2007 and 2012."[15]

5. Citibank/Banamex USA (2017)

"From at least 2007 until at least 2012, Banamex USA processed more than 30 million remittances to Mexico valued at more than $8.8 billion. Those remittances prompted more than 18,000 alerts involving some $142 million in potentially suspicious transactions…However, the bank conducted fewer than 10 investigations and filed only nine suspicious activity reports stemming from the alerts because its compliance unit was seriously understaffed with only two employees." [16]

Criminal violations totaled $97 million in fines, but the US DoJ didn't pursue criminal prosecution. Upon settlement, Citi announced that:

"(I)t was pleased to resolve the Justice Department investigations and said having "the strongest possible system for anti-money-laundering" was among its most serious obligations."

As you read Citigroup's "pleasure" in settling the case without admission of guilt, consider Judge Rakoff's rightful quest for the truth.

---

15   The Guardian, *"Citigroup to pay $425m in latest action against global banks,"* May 25, 2016. https://www.theguardian.com/business/2016/may/25/citigroup-fine-foreign-exchange-interest-rate. Retrieved November 16, 2020
16   Darmiento, Lawrence, "Citigroup to pay nearly $100 million to settle Banamex money-laundering claims." *Los Angeles Times*, March 22, 2017 - https://www.latimes.com/business/la-fi-banamex-settlement-20170522-story.html. Retrieved November 16, 2020

6. Citigroup (Banamex) Internal Accounting Control Weaknesses (2018)

The US Securities and Exchange Commission issued a cease-and-desist order against Citigroup, Inc. for:

> "...failure to devise and maintain a sufficient system of internal accounting controls concerning a wholly-owned subsidiary (Banamex) ... sufficient to provide reasonable assurances that Banamex's transactions were recorded as necessary to permit the preparation of Citigroup's financial statements in accordance with generally accepted accounting principles (GAAP) and to maintain accountability for assets... without admitting or denying the findings." [17]

To clarify, between 2008–2014, Mexico City-based Banamex embarrassed Citigroup by losing more than $500 million on fraudulent loans to a supplier to the state-owned oil company. In addition, it didn't have internal accounting controls to capture the manipulation of books and records, and it never escalated the problems to the Citigroup head office.

7. Citibank and Citigroup Cease and Desist Orders (October 2020)

> "The Office of the Comptroller of the Currency (OCC) today assessed a $400 million civil money penalty against Citibank, N.A.... related to deficiencies in enterprise-wide risk management, compliance risk management, data governance, and internal controls... The OCC took these actions based on the bank's unsafe or unsound banking practices for its long-standing

---

17   US Securities and Exchange Commission. "In the Matter of Citigroup, Inc., Respondent," Order Instituting Cease-and-Desist Proceedings Pursuant to Section 21C of the Securities Exchange Act of 1934 . . . August 16, 2018 - https://www.sec.gov/litigation/admin/2018/34-83858.pdf. -Retrieved November 16, 2020

failure to establish effective risk management and data governance programs and internal controls."[18]

"Among other things, the firm has not taken prompt and effective actions to correct practices previously identified by the Board in the areas of compliance risk management, data quality management, and internal controls."[19]

8. Continued Internal Control Blunders: Revlon Payment (August 2020–May 2021)

In August 2020, an "operational error" caused Citigroup to send $893 million of its own funds to the lenders of Revlon, the cosmetic company, appearing to pay off a loan not due until 2023, when it intended to send only a $7.8 million interest payment.

To date, $389.8 million had been repaid to the bank at its request, but some of Revlon's lenders held on to the funds, prompting Citigroup to wage a legal battle against a group of hedge funds to recover the remainder. In February and May 2021, a federal judge rejected Citigroup's request to extend a freeze on the remaining amount over $500 million. As the court stated in its ruling, "To believe otherwise—to believe that Citibank, one of the most sophisticated financial institutions in the world, had made a mistake that had never happened before, to the tune of nearly $1 billion—would have been borderline irrational."

Citigroup had to record an additional $390 million in operating expenses in the 2020 fourth quarter because of the blunder. As a result, Citigroup revised its fourth-quarter earnings to $1.92 per share, down

---

18   US Comptroller of the Currency. OCC Cease and Desist Order: Citibank, NA, October 7, 2020 Press Release: https://www.occ.gov/static/enforcement-actions/ea2020-056.pdf. Retrieved November 16, 2020

19   Federal Reserve Board Cease and Desist Order: Citigroup, Inc, October 7, 2020 Press Release - https://www.federalreserve.gov/newsevents/pressreleases/files/enf20201007a1.pdf. Retrieved November 16, 2020

from $2.08, according to a filing. Some add that "[s]hortfalls in Citigroup's internal controls were a factor in chief executive Mike Corbat's planned early retirement in 2020."[20]

Pulling It All Together

As noted by *The Wall Street Journal*, "Regulators have long fretted that the hodgepodge of systems, a legacy of a string of deals in the 1990s that turned Citigroup into a financial powerhouse, could make the bank vulnerable to costly and potentially damaging missteps."[21]

Although the names and faces have changed, perhaps Citigroup should apologize again, as they did in Japan in 2004. Not only to regulators, but to shareholders, employees, and other long-term stakeholders for years of corporate cultural misconduct, short-term personal financial benefit at the expense of markets and customers, executive lack of accountability, and neglect of fundamental internal controls over people, process, and technology.

As reported in the press and analyzed by academia, what's even more appalling is that if it weren't for support obtained by Citigroup's co-chairmen John Reed and Sandy Weill from US President Clinton, Federal Reserve Chairman Greenspan, and US Treasury Secretary Robert Rubin, Citigroup itself would have been illegal.[22] Prior to 1999, Citicorp was a bank holding company which owned a "commercial bank." Travelers Group was an insurance company regulated by individual states, and

---

20   Moise, Imani, "Citigroup revises earnings lower after losing Revlon case," February 26, 2021, *Reuters*. https://www.reuters.com/business/citigroup-revises-earnings-lower-after-losing-revlon-case-2021-02-26/; Stempel, Jonathan, "Judge denies Citigroup a longer freeze on botched Revlon transfer," May 12, 2021, *Reuters*. https://www.reuters.com/business/legal/citigroup-fails-obtain-longer-freeze-botched-revlon-transfer-2021-05-12/
21   Benoit, David. "Regulators Fine Citigroup $400 Million Over 'Serious Ongoing Deficiencies' Fed, OCC order the nation's third-largest bank to fix its risk-management systems," *The Wall Street Journal*, October 7, 2020 - https://www.wsj.com/articles/federal-reserve-finds-serious-ongoing-deficiencies-at-citigroup-11602103099#:~:text=Federal%20banking%20regulators%20on%20Wednesday%20fined%20Citigroup%20Inc.&text=In%20a%20consent%20order%20agreed,regulatory%20reporting%20and%20capital%20planning. Retrieved November 16, 2020
22   Wilmarth, Arthur E., The Road to Repeal of the Glass-Steagall Act (2017). GWU Law School Public Law Research Paper No. 2017-61; GWU Legal Studies Research Paper No. 2017-61. Available at SSRN: https://ssrn.com/abstract=3026287. Retrieved November 16, 2020

Salomon Brothers was a registered broker-dealer and investment bank regulated by the SEC and Financial Industry Regulatory Authority (FINRA). US laws required a separation between these types of businesses because at the time of its passage in 1934, risky non-banking activities such as investment banking and insurance were considered "unsafe and unsound" for government-insured deposit-taking activities of commercial banks. Nevertheless, the Citi/Clinton/Greenspan/Rubin agreement compelled the Federal Reserve staff to grant a one-year reprieve, which lasted until the US Congress passed the Gramm-Leach Bliley Act, which resulted in "universal, one-stop-shopping" super banks such as Citigroup and JP Morgan Chase.

Citi had achieved its strategic goals through regulatory arbitrage.

What *didn't* follow was a corresponding integration of Citigroup's system of internal controls, enterprise risk management (including compliance risk management), and data controls to enable Citigroup (and perhaps other universal banks such as JP Morgan Chase), and instead a continuation of fragmented, siloed people, process, and technology—and a continuation of a corporate culture of short-term profit maximization and cost minimization.

Enterprise Risk Management including Compliance Risk Management

As noted in earlier chapters, Fed Governor Susan Bies' said in 2003 that large, complex banking organizations required corporate-wide (enterprise) compliance risk management. The following year, The Committee of Sponsoring Organizations (COSO) issued its Enterprise Risk Management principles, which was followed in 2008 by the Fed's Compliance Risk Management guidance over large, complex banks.

I have argued that together with the US DoJ Corporate Sentencing Guidelines, integrating these compliance risk management principles enables all companies across all industries to manage their compliance risks

effectively and sustainably, regardless of their clients, industry, geography, or compliance risk profile. Combined with a system of internal accounting controls, the corporate culture of the firm should enable companies to manage their compliance risks, including manipulation of their books and records to violate laws such as the Foreign Corrupt Practices Act.

More recently, on November 11, 2020, COSO and the Society of Corporate Compliance and Ethics (SCCE) issued a publication promoting the linkage between enterprise risk management and compliance risks. Finally, after a forty-year career as a CCO, there is an official acknowledgement of the importance and need for an enterprise compliance risk management program across industries.

What I've described here—a series of examples of how poor culture leads to bad strategy—could happen (and is, undoubtedly happening right now) globally. Citigroup is a harsh lesson learned of what not to do culturally and strategically. Board members and chief executive officers need to actively know how well their compliance risks are being managed. They can no longer say or believe or hide behind a defense of neglect that "I didn't know." And where *was* the Citigroup board?

The point here is that compliance must be empowered, with authority and stature, to declare independence and act accordingly. It must also have the ability to escalate compliance risk issues directly to the board so that the board can fulfil its fiduciary duties of care and loyalty.

Introduction to the Compliance Hexagon and Honeycomb and Six Recommendations for a "Clean" Organization, Industry, and Infrastructure

This chapter previews my six recommendations that are designed to create a truly independent compliance & ethics function, one that isn't beholden to any other department or executive, and one that is a value-added, strategic partner with the board of directors to hold management accountable.

To summarize in advance, the six recommendations are:

1. Educate and Enlighten the Board of Directors
2. Hold Management Accountable and Culpable
3. Declare and Enable Compliance Independence
4. Invest in Compliance Resources
5. Transparency ("Sunlight is the Best Disinfectant")
6. Protect and Enable Whistleblowers

Implementing all six of these recommendations will provide and sustain a path to a "cleaner,[1] more efficient, and effective organization."[2]

---

1   "Cleaner" as in more ethical and compliant.
2   A quote by Alexander Fleiss, CEO of Rebellion Research during his Rebellion TV Education Series interview of me on February 10, 2021: https://www.youtube.com/watch?v=E_e4nLeV-xA&feature=youtu.be

And by extension, a cleaner industry and global infrastructure. That said, I know it may not be easy and that it won't happen overnight.

Admittedly, some of these recommendations are provocative and controversial. But meaningful change isn't always going to be easy. Despite decades of legal and regulatory "efforts," financial crimes and external frauds have not abated. Internal fraud including the manipulation and/or inaccurate financial information driven by greedy, desperate and/or corrupt business leaders continue to maximize profits or mask losses. Bribery and corruption in many forms persist. Customers and markets continue to be abused across all sectors.

I applaud Columbia University Law Professor John C. Coffee, Jr.[3] for emphatically highlighting that there is a crisis of underenforcement for the lack of effective prosecution of corporate senior executives. He's right. Shifting paradigms to change and sustain the right corporate culture—however unpopular—is vital. My recommendations are simple but require courage by Congress, the board, and the chief compliance officer to hold management accountable. Why?

Powerful lobbies continue to influence legislators to insulate board members, CEOs, and the C-suite from prosecution. Personal liability laws need to be changed to expose misconduct or neglect. Meanwhile, carefully structured layering of the legal and risk functions prevents the CCO from interacting with the board of directors meaningfully, while also enabling the C-suite to be sufficiently insulated to legally claim that "they didn't know" how weak and ineffective their compliance programs are.

---

3   Coffee, John C., Jr. "Corporate Crime and Punishment: The Crisis of Underenforcement." 2020, Berrett-Koehler Publishers, Inc.

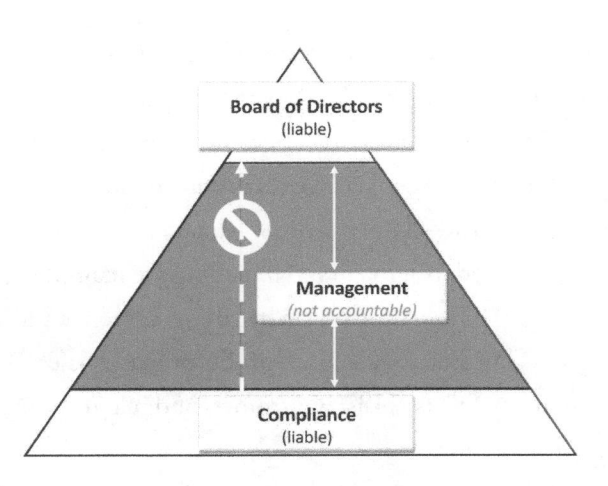

Source: author

The Directors & Compliance Hexagon©

The Directors & Compliance Hexagon embodies my six recommendations to expose and disinfect management misconduct or inaction, and hold them personally accountable, while enabling board members to fulfill their fiduciary duties of loyalty and duty of care.

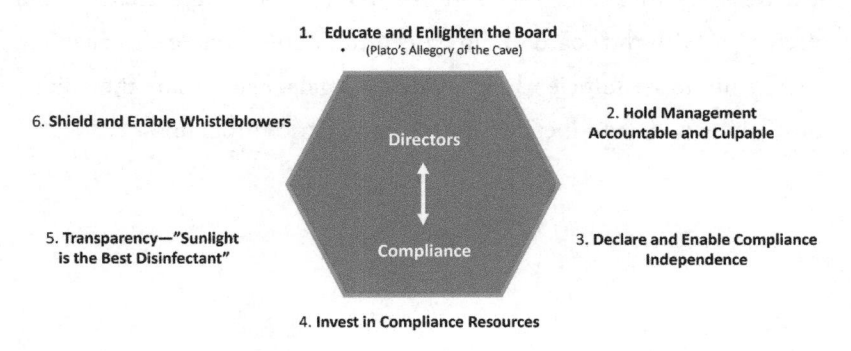

Source: author

For example, a board's independent, continuous, and candid dialogue with the CCO would provide documentary evidence to regulators, enforcement agencies, and plaintiffs that the directors are not "utterly failing" in executing their fiduciary duty of care. Discussions would cover compliance risk assessments, metrics, policies, and controls, and whether the company is operating within its compliance risk appetite (including emerging risks, which could give rise to material events causing reputational damage).

The Essential Role of the Board and Chief Compliance Officer

As noted in part 1, the Delaware Supreme Court's June 2019 opinion in *Marchand v Barnhill* found that Blue Bell, the ice cream manufacturer, had for years been deficient in food safety and alleged compliance weaknesses. The Court found not only its CEO and CFO in breach of their fiduciary duties and knowingly in violation of safety and contamination laws, but also that Blue Bell's directors cannot be absent from or disregarding the fundamental matters of the corporation. The standard of a director's duty was lowered (that is, the expectation is higher) that such absence or disregard for fundamental duties creates a risk of significant liability, and an "'utter failure to attempt to assure a reasonable information and reporting system exists' (to the point that it) is an act of bad faith of the duty of loyalty."[4]

The CCO is essential and critical to overseeing the enterprise-wide activities and risks of the corporate body and informing the board of directors, independently, whether management including its revenue generating businesses, the CFO, and the CEO are fulfilling their compliance responsibilities.

The CCO must also inform the board that employees' reports of integrity or compliance issues are escalated, investigated, measured, benchmarked, analyzed, and reported in a meaningful way for the board to

---

4   https://courts.delaware.gov/Opinions/Download.aspx?id=291200 – last retrieved July 6, 2021

understand the company's risks easily and comprehensively. Otherwise, the company will not only be subject to civil and possibly criminal violations and enforcement actions, but it will also subject its board of directors to personal liability and potential criminal prosecution.

By remaining calm, confident, credible, clear in articulation, and especially courageous to escalate integrity, budget, technology, and other compliance, conduct and control concerns, the chief compliance officer will enable the company to remain healthy, and its board of directors governing over the company's management, effectively.

The Compliance Honeycomb©

As you'll see in the following chapters, the board of directors and CCO can effectively address these heightened compliance risks through my six overarching recommendations, collectively known as the "Compliance Hexagon." If each of the sixteen critical infrastructure sectors adopts the Compliance Hexagon, those Hexagons will come together to create the Compliance Honeycomb (honeycombs, by the way, are one of the strongest and most stable structures known to science).

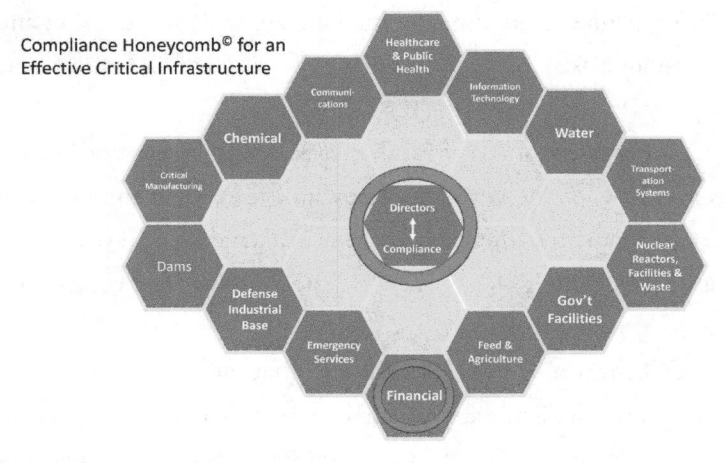

Compliance Honeycomb© for an Effective Critical Infrastructure

Source: author

Degree of Difficulty

Implementing, let alone visualizing, the Compliance Hexagon is a monumental lift. But I urge you[5] to persevere and implement as many as you can as soon as you can and set your sights on implementing all six. If you need any help, feel free to contact me at eric@ethicalpebble.com.

---

5   Directors, chief compliance officers, legislators and regulators, and all employees including integrity raisers (otherwise known as whistleblowers)

Recommendation No. 1:
Educate and Enlighten the Board

A s we've seen throughout this book, in many organizations large and small, management is not personally accountable enough for their activities. Far too often, this lack of accountability—and legal liability—emboldens businessmen and women and their supervisors to break laws and/or violate their ethical and compliance responsibilities. It's as though they're thinking, "If I *do* get caught, the company will just write a check." Untethered by accountability, misconduct and violations can spread like a virus throughout the organization, becoming part of, or dominating the corporate culture.

1A: Educate and Enlighten the Board of Directors. If you're a board member, you have a fiduciary duty of care,[1] which means that you could get prosecuted if you're seen as not challenging management over their compliance responsibilities. But how can you fulfil that duty of care if you're not fully aware of your record of compliance and ethical behavior, or enlightened as to the rules that the C-suite needs to follow? In other words,

---

1   A board's duty of care is typically defined as exercising the same due care in the management of the corporation's business as a prudent person would exercise in the management of his or her own affairs.

how will you (and your fellow directors) know what good looks like? The more enlightened your board is, the more accountable management will be.

The CCO and his or her compliance & ethics department must regularly train and educate the board of directors on how to challenge management effectively and powerfully on whether they're fulfilling their enterprise compliance risk management responsibilities.

By "train and educate," I don't mean death by PowerPoint or drowning your directors in a sea of data (although data and PowerPoint, in reasonable amounts, are often helpful). Instead, aim to provide meaningful, enlightening "storytelling" based on data, illustrated with charts and graphs only as needed.

VALUE TO THE BOARD: The more board members understand how compliance and their duty of care are inextricably linked, the more confident they'll feel in overseeing and challenging (not just agreeing with or relying upon) management's investment in and effectiveness of its compliance program.

1B: Produce and Present Annual Fiduciary Duty of Care Training. Annually, the general counsel and CCO should conduct fiduciary duty of care training to educate new (and remind existing) board members about their fiduciary oversight and corporate governance responsibilities over compliance & ethics risks and how they impact the company's reputation, particularly with regard to the environment, social responsibility, customers, markets, and employees.

As part of this annual training, the CCO should describe—and have the full board review and approve—its overall Compliance Risk Management Program (CRMP), which includes an Annual Compliance Plan (ACP) that:

1. Defines "compliance & ethics risk" and "compliance risk appetite" for board consideration and approval

2. Describes its compliance & ethics risk assessment methodology

3. Provides a year-over-year comparison between the firm's residual compliance & ethics risk rating as an enterprise, as well as by topic, law, and product/division, in prioritized order (with quarterly updates)

4. Identifies—with timeline, action, and owner—how each compliance & ethics risk will be managed in a satisfactory and sustainable manner within the board-approved compliance risk appetite, which will be measured and reported quarterly to the board with progress and material exceptions provided quarterly.

VALUE TO THE BOARD: Instituting this type of ACP will enable the full board to discuss and challenge management about whether its overall CRMP program is, according to regulators and the DoJ, "adequately resourced" to keep within its compliance risk appetite, invest in the technology tools necessary to effectively monitor compliance risks in accordance with the board's duty of care, and assess its compliance risks in an intelligent manner.

1C: Reinforce US Department of Justice Corporate Sentencing Guidelines, and US DoJ Evaluation of Corporate Compliance Programs Expectations (DoJ Compliance). Annually, have the CCO provide board members with DoJ Compliance training. I've often described the DOJ Evaluation of Corporate Compliance Program guidance as an open-book test, because the three questions[2] are publicly available, and regulators assume that corporate entities will have read and can honestly answer Yes to all three. There are no trick questions and no surprises. Actually, the only surprise is if the US DoJ concludes that the open-book test was ignored. For that reason, the board's DOJ Compliance training should include

2   US DoJ Evaluation of Corporate Compliance Programs. https://www.justice.gov/criminal-fraud/page/file/937501/download, June 2020

compulsory completion and what I call: "enlightenment validation," that is, a three-question quiz which each director must complete and pass:

- Is the corporation's compliance program well designed?

- Is the program being applied earnestly and in good faith? In other words, is the program adequately resourced and empowered to function effectively?

- Does the corporation's compliance program work in practice?

In addition, you should provide quarterly US DoJ-topical training,[3] with each session covering one of the following topics, on a rotating basis:

- Foreign Corrupt Practices Act

- Third-party (vendor) risk management

- Anti-trust

- Mergers and acquisitions

- Cyber-security (together with your chief information security officer)

- Key regulatory risks expressed through key compliance risk indicators and trends, supported by quarterly commentary to address whether or not the level of risks is acceptable and within board-approved risk appetites.

VALUE TO THE BOARD: You'll not only be educated but also armed to challenge the CEO (who should be just as educated if not more so on whether they're passing or failing the "open-book test").

1D: Review the UK Serious Fraud Office (SFO) Program: "Evaluating a Compliance Program."[4] While not all firms are multinational, large, or

---

3   Some of these topics might already be given in siloes, but not comprehensively as part of the DoJ Compliance program.
4   UK SFO. "Evaluating a Compliance Program." January 2020. https://www.sfo.gov.uk/publications/guidance-policy-and-protocols/sfo-operational-handbook/evaluating-a-compliance-programme. Retrieved February 28, 2021

complex, it's always prudent to compare and contrast various jurisdictions' treatment of organizational compliance and ethical behavior, and lessons learned from those jurisdictions. Although the principles are often similar, there may be significant differences in how (and whether) they're enforced and the consequences for not following them.

VALUE TO THE BOARD: Know your markets and know your regulators! More on this in Recommendation 2. The UK, Hong Kong, and Singapore in particular, are tougher on individual CEOs and their C-suite than the United States is.

1E: Customize and Annualize Bank Regulators' Compliance Risk Management Guidance for Banks and Commercial Enterprises. For financial institutions (but equally beneficial for commercial enterprises), provide annual enterprise compliance & ethics risk management training formulated around the:

- Federal Reserve Supervision and Regulation Letter (SR 2008-08)[5]

- Basel Committee Paper[6]

- SCCE Compliance Risk Management guidance,[7] which applies the Committee of Sponsoring Organizations of the Treadway Commission's (COSO) Enterprise Risk Management Framework (ERM)

VALUE TO THE BOARD: The benefit of these regulatory, internal control, and industry frameworks is that corporations can use them to customize their own compliance risk management programs, ensuring that they're fit for their purposes, business lines, and compliance risks and that they meet regulatory expectations before they become criminal violations.

---

5   Specifically, "Compliance Risk Management Programs and Oversight at Large Banking Organizations with Complex Compliance Profiles." See chapter 2.8 for more.
6   Specifically, "Compliance and the Compliance Function in Banks" (also known as the Enterprise Regulatory Compliance Risk Framework).
7   SCCE - Compliance Risk Management: Applying the COSO ERM Framework, November 2020. https://www.coso.org/news/Pages/compliance-risk-management-applying-the-coso-erm-framework.aspx. Retrieved February 28, 2021

Use Young's Vision as the basis to provide the Fed SR 2008-08 Compliance Risk Management training combined with the DoJ Sentencing Guideline training.

1F: Conduct Risk Management Training. Jointly with the CEO and/or designee (e.g., the head of HR, business, or the CFO), provide annual Conduct Risk Management training, which includes case studies involving workplace and sexual harassment as well as business and ethics dilemmas. This training may be combined with the training noted above and/or training (that should be provided to the board) on the importance of maintaining accurate books and records and an effective system of internal controls.

VALUE TO THE BOARD: At a minimum, the above training will arm the board with an understanding of key compliance, ethics, and conduct objectives; risks and priorities; whether the company's compliance budget and resources are adequate; and whether compliance risk appetites (which need to be approved annually and measured at least quarterly) are being satisfied at acceptable residual levels.

1G: Compulsory Training. Other corporate functions should also be involved. For example, human resources and compliance should, together, enlighten board members about the correlation between ethical behavior, performance, and compensation. The chief information security officer should conduct training on how cyber breaches can lead to compliance violations and reputational damage; the chief financial officer should discuss how material inaccuracies in the firm's financial statements could reflect a poor system of internal controls.

VALUE TO THE BOARD: Educating the board will enable its members to challenge the CEO, CFO, and other executives and their business managers and hold them accountable for actions (or inactions) that are questionable, unethical, or violate a law, regulation, or policy. And having

the CCO take the lead with support from HR and other functions will prompt more collaboration and ownership of compliance & ethics issues across the organization.

Recommendation No. 2: Hold Management More Accountable and Culpable

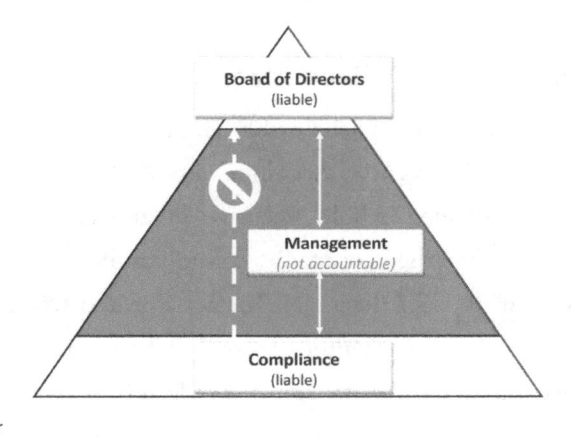

Source: author

Under current US law, both corporate boards of directors and chief compliance officers (CCOs) may be held personally liable for the misconduct and/or illegal acts of chief executive officers and their corporate and business executives. As we've discussed throughout this book, management's lack of accountability and culpability has the potential to reduce any incentive for managers and executives to do the right thing. It also makes it harder for management to make the right decision when

choosing between short-term profit maximization (through aggressive cost reductions to maximize shareholder returns) and being more ethical (by supporting the company's non-shareholder stakeholders, such as the community, employees, and society as a whole). This may produce lower profits in the short run, but absolute benefit in the medium and long run.

It's essential that corporate executives and their mid-level managers be held more accountable, culpable, and personally liable. Doing so sets the company on a more ethical path to meet non-shareholder stakeholder expectations. The recommendation in this chapter consists of five distinct parts. Some of them require legislative action at the US federal or state level, while others can be implemented internally by the corporate entity itself. Before we get to the recommendation itself, let's take a minute to go over some important background.

Prosecuting Corporate Executives for Negligent Conduct

In April 2019, United States Senator Elizabeth Warren (D-Mass.) introduced the Corporate Executive Accountability Act[1] (the Accountability Act), which was intended to hold executives of large corporations criminally responsible when their companies commit crimes, harm customers, or repeatedly violate US federal law. The Senator also reintroduced the Ending Too Big to Jail Act, a comprehensive bill designed to hold big bank executives accountable when the banks they lead break the law. Neither law passed at the time, but both should be re-introduced in whole or in part. As of the writing of this book (mid 2021), in the US, Democrats control the presidency and both houses of Congress. If there's a window of opportunity to enact this type of accountability on corporate executives, now is the time.

Historically, prosecuting corporate executives (in particular, CEOs) has been a major challenge, because they sit multiple layers above an

---

1   Press release of Senator Elizabeth Warren (D – Mass), April 3, 2019. "Senator Warren Unveils Bill to Expand Criminal Liability to Negligent Executives of Giant Corporations"

offending employee. Typically, the executive will claim no knowledge of the wrongdoing or to have not been directly involved in the decision-making process that resulted in that wrongdoing. Senator Warren recommended—and I concur—that the Accountability Act widen and extend its scope to include *negligence*,[2] in other words, a he-or-she-should-have-known standard. Here's my five-part recommendation:

2A: CEOs and, by Extension, Their Direct Reports, Must Be Held Criminally Liable and Culpable for Not Having an Effective Enterprise-Wide Compliance Program. They must also be held criminally liable if they've been *neglectful* of their fiduciary duty of loyalty and/or duty of care to ensure that adequate compliance & ethics resources (people, budgets, and tools) are in place, effective and sustained, and that the escalation and reporting to the board of directors of material compliance & ethics issues and associated remedial actions are both meaningful, regular, and actionable.

2B: Apply and Increase the Use of the US Racketeer Influenced and Corrupt Organizations Act (RICO) to Criminalize Corporate Misconduct and Incent the Right Behavior. This process has, to a limited extent, already begun. For example, the US Department of Justice recently cited the RICO Act in filing charges against a former JP Morgan precious

---

2   Senator Warren's April 3, 2019 press release states, among other things, that while the Accountability Act was not enacted in its proposed form, it "was built on existing federal statutes and was intended to make it easier to send executives to jail for serious crimes by expanding criminal liability to negligent executives of corporations with more than $1 billion in annual revenue that:

- Are found guilty, plead guilty, or enter into a deferred or non-prosecution agreement for any crime.
- Are found liable or enter a settlement with any state or Federal regulator for the violation of any civil law if that violation affects the health, safety, finances, or personal data of 1% of the American population or 1% of the population of any state.
- Are found liable or guilty of a second civil or criminal violation for a different activity while operating under a civil or criminal judgment of any court, a deferred prosecution or non-prosecution agreement, or settlement with any state or Federal agency.

Punishment for such a violation will be up to a year in jail, while a second violation carries up to three years in jail, consistent with the Food, Drug, and Cosmetic Act."

metals salesman, who, along with JP Morgan traders, allegedly manipulated precious metal futures markets.[3] More recently, private litigants may proceed in a RICO lawsuit predicated on violations of the Anti-Kickback Statute (AKS). In one case, plaintiffs alleged that rebates paid by EpiPen manufacturer Mylan to various pharmacy benefit managers violated the AKS and led to increased list prices for wholesale purchasers.[4]

In addition—and perhaps more importantly—I recommend that, as soon as a RICO indictment has been filed against a company, the CEO should be indicted for negligent *criminal conduct*. Doing so would provide a nexus between an employee's criminal misconduct and the CEO's negligence and would make it clear that the CEO should have known of the activities and level of compliance throughout the corporate enterprise. Together with Recommendation 2A, CEOs will have much more incentive to ensure that their fiduciary duty of care over compliance is robust and enterprise wide.

2C: In Applying, Expanding, and Customizing the Enterprise Crime Principles of the US RICO Act for Regulatory and Civil Violations, Regulators Should Adopt a Civil Regulatory-RICO Equivalent for Corporate Employee Misconduct. All too often, mid- and junior-level staff are thrown under the corporate, regulatory, and prosecutorial "bus," allowing executive management (including the CEO) to remain shielded from personal accountability. Since corporate culture and conduct generally start at the top and are emulated throughout the organization, there need to be both incentives and consequences to ensure that executives conduct themselves within the spirit and the letter of laws, regulations, and policies, including codes of ethics and conduct.

---

3   https://www.justice.gov/opa/pr/superseding-indictment-charges-former-precious-metals-salesman-racketeering-conspiracy. Retrieved September 30, 2020
4   JD Supra podcast. "EpiPen RICO Ruling Opens Door for Private AKS Enforcement." Trautman Pepper, February 2021. https://www.jdsupra.com/legalnews/epipen-rico-ruling-opens-door-for-privat-02003. Retrieved March 10, 2021

As we've discussed earlier, CEOs and other executive officers frequently try to insulate themselves from regulatory and legal exposure by inserting layers of personnel between themselves and the CCO. That allows them to claim that they "already have too many direct reports" or that they "didn't know" of an individual employee's misconduct or even the divisional misbehavior or dysfunction that ultimately led to legal or regulatory violations.

For that reason, I recommend that no matter how junior a staff member may be or in which part of the organizational enterprise he or she works, if he or she violates in a material manner a law, regulation, and/or code of ethics and conduct, the senior most executive (that is, the CEO) should also be held negligent (and liable) for that employee's misconduct. Together with 2B, this recommendation will incentivize the right behavior, particularly at the top, but also of middle management.

2D: Adopt the UK's Financial Conduct Authority Senior Manager and Certification Regime (UK FCA SMCR), Which Holds the CEO and Management Directly Accountable for Violations of Law, Regulation, and/or Misconduct. As described in chapter 2.9, the UK FCA SMCR holds executives much more accountable than does corresponding law in the US. This regulatory regime has helped shape and incent improvement in executive and employee conduct in the UK as well as compelled the FCA and the UK Serious Fraud Office (SFO) to prosecute violations of the UK's conduct rules. To impose even more accountability onto the CEO and his or her senior managers, the United States must pass legislation to require a comparable regulatory expectation of qualification, certification, and accountability of these officers. Some question the efficacy of the SMCR and SFO regimes, but they do hold executives more individually accountable than in the US. Accountability matters.

2E: Change from "Duty of Responsibility" to "Presumption of Responsibility." Executives too easily delegate not only activity but also responsibility, which serves to get executives off the hook. In 2015, when the UK SMCR was first proposed, it—to the relief of the UK banking industry—defaulted to the prescriptive (but also more lenient) "duty of responsibility."[5] Imposing a *presumption* of responsibility would be more consistent with the negligence provisions described above in 2A and 2B. Otherwise, executives and other business leaders will still argue that they "didn't know" or "weren't responsible" for their staff's actions or inactions.

VALUE TO THE BOARD: If the CEO, C-suite, and management are held more accountable, an enlightened board and accountable management will more likely create an effective compliance program that's fit for long-term purposes, including stronger reputation and lower likelihood of ethical and regulatory violations.

5   Ruck, Michael. "Does the SMCR need more 'teeth'? FCA priorities series part 2." Lexology. com, May 16, 2019. https://www.lexology.com/library/detail.aspx?g=19c8d2c3-d6a0-470a-8fa3-96a5f881127e. Retrieved March 10, 2021

Recommendation No. 3:
Declare and Enable Compliance Independence

T his recommendation has five parts. But before we jump in, let's define the word "independent."[1]

- Not subject to control by others
- Self-governing
- Not affiliated with a larger controlling unit
- Not requiring or relying on something else
- Not looking to others for one's opinions or for guidance in conduct
- Showing a desire for freedom

Okay, now let's break down this recommendation into tangible steps.

3A: Separate the Position of Chair of the Board of Directors from the CEO. In many organizations in the United States, the positions of CEO and chair of the board of directors are held by the same person. As of June 2021, only 60% of S&P 500 companies have separated their chair

---

1   Merriam-Webster.com/dictionary/independent. Retrieved October 3, 2020

from the CEO. And recently, Microsoft bucked that trend by reaffirming the combined position of CEO and Chair Satya Nadella.[2] Are Big Tech companies better at corporate governance than non-technology firms?

Separating the two positions would effectively make the non-executive board much more independent of the CEO and his or her short-term profit maximization priorities. That independence will, in turn, enable the board to govern, oversee, and challenge management, as well as better fulfill its fiduciary duties of care and loyalty.

3B: Leverage and Strengthen the Independence of the CCO. As we've discussed throughout this book, management can (and does) severely limit—or even suppress—the CCO's and the compliance & ethics department's ability to escalate and report key compliance metrics and other related C&E integrity issues to the board. That, in turn, can (and often does) ultimately cause harm to customers, markets, employees, and other stakeholders and could interfere with the board's ability to fulfill its fiduciary duties of care and loyalty.

A truly independent CCO and compliance & ethics function would unshackle the CCO from management, general counsel, chief financial officer, or chief risk officer. That would allow the CCO to:

- Control his or her own compliance & ethics budget, including the adequacy of the quantity and quality of critical resources, such as staffing and investment in compliance technology.

- Execute a compliance program specifically designed to help the corporate organization manage its compliance and reputational risks while enabling the firm to execute its strategic objectives safely.

- Strengthen the partnership between the independent board of directors and CCO to more successfully hold the CEO and

---

2   Sun, Mengqi, "Microsoft's Combination of CEO and Chairman Roles Goes Against Trend," *The Wall Street Journal,* June 17, 2021 - https://www.wsj.com/articles/microsofts-combination-of-ceo-and-chairman-roles-goes-against-trend-11623970653 - last retrieved June 29, 2021

management more accountable, which in turn strengthens the effectiveness and sustainability of an effective compliance program.

- Escalate and report to the board of directors and management the level of residual compliance risks and action plans, timelines, and owners if such risks exceed the board-approved compliance risk appetite.

- Meet and sustain the DoJ's seniority, stature, and authority[3] expectations, and enable the company to meet its multiple regulatory expectations (which will vary by industry and sector).

3C: Have a Direct Reporting Line and Dialogue Between the Independent CCO and the Independent Board.[4] Unfortunately, management, including the general counsel and corporate secretary, is too often the obstacle and/or gatekeeper that separates the board of directors from the CCO because the CEO and his or her executive team's primary objective is to maximize short-term profits and shareholder value. This continues despite the current (and likely enduring) trends of ESG (environmental, social, and governance) and stakeholder capitalism. As we've discussed, CEOs rely on their chief financial officers to streamline costs, budgets, and long-term investments to accomplish that short-term, myopic objective. Too often, this creates a corporate culture that is completely antithetical to the effectiveness of any compliance & ethics program, which is designed to focus on long-term adherence with laws and regulations.

Giving the CCO a direct line to the board provides an opportunity for board members and the CCO to regularly partner and dialogue.

---

3   For example, see page 11 of the DoJ, Evaluation of Corporate Compliance Programs; June 2020.
4   Alternatively, have the CCO report into the board governance committee, or board risk committee (if it exists), or even the board compensation committee (given the relationship between misconduct and employee compensation). Ideally, a board compliance committee.

3D: Establish a Compliance Committee (or Subcommittee) of the Board of Directors[5] to Discuss, at Least Quarterly, Key Compliance Risk Indicator (KRI) Metrics and Key Performance Indicators (KPIs). These include:

- Compliance Risk Assessment ratings

- Status and trend against board-approved compliance risk appetite

- Lessons learned from industry enforcement actions, audit and regulatory findings, and recommendations

- Status and trend against remediation projects and programs

- Education and enlightenment programs (see Recommendation #1)

- A report of whistleblowing metrics including trends, root causes, and levels of retaliation (see Recommendation #6)

- A statement, at least annually, of the state of compliance resource adequacy including investment in compliance technology

- Quarterly CCO reporting and dialogue, without management, on the effectiveness of the compliance & ethics program.

3E: Require that Risk Management Skill Sets, Particularly Compliance & Ethics Risk Management Be Included in Board Members' Job Description. This would be consistent with the definition of "diversity and inclusion." Diversity of thought and skills is just as important as race, gender, and other more-visible attributes. If opinions and risk management skills are excluded, where's the diversity?—particularly when it comes to protecting a firm from abuse of customers, markets, and ethical behavior.

VALUE TO THE BOARD: Enacted in all its parts, this recommendation will enable a much stronger partnership and relationship between board members and the CCO, thereby enabling them to hold

---

5   Preferably, its own committee. However, if a subcommittee it could be of the audit committee, governance committee, risk committee, or compensation committee.

management accountable, which in turn will make the C&E program more robust and sustainable, leading to a more profitable, thriving, and ethical company.

Recommendation No. 4:
Invest in Compliance Resources, Including GRC and Artificial Intelligence Tools

"[T]he boards and senior management of every financial institution must foster and implement a sustainable strong culture of compliance, as it is the foundation of the entire organization...

"To do this, leadership needs to empower compliance officers and put them on par with the bankers. They need to be independent—fully supported and properly resourced. It is the responsibility of senior management to ensure that compliance recommendations are appropriately reviewed and given substantial weight."

— LINDA LACEWELL[1]

Throughout this book, I've drawn an analogy between the fictional Cinderella and the way CCOs (and the entire compliance function) are often treated—like second-class citizens, unable to make their own decisions, and subject to the whims of the evil stepmother (whichever department controls compliance's budget). But nowhere is this analogy more apt than when it comes to resources.

---

1   New York State Superintendent Linda Lacewell Press Release, September 29, 2020. https://www.dfs.ny.gov/reports_and_publications/press_releases/pr202009291. Retrieved October 5, 2020

Since compliance is a non-revenue-generating function, it's often seen as an impediment to the mission of the organization: to make money. So, when the CEO and CFO are looking for expenses to slash, the compliance budget is one of the first to go. This, of course, severely limits the chief compliance officer's ability to perform his or her duties, which is, at the core, to protect the corporation, customers, markets, and the broader community.

But even when budgets aren't being cut, while most other departments get the latest and greatest resources—financial (including humans and IT)—that they need to do their jobs and improve their performance, the typical CCO is forced to use 20th century tools to deal with 21st century problems, such as the growing number of sophisticated cyber and financial crimes; escalating levels of management and employee misconduct, fraud, and illegal behavior; and the looming threats associated with the growing popularity of cryptocurrencies, which very few people truly understand. As a result, compliance is not only unable to fully protect the organization and its reputation, but it's also unable to satisfy the ever-changing demands imposed by the DoJ and other enforcement agencies and regulators.

The following five-part recommendation addresses these issues and is aimed at transforming (without the use of a Fairy Godmother) the Cinderella CCO into a meaningful princess (or prince) who has all the necessary resources, not only to attend the reputational ball, but also to protect it and enable the company to thrive. But before we get to the recommendation itself, let's take a look at the three types of resources that compliance & ethics departments need:

1. **People**. Invest in not only the appropriate number of compliance personnel, but also ensure that they have the right skill sets to meet the demands of an end-to-end enterprise compliance risk management program. These are:

   a. **Operational and project management skills.** Being an attorney is no longer a sufficient or even necessary qualification

for a 21st century compliance officer. It's great to know the law and to eloquently articulate and give training about policy, but businesses and executive management expect decisive, operational knowledge as well as the ability to translate technical laws into easily understandable, documented procedures that can be implemented operationally. Sadly, many compliance officers are tremendous subject matter experts in specific laws and regulations but are horrible managers of process, time (deadlines), and even taking responsibility. Project management skills add time management and ownership skills.

b.   **Data.** 21st century compliance & ethics officers don't need to know how to code, but they definitely need to be comfortable with data in multiple forms (numeric, risk appetite, flows, trends, data integrity, and what all of those mean with respect to input and especially, output). This is especially true given that they're the ones who need to articulate it clearly and simply to the board of directors.

c.   **Investigative and analytical skills.** Being comfortable with data is just the beginning. C&E officers must also be able to analyze that data (either on their own or via artificial intelligence) and make thoughtful, intelligent decisions (as opposed to those that might be demanded by individuals or business units that would be pressured into those decisions).

2.   **Process.** At GE, our chief information officer used to say, "Lean before digitizing." He was referring to the Lean Six Sigma methodology, which seeks to identify an organization's processes and then improve performance by reducing waste. And what he was saying was absolutely right: before introducing or enhancing automated tools, it's essential to fully understand how things work; what you're trying to accomplish; and how the customer experience

is a product of end-to-end steps with owners, controls, and gaps and weaknesses that are identified and addressed. Without that basic, background knowledge, technology will simply accelerate flawed processes with unclear owners.

Analyses to change processes take time and money, which management must be willing to invest. Compliance & ethics officers, as change agents, can oversee the appropriate project management disciplines to enable smooth execution of this simplification process across the organization.

3. **Technology**. The obsolete but sadly, typical compliance tools (Excel and PowerPoint) are 20th century solutions, painfully slow, shallow, and narrow in data collection. As such, they're unable to keep up with the near-instant pace of cyber-, viral-, and social-media change and attacks and the accelerating proliferation in crime, fraud, terrorism, and other reputationally damaging events. These attacks not only pose individual entity threats but can also happen simultaneously on multiple fronts and in multiple industries, jurisdictions, and governments. Simply identifying threats (let alone analyzing, escalating, and addressing them) could take weeks or longer if C&E officers aren't equipped with the most cutting-edge tools.

Now that you know what resources CCOs and C&E officers need to do their job, let's take a look at my specific recommendations.

4A: The Compliance Budget Should Be Reviewed, Benchmarked, and Approved By the Full Board of Directors, with Input from the Audit Committee, Compensation Committee, Risk Committee (if One Exists), and the Governance Committee. As we've discussed, too often the compliance budget is controlled by the general counsel or chief risk officer and is held hostage to the short-term deliverables of the CEO and

CFO. Having a straight line to the board unshackles the CCO from the short-term pressures and cuts of the C-suite.

4B: To Preserve the CCO's and Compliance & Ethics Function's Authority and Independence, Ensure that the Firm's Operating Principles Include—in Writing—That the CEO, CFO, and Business Lines Are Aware of, But Do Not Have Veto Power Over, the Compliance Budget and Resources. The CCO must have sole authority to hire, fire, evaluate staff (and quality of skill sets), and a compliance-dedicated technology team and process to implement the needed surveillance, governance-risk-compliance (GRC) tools to monitor, track, inventory, measure, and ultimately analyze the results and report them to the board of directors.

4C: Codify, with Board Approval, Within the Firm's Overall Charter or Articles of Association and Code of Ethics, that Only Compliance Has the Authority to Control and Manage Its Resources. These resources include people, processes, and especially a robust technology platform, which should include artificial intelligence and machine learning tools to monitor and test for misconduct and violations before they occur in order to facilitate timely responses.

a.   The board should also enable the investment in GRC regulatory technology, including the use of artificial intelligence and robotic tools so that multiple control functions, including C&E officers, can utilize case management tools, issue trackers, and policy and training repositories to assess employee diligence and behaviors, monitor behaviors through surveillance and monitoring tools including behavioral and contact tracing mechanisms to identify and quantify aberrations in behavior.

b.   By investing in GRC tools powered through artificial intelligence, cloud, and SaaS capabilities, C&E officers and ultimately, board members, would be armed with a better toolkit that will help them

identify exceptions with much greater efficiency and effectiveness. This in turn, enables more promptly, for the board to understand both current and predictive states of risk against its approved risk appetites.

4D: Quarterly, the CCO Should Brief the Board Audit, Risk, and Compensation Committee Chairs and the Full Board of Directors on the Progress of Compliance IT Investment, Implementation, and Adequacy. Investing in compliance technology is one thing; ensuring that the technology is actually being implemented is another. Informing the board keeps a spotlight on management and ensures that the company will have the IT support it needs to monitor compliance, reputational, and ethics risks into the 21st century.

4E: If Behavioral Science Data Management Is Housed in the Company's Risk Function, the Overall Compliance Budget Should Include a Shared Item with Risk Management So that Operational Risks, Including Fraud, Are Also Measured and Collaborated in an Effective Yet Efficient Manner. Behavioral science, embedded into compliance & ethics is critical. That said, the key is for the board and the CCO to take *action* from the behavioral metrics.

VALUE TO THE BOARD: Investing in compliance & ethics resources (people, process, and technology) enables the organization to navigate the information superhighway with a fully functional steering wheel, a compliance dashboard, and working brakes that will help the board and C-suite avoid catastrophic disasters.

Recommendation No. 5:
Transparency (Sunlight is the Best Disinfectant)

*"**Sunlight is said to be the best of disinfectants...** electric light the most efficient policeman... But the disclosure must be real. And it must be a disclosure to the investor... To be effective, knowledge of the facts must be actually brought home to the investor." (1914)[1]*

— LOUIS BRANDEIS, *(three years before he was confirmed to be Associate Justice of the US Supreme Court (emphasis mine))*

"We are transparent and candid." (2015)[2]

*"This Committee staff report **shines a much-needed spotlight** on 'The Real Wells Fargo,' a reckless megabank with an ineffective board and management that has exhibited an egregious pattern of consumer abuses." (March 2020)[3]*

— HOUSE FINANCIAL SERVICES COMMITTEE REPORT ON WELLS FARGO *(emphasis mine)*

---

1   Former Associate Justice of the US Supreme Court Louis Brandeis, first quoted in a 1913 *Harper's Weekly* article (while still in private practice), entitled *"What Publicity Can Do,"* and then published as a series of essays in 1914 in his book, *Other People's Money and How the Bankers Use It: The Classic Exposure of Monetary Abuse by Banks, Trusts, Wall Street, and Predator Monopolies.*
2   Wells Fargo. "Our Code of Ethics & Business Conduct" (2015), signed by then-CEO John Stumpf. https://www.sec.gov/Archives/edgar/data/72971/000119312516482046/d149067dex9911.pdf. Retrieved June 29, 2021
3   Joint House Financial Services Committee and Subcommittee on Oversight and Investigations Report and Press Release, March 4, 2020. https://financialservices.house.gov/news/documentsingle.aspx?DocumentID=406382

Background for Context for Recommendation No.5

Members of the US Congress and the public were outraged that it took literally *years* before the public was made aware that Wells Fargo's sales force had created more than 3.5 million fake accounts and committed numerous other legal and regulatory violations at customers' expense. Even more shocking was the revelation that these violations had happened because Wells' corporate culture—starting at the very top with former CEOs John Stumpf and Tim Sloane—supported it by encouraging, financially incenting, and pressuring employees to commit fraud. Even worse, public Congressional testimony and Committee reports revealed that although Wells' primary bank regulators (the Federal Reserve Bank of San Francisco and the US Treasury Office of the Comptroller of the Currency) had repeatedly criticized Wells' board of director governance over management's sales practices and weak regulatory compliance program, they had known about "serious, enterprise-wide deficiencies at Wells Fargo for years, without alerting the public." The House Committee further found the following:

- "Wells' Board of Directors failed to ensure that management could *competently address* the company's risk management deficiencies.

- "Wells and political appointees at the Consumer Financial Protection Bureau (CFPB) had backchannel communications regarding CFPB's Compliance Risk Management Consent Order (a situation that lacked transparency and violated protocol).

- "Wells' Board of Directors allowed management to repeatedly submit materially deficient plans in response to the Fed, OCC, and other regulatory enforcement actions.

- "Wells' Board of Directors and management *prioritized financial and other considerations above fixing issues identified by regulators.*

- "Wells' Board of Directors *failed to hold senior management accountable* for repeatedly not meeting regulators' expectations under the consent orders.

- "…the potential for widespread consumer abuse at Wells remains."[4]

- According to the Federal Reserve, "[t]he primary reason for the downgrade is the *inability of the board to oversee, and senior management to implement*, the changes necessary to bring compliance risk management to an acceptable level *over the past six years.*"

"Again, according to the Federal Reserve, there were similarities between the root causes of the 2016 sales fraud scandal at Wells Fargo Bank, and other sales practices *issues identified in a 2011* Federal Reserve enforcement action against Wells Fargo Financial, a former non-bank subsidiary of WFC"[5] (emphasis mine).

Attach and Publicize "Mens Rea"[6] to Individual Chief Executive Officers, Chief Financial Officers, and Others

Mens Rea is Latin for "*guilty mind*" and comes in four flavors: purpose (intent), knowledge, recklessness, and negligence. As described by Cornell University: "The *mens rea* requirement is premised upon the idea that one must possess a guilty state of mind and be aware of his or her misconduct; however, a defendant need not know that their conduct is illegal to be guilty of a crime. Rather, the defendant must be conscious of the 'facts that make his conduct fit the definition of the offense.'"[7]

Although attaching a publicly disclosable *mens rea* label to a CEO or CFO warrants further investigation and conclusion as to whether to prosecute, the importance of early timing and the full disclosure to

---

4   Ibid, pages 14 - 15
5   Ibid, page 28
6   Legal Information Institute, Cornell Law School - https://www.law.cornell.edu/wex/mens_rea. Retrieved March 3, 2021
7   Ibid, second paragraph.

shareholders and the public at large is essential to sending a clear message that misconduct and violation of laws and regulations will not be tolerated. Disclosing *mens rea* provides the transparency needed to deter such actions.

There is precedent to publicly disclosing a warning of material US securities violation(s). A "Wells Notice" (no relation to Wells Fargo) is a letter sent by a securities regulator to a prospective respondent individual or firm, laying out the substance of charges that the regulator intends to bring, and affording the respondent the opportunity to submit a written statement to the ultimate decisionmaker.[8]

Some industries, such as food and agriculture, manufacturing, pharmaceuticals, and healthcare allow a relatively short period of time between discovery of a breach and public disclosure. This is likely because of the need to inform consumers and communities of a public safety hazard (such as contaminated or poisonous food); safety issues (such as those that put the lives of children and others at risk); nuclear radiation, etc. However, powerful lobby groups and law firms continue to combat and litigate against public disclosure of alleged violations of law because they fear class-action lawsuits by shareholders and reputational damage. As a result, years often pass before the public (and shareholders) learn the truth, usually thanks to a whistleblower.

Attaching a *mens rea* label to the CEO and CFO (and/or general counsel) would cut through the attempts by lobbyists and external law firms to deflect and delay disclosure. Although market reaction might be swift, again, by precedent and comparison, Wells Notice disclosures demonstrate that markets can digest the potential for misconduct and material violations. And regulators and enforcement agencies should assess and attach the label of a *mens rea* to CEOs and CFOs (and where necessary, the general counsel) when material violations are initially discovered by compliance testing (through voluntary self-disclosures to the regulators),

---

8   "Wells Notice." https://www.law.cornell.edu/wex/wells_notice. Retrieved October 7, 2020

internal audits (through their private regulator conversations), regulatory examiners, and/or escalated by whistleblowers.

5A: Pass Legislation to Require Regulatory Attachment—and Public Disclosure—of *Mens Rea* Labels to Individual CEOs, CFOs, and/or General Counsels Upon Early Discovery of a Potential Legal or Regulatory Violation. Such public disclosures may include a disclaimer to inform the public that the *mens rea* label is preliminary and that it could be lifted if, after further investigation, the allegation is dismissed. Furthermore, board members (other than the CEO) should also have the *mens rea* label attached to them personally, compelling the board's duty of care responsibilities to pay closer supervision of the CEO's, CFO's, and general counsel's actions to address and remediate the allegation of material violation.

5B: As is Already Done on an Aggregate Basis with Credit Rating Agencies Such as S&P Global Ratings, Inc. and Moody's Analytics, All Financial Services Regulators (as Well as Those in Consumer Protection, Anti-Trust, Privacy, and Elsewhere) Should Publicly Disclose Certain, Selective Examination and Audit Findings/Weaknesses. This will allow the investing community, markets, and consumers to understand the strengths and weaknesses of a corporation's board governance, corporate culture, and internal controls to manage compliance & ethics risks. This disclosure should be made at least annually.

Public disclosure of an individual bank's compliance is already made for the Community Reinvestment Act (regarding discriminatory lending practices) and a less-than-satisfactory rating negatively affects any plans a bank may have for strategic expansion. Therefore, public disclosure of examination ratings (for banks *and non-banks* alike) should be expanded to include:[9]

---

9   This recommendation can be conducted based on organizations' asset or capitalization size, major client base, or type of business.

1. Corporate culture and governance rating, as reinforced by the board of directors

2. Aggregated disclosure of employee (and vendor) misconduct (number of investigations, aggregate outcomes of consequences, etc.)

3. Aggregated whistleblowing allegations and statistics (without compromising the confidentiality or privacy of specific individuals or cases but highlighting thematic issues or problems)

4. Customer protection and market integrity examination ratings

5. Satisfaction of remediation (as summarized either by independent monitors and/or regulators)

6. Disclosure (in full or in limited form) of qualified financial audit opinions relating to their annual reports and/or SEC (or equivalent) 10-K filings

7. Orange flags to designate violations that are not as severe as SEC-defined red flags, which are for material disclosures and must be covered in the management discussion and analysis section of the 10-K and annual report

8. Material excess risks beyond a board-approved risk appetite

9. Sustainability of managing residual compliance & ethics risks including:

    a. Adequacy of compliance resources

    b. Data integrity and governance

    c. Level of alert backlogs and case investigation over suspicious activities, including fraud, trading and sales, retail sales, and financial crimes, such as money laundering, terrorist financing, bribery, and corruption

   d.   Data privacy and integrity controls, including physical security, cyber security and cyber risk assessment, and crisis management readiness

   e.   Health and safety inspection results of the food and drug, energy, industrial, and manufacturing sectors

Although some of the above disclosure of examination findings could be considered strictly "confidential supervisory information" (CSI) by banking regulators for fear of causing a liquidity crisis or a run on bank deposits, the financial crisis of 2007–2010 and the COVID-19 financial and economic shutdowns taught us that there is a lower likelihood of such liquidity runs, thanks to stricter liquidity coverage ratio requirements and extreme stress-testing scenarios, which have demonstrated sufficient safeguards to prevent such runs.

The information gathered and released to the public under Recommendation 5B can therefore be done on an individual bank-by-bank basis. This would serve two important purposes:

1.   Place accountability on each bank to be transparent before regulatory criticism is warranted.

2.   Early disclosure of systematic and potentially widespread industry-wide cultural and/or control weaknesses, which could risk the safety of the public, consumers, employees, and markets.

Recommendation No. 6:
Protect and Enable Whistleblowers

As described in chapter 2.10, a whistleblower is "[o]ne who reveals wrongdoing within an organization to the public or to those in positions of authority."[1] In the United States and many other countries, whistleblowing laws and regulations have been enacted to support, strengthen, and protect the ability of public- and private-sector individuals to raise integrity, ethical, and compliance issues (e.g., fraud, bribery, and corruption) against colleagues, vendors, corporations, and other entities on a named or anonymous basis (if preferred).

Unfortunately, "current federal law largely ignores this problem, and protections for job applicants with whistleblowing histories have been severely lacking in some of the most prominent whistleblowing statutes," according to professors Leora Eisenstadt and Jennifer Pacella.[2] Worldwide, the situation is much the same. According to the National Whistleblower Center (NWC), "(w)ithout adequate protections and rewards, however,

---

1   American Heritage Dictionary. Retrieved October 9, 2020
2   Eisenstadt, Leora F. and Pacella, Jennifer M., Whistleblowers Need Not Apply (February 1, 2018). American Business Law Journal, 2018, Fox School of Business Research Paper No. 18-013, Baruch College Zicklin School of Business Research Paper No. 2018-05-02, Available at SSRN: https://ssrn.com/abstract=3129731

many laws still fall short of supporting effective whistleblowing."[3] As a result, retaliation and blacklisting are on the rise.

An effective corporate compliance & ethics program depends heavily upon the ability of employees and others to raise integrity and other issues alleging wrongdoing, fraud, other misconduct, or illegalities—including workplace and sexual harassment—without hesitation or fear. Third-party, independently managed integrity hotlines are increasingly prevalent, and they investigate claims and make reports to boards of directors. However, not enough is being (or has been) done to enable and shield whistleblowers, who expect that the "right thing" will be done to address concerns they raise in good faith.

Therefore, I recommend that lawmakers enact legislation that would categorize whistleblowers as a protected class of employees when applying for future employment, and that more severe action be taken to discipline individuals and their employers for retaliating against whistleblowers.

Embracing, Rather Than Hiding Whistleblowers

Ironically, keeping whistleblowers anonymous does more harm than good, both to firms and individuals, because rather than calling out wrongdoers, it demonstrates that employees are afraid that if they identify themselves, they'll be subjected to retaliation. Whether compelled by regulation or prosecution, or through self-governance, whistleblowers should be identified and hailed (and protected) as heroes, not kept in the shadows. And those who condone, act, or create a workplace of fear and retaliation need to be exposed. Unless there is a culture and environment of safety, keeping anonymity actually reinforces retaliation—once issues are raised, companies can isolate whoever raised the complaint.

The following recommendations are meant to enable whistleblowers, also known as "integrity escalation individuals," to have a secure path to

---

3   National Whistleblower Center. "Whistleblower Laws Around the World." https://www. whistleblowers.org/whistleblower-laws-around-the-world. Retrieved October 10, 2020. The NWC is the leading nonprofit in the U.S. dedicated to protecting and rewarding whistleblowers.

future employment and security and to ensure that they are not punished for the courage they displayed at their prior employer.

6A: The US Senate, House of Representatives, Executive Branch Agencies, State and Local Governments Should Declare October as "Whistleblower Appreciation and Protection Month."[4] Declaring October as an annual appreciation and protection period reminds executive management—in the heart of most Fortune 1000 companies' budget cycle—that fraud and illegal acts cost companies billions in lost revenue and reputational damage, and that without whistleblowers, even more could be lost (and much more could be saved through preventative measures).

6B: Companies Should, Without Threat of Retaliation, Encourage Whistleblowers to Identify Themselves. Self-identification could be encouraged through significant financial incentives awarded by companies but also through encouragement by regulators and prosecutors (beyond regulatory bounties). Identification, in and of itself, also enables whistleblowers to protect themselves further from retaliation. Furthermore, there should be a requirement that companies submit a quarterly registry of whistleblowers to their board of directors, the US Securities and Exchange Commission (or local government equivalent), and the companies' primary supervisory regulator.

The burden of proof should also formally shift from the fearful, anonymous whistleblower to the accused for fraudulent (e.g., mispricing, financial statement, or tax evasion), customer protection, market abuse allegations/violations, and for non-workplace harassment allegations.

---

4   On July 30, 2013, the US Congress made a halfhearted attempt to recognize whistleblowers by declaring National Whistleblower Appreciation Day. But that was a one-off event that barely anyone noticed at the time. There have also been a World Whistleblower Day and an International Whistleblower Day.

Allegations must still be made in good faith, however, and making bad faith or false allegations should carry a heavy penalty.

For workplace harassment/environment and other human resource allegations including sexual harassment, the burden of proof already falls on the accused. The intent of the public disclosure of the whistleblower is to demonstrate that the CEO and C-suite have zero tolerance for these issues.

Disclosing the name of the accuser serves two purposes: (1) it protects the whistleblower formally and visibly from retaliation; and (2) it acts as a disincentive for making false allegations.

6C: Whistleblowers Should Be Recognized and Rewarded. This is a major paradigm shift that must be made in order for the broader corporate culture to change to ferret out fraud, customer and market abuse, and workplace harassment.

To induce both the individual and the company, whistleblowers should be identified and "tagged" in their human resources records as a protected class from the time an allegation is made, throughout the investigation period, and for two years thereafter (with a renewable option every two years). Protection would shield the whistleblower from retaliation, whether direct or indirect, explicit or subtle. The whistleblower's claim that the protection has been violated would trigger disclosure to the board of directors, the SEC (or foreign equivalent) and to the primary supervisory regulator. A quarterly status report based on the whistleblower registry would also be provided by the chief compliance officer to the board.

6D: Prevent and Prohibit Blacklisting. Professors Eisenstadt and Pacella analyzed, compared, and contrasted international whistleblowing standards and went on to astutely parallel the US civil rights laws[5] of individuals with the civil rights of whistleblowers. They note that:

---

5   For example, the US Civil Rights Act of 1964, [42 U.S.C. Chapter 21 Subchapter VI], and US Americans with Disabilities Act [42 U.S.C. § 12203(a)]

"These examples are representative of the struggles that nearly *two-thirds of job applicants with whistleblowing histories face in finding future employment...* (and that) that an entire subset of whistleblowers—job applicants—have an exceedingly difficult time maintaining their livelihoods and moving forward after their courageous disclosures."[6] (emphasis mine)

Professors Eisenstadt and Pacella go on to holistically recommend that whistleblowers who are job applicants be afforded the same rights as all applicants who are already protected under Title VII of the Civil Rights Act of 1964:

"We recommend statutory amendments to SOX,[7] Dodd-Frank, and the FCA[8] to explicitly include job applicants among those eligible for retaliation protections and to provide at least the same level of protection afforded job applicants under the civil rights laws. Given the comparison to Title VII's retaliation provision and its comprehensive coverage of applicants, it makes sense to use the statutory language in Title VII as a model for proposed statutory amendments to SOX, Dodd-Frank, and the FCA. In fact, not only do we recommend using Title VII's language as a guide, but we also propose that it be explicitly referenced in any statutory amendments to this effect."[9]

---

6   Eisenstadt, Leora F. and Jennifer M. Pacella. "Whistleblowers Need Not Apply." *American Business Law Journal,* volume 55, Issue 4, 665–719, Winter 2018; p 669; and their footnote citing: Gideon Mark, *Confidential Witnesses in Securities Litigation,* 36 J. CORP. L. 551, 596 (2011), (discussing the occurrence of blacklisting as a common repercussion of blowing the whistle). Retrieved October 9, 2020
7   Sarbanes-Oxley Act 18 U.S.C. §1514A
8   False Claims Act 31 U.S.C. §§ 3729
9   Ibid, pg. 709, Section IV – "*Proposals for Reform*"

I heartily endorse professors Eisenstadt's and Pacella's recommendations, specifically, that:

- The language of Section 806 of the Sarbanes-Oxley Act (SOX) be modified to add the following italicized language: "No [public] company [or other enumerated entity] … may discharge, demote, suspend, threaten, harass, or in any other manner discriminate against an employee in the terms and conditions of employment, *or an applicant for employment,* because of any lawful act done by the employee or applicant for employment [to blow the whistle] …."[10] (bracketed text is in the original)

- The Remedies section of the Dodd-Frank Act be modified to add the following italicized language: "Relief for an individual prevailing in an action brought [hereunder] shall include—(i) reinstatement with the same seniority status that the individual would have had, or hiring to the position such applicant for employment would have had, but for the discrimination; (ii) 2 times the amount of back pay otherwise owed to the individual, with interest; and (iii) compensation for litigation costs, expert witness fees, and reasonable attorneys' fees"[11]

- The Retaliation section of the False Claims Act should be amended to read: "Any employee, contractor, or agent shall be entitled to all relief necessary to make that employee, contractor, or agent whole, if [such person] is discharged, demoted, suspended, threatened, harassed, or in any other manner discriminated against in the terms and conditions of employment, *or, as an applicant for employment,* because of lawful acts done by the employee, contractor, agent or associated others in furtherance of an action under this section…"[12]

---

10   Ibid, Pg. 710
11   Ibid, Pg. 711
12   Ibid, Pg. 711

6E: To Strengthen and Enforce the Protection of Job Applicants, Comparable to the Boxes Checked Seeking Information of the Applicant's Race, Color, Gender, and Other Protected Classes, Provide an Optional Box for "Integrity Escalation Individual" (Or IEI). The job application should also include IEIs explicitly, in the standard language specifying how certain classes of applicants are protected under Federal, state, and local laws.

6F: Extend Comparable Language, If Not Already in Existence in International and National Laws That Contain (or Should Contain) Whistleblower Protection Provisions to Include Prospective Job Applicants.[13] Encouraging, enabling and shielding whistleblowing by employees and others is a critically important component of, and process for sustaining an effective compliance program. An army of compliance officers would not equal the impact of a single whistleblower who, in good faith, raises an integrity issue. Whistleblowers face tremendous pressure before, during, and especially after they raise their hands, regardless of whether they voluntarily self-identity or make their claims anonymously.

---

13   An insightful article about the retaliatory fate of whistleblowers and blacklisting of them can be found in Charlie Middleton's "Whistleblower v. Anti-Whistleblower – Don't Sue Me; It's True", April 9, 2020 - https://www.linkedin.com/pulse/whistleblower-v-anti-whistleblower-dont-sue-me-its-true-middleton/. Retrieved June 29, 2021

The Way Forward: Cross Pollenating the Hexagon into the "Compliance Honeycomb"©

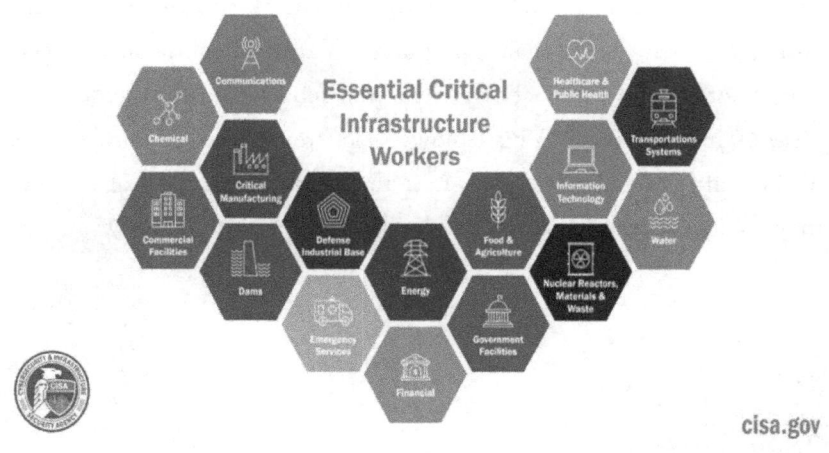

Source: US Department of Homeland Security-Cybersecurity & Infrastructure Security Agency (CISA)

I n two parts, I've written about corporate and professional lessons learned, and why companies fail to integrate culture with strategy to protect their long-term reputations and stakeholders. Companies' short-term culture often leads to long-term damage to themselves and worse, beyond. The DoJ Sentencing Guidelines or Fed's SR 08-08 compliance guidance individually, aren't enough (nor are their international counterparts) to build an effective compliance & ethics program.

Young's Vision, which integrates and consolidates the Sentencing Guidelines and Fed SR 08-08 works well to achieve an effective compliance program—but only until management cuts the budget or refuses to invest meaningfully in compliance technology. It's a vicious cycle. Management's short-term thinking and lack of culpability is the problem.

My six Compliance Hexagon recommendations will lead you to a cleaner and more efficient organization. Your individual company will break that vicious management myopia on a *micro*-economic basis. For example, your board and CCO will partner regularly, and your compliance program will be robust—and sustainable. But on an industry-wide basis or across industries, what if your competitors aren't so "clean," or act like lemmings, ultimately driving some of you over the proverbial cliff? What then? Please read on.

Close your eyes, and imagine the following scenario (which is both possible and essential for the sake of national and global security): on a macro level, our national and global economies are culturally, ethically, and compliantly cleaner, safer, and more efficient. And all companies are disinfected with sunshine and transparency, are protecting and enabling whistleblowers to raise issues in good faith and are arming their boards and CCOs with tools to oversee and manage compliance & ethics risks more predictably and meaningfully. Why is this so important for our national security?

Homeland Security's "Essential Critical Industries"

Since March 2020, the US Department of Homeland Security's Cyber-security and Infrastructure Security Agency (CISA)[1] and other agencies identified sixteen "essential critical industries and workers" to continue functioning throughout the COVID pandemic and beyond. These sectors are the foundation of American industry and finance. Other nations likely

---

1   *Identifying Critical Infrastructure During COVID-19*. CISA. December 20, 2020. https://www.cisa.gov/identifying-critical-infrastructure-during-covid-19. Retrieved April 10, 2021

have (or should have) comparable designated business and financial sectors. These sixteen CISA sectors are symbolized in CISA's hexagonal shapes, shown on page 150, and listed below:

Chemical	Dams	Financial services	Information technology
Commercial facilities	Defense industrial base	Food and agriculture	Nuclear reactors, materials, and waste
Communications	Emergency services	Government facilities	Transportation systems
Critical manufacturing	Energy	Healthcare and public health	Water and wastewater

Homeland Security states that these "… critical infrastructure sectors … are considered so vital to the United States that their incapacitation or destruction would have a debilitating effect on security, national economic security, national public health or safety, or any combination thereof."[2]

Each of these sixteen industries is highly regulated. Accordingly, government agencies should already have internal control and compliance & ethics expectations of their constituent companies and employees. Furthermore, with the 2020–2021 "public-private" partnerships for all things COVID, many "essential critical" companies such as yours are re-calibrating your compliance program to operate with higher compliance risks and lower regulatory tolerance for violations. Employee safety and health, nursing home care, healthcare and life sciences, and financial services compliance are also under a newer, more powerful level of pandemic

2   Ibid.

and post-COVID scrutiny and risk. Your stakes are much higher. Your business model paradigm to maximize profit for the short-term won't work anymore.

Post-COVID and the Threat of Cyber-Attacks

With COVID vaccines now available and widely distributed across the US and increasingly across the globe, your COVID triage mode has likely abated though variant mutations and government lockdowns recur. Even if the severity of COVID diminishes, CISA "essential critical industries and workers" still face national security risks from external cyber-driven enemies. For example, your corporate boards, CCOs and chief information security officers and companies already face the following[3]:

- Globally, 30,000 websites are hacked daily.

- 64% of companies worldwide have experienced at least one form of a cyber-attack.

- There were 20 million breached records in March 2021.

- In 2020, ransomware cases grew by 150%.

- Email is responsible for around 94% of all malware.

- Every 39 seconds, there's a new attack somewhere on the web.

- An average of around 24,000 malicious mobile apps are blocked daily on the internet.

In addition, most, if not all of the sixteen CISA critical infrastructure industries remain commonly vulnerable to risks of bribery and corruption, anti-trust, external and insider fraud, money laundering, terrorism, and OFAC sanctions. Another cyber-attack occurred over the July 4th, 2021 holiday weekend. And the Colonial Pipeline and JBS attacks in May 2021

---

3   Bulao, Jacqueline, "How Many Cyber Attacks Happen Per Day in 2021?", June 17, 2021. https://techjury.net/blog/how-many-cyber-attacks-per-day/#gref., Retrieved June 30, 2021

demonstrate just how vulnerable our critical infrastructure is[4] and steps needed to address these risks.

And don't forget how Big Tech is blurring and disrupting our essential critical industries.

Big Tech Monopolies, the Convergence of Industries, and the Nano-Second Speed of Social Media is Increasing Compliance & Ethics and Reputational Risks

Compliance & ethics risks have not been put on hold (nor can they ever be) because of COVID-19 or its variants, or because of technology and cybersecurity vulnerabilities. These risks have increased exponentially because of:

1. The government-induced trend to converge banking and commercial industries through the introduction and disruption of technology players, including start-ups, social media, crypto, and Big Tech (Amazon, Apple, Google, Facebook, Microsoft, and Twitter).

2. The growing power of today's Big Tech "monopolies," including how they've blurred the lines—and inherent risks—between banking, healthcare, food, pharma, energy, and other industrial sectors. Our great grandparents' monopolies of JP Morgan and Carnegies to control money, has been replaced with an even greater dominance over money and more dangerously, data and information.

Big Tech's control over data, information, and money is rapidly re-shaping our environment, society, and way of governing. It's indeed the fourth (if not, fifth) industrial revolution. It's as if we're driving a Ferrari on a re-built, much faster, possibly more dangerous "information

---

4   Isenberg, Rich, Kristensen, Ida, Mysore, Mihir, and Weinstein, David – "Building Cyber Resilience in National Critical Infrastructure," McKinsey Insights, June 30, 2021 - https://www. mckinsey.com/business-functions/risk/our-insights/building-cyber-resilience-in-national-critical-infrastructure – retrieved July 6, 2021

highway" with safety equipment from the 1990s when the internet was new. Better yet (or worse?), we humans aren't even driving the Ferrari—it's self-driving with Siri, Alexa, and other machines!

If a self-driving Ferrari is hurtling down the information highway to maximize profits and share price, how can we ensure that the Ferrari doesn't crash and bring down all industries, markets, customers, communities, and society overall? And how will your board directors fulfil their duties of care and loyalty in this nano-second world?

The Perfect Storm, Duty of Care, and the Role of the Board and CCO

A perfect storm is in play. The pandemic, social, and political unrest, and an uneven global, regional, and local economic recovery continue to invite major cyber-attacks, management misconduct, fraud, and compliance violations—across banking and commercial industries. And the inherent risks below are not new, but exponentially greater—and blurrier—and are faced by *all* industries as Big Tech disrupts and clouds our industries:

1. Health and safety

2. Anti-trust and price fixing

3. Bribery, corruption, and financial crimes[5]

4. Cyber-security, data privacy and protection of personal data

5. Consumer protection

6. Market abuse

7. Workplace and sexual harassment

8. Fraud and misconduct (which can be found in each of the above)

---

5   "Financial crimes" include money laundering, terrorist financing, and economic sanctions (e.g., OFAC). Please also note that under many international anti-money laundering laws, financial institution can include many commercial enterprises.

Will board members and C-suites of one industry understand the new risks of a blurrier industry? If we've played corporate "baseball" all our lives, how will we know how to play "football"? Will we know how and where the foul lines *and* goal posts will be in our hybrid world? And if the rules once again aren't clear, the odds are good that an aggressive CEO, CFO, or business leader will arbitrage the blurry rules again. Will directors be willing to account for an overly aggressive C-suite with a (justifiably) more aggressive DoJ that's seeking tougher, criminal guilty pleas?

For Business Schools Globally, to Consider and Teach: Executing the Compliance *Hexagon* Within the Broader "Compliance *Honeycomb*"©

The honeycomb structure is one of the strongest and most efficient structures in the fields of physics, medicine, engineering, molecular science, nature,[6] and aerospace.[7] As Big Tech, fintech, social media, cryptocurrencies, and cyber-attacks simultaneously blur and magnify compliance and reputational risks across industries, directors and CCOs must together execute their Compliance Hexagons, to clean their individual companies.

As illustrated below, a collection of corporate hexagons need to be executed together so that individual micro-driven cultures of any one company will align with the macro-driven cultures of multiple companies across their industry. As multiple industries, cultures, and hexagons are executed and aligned, these hexagons become a Compliance Honeycomb.

---

6   Multiple authors, scientists, "Honeycomb Structures," Science Direct (through 2019) - https://www.sciencedirect.com/topics/engineering/honeycomb-structures - retrieved July 1, 2021
7   Continental Steel and Tube Company, "The Benefits of Aluminum Honeycomb in Aerospace Applications," February 15, 2017 - https://continentalsteel.com/blog/aluminum-honeycomb/ - retrieved July 1, 2021

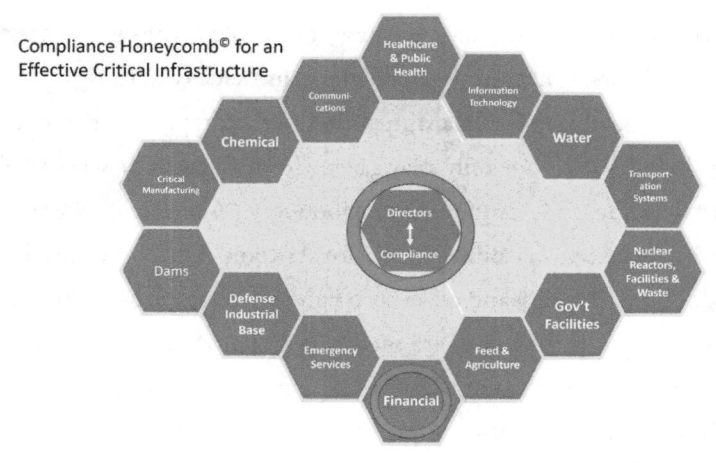

Compliance Honeycomb© for an Effective Critical Infrastructure

Source: author

Just as a bees' honeycombs are built to last (and to survive attacks from a variety of external threats), the Compliance Honeycomb can be equally strong in protecting our individual, siloed industries and our aggregate, global economic infrastructure from cyber and reputational risks. But only if individual directors and their CCOs first work together to execute their own Compliance Hexagon (especially if they're in the financial services sector, which fuels all other industries).

The Way Forward: Executing the Honeycomb with the Right Compliance & Ethics Skill Sets

Are CCOs and today's compliance & ethics officers fit for purpose for tomorrow? Sadly, no. With all due respect to my lifelong friends who are lawyers, lawyers aren't tomorrow's compliance & ethics officers. We need our future compliance officers to have backgrounds in STEM (science, technology, engineering, and math) as well as bona fide compliance risk management skills. They need to be creative project managers, data governance, process engineers, long-term thinkers/strategists to guide and enlighten their partners—the board; they need to be philosophically and artistically minded, thinking creatively and thoughtfully. We need chess

players who know how to win—and how to enable a win-win strategy that benefits clients, communities, regulators, and society in the long run.

We need equally skilled board members with compliance risk management skill sets who not only play chess (so to speak) but who aren't afraid to say to the CEO as they do in Monopoly, "Go to jail!" We need to invest in and empower our CCOs with AI tools. Finally, we need to remember Plato's Allegory and never stop fighting to escape our corporate caves so we can enlighten our board members and protect our employees, customers, markets, and society. Leaving the cave takes courage and long-term thinking. And the results—profiting safely and responsibly—are compellingly achievable.

Acknowledgements

Writing acknowledgements for my first book is almost more difficult than writing the book itself. Where to start, whom to include—or not, and how to thank them and why. Especially after an intense yet fulfilling career and life so far.

Faith

I thank God. My faith is very personal and important to me.

Family

God sent me a beautiful, guardian angel: my wife. She fiercely protects me and loves me as I do her. We laugh like children every day, which keeps us young. She finds humor in most things in life. We're always on an adventure together wherever we are and along the way, we always have fun! She's also my compass, pointing to our ethical north. We've known each other most of our lives. I'm very blessed to have met and married her. Thank you!

I also want to thank my parents whom I will always love. They're in Heaven now in a better place and hopefully, looking down with a smile. I miss them very much. I also thank my sister and her family. She's shown an inner strength throughout and raised two wonderful boys. Good wishes

as well to my brother and his family. I also honor my father-in-law and mother-in-law. My wife's father was wise and so humane. They both loved me and treated me like a son. I love and miss them very much.

Friends (and colleagues)

The term "friend" can have so many meanings. "Forever friend," "ally," "colleague," and most importantly, "mentor."

Mentors

Beyond my dad who taught me so much, I honor and remember the late George Mah, Vice President and Head of Internal Accounting Controls at JPMorgan Chase. He shaped my early career and provided me with incredible opportunities. I'm especially grateful to George's daughter, Amy, who graciously and patiently reviewed my draft chapters and references about George. Writing about and discussing George with Amy brought back so many fond memories for both of us. We miss him very much.

Thank you, David Aufhauser, former General Counsel of the US Department of Treasury. Learning from David is an honor. Like George, he threw me into the deep end of the pool when we worked together at UBS. I loved it. I'm also very grateful to Gene Ludwig, former US Comptroller of the Currency and Founder & CEO of Promontory Financial Group. I've known Gene for twenty years and he's always been kind, wise and generous with his time for me. For this I'll always be grateful.

Who says I don't like or get along with attorneys? (Smile). Some of my best friends are lawyers. Ron Mayer in particular is one whom I first met at Chase after leaving the Fed (where he was also previously an attorney). As Chase's regulatory attorney and then, corporate secretary, he taught me so much about the Fed's and other regulators' expectations and he epitomized how mutually beneficial a strong legal and compliance partnership can be. Always responsive, never dismissive, continuously kind, genuine, and patient, to this day. Thank you, Ron!

Colleagues

My dad always said, "Those that work for you are more important than those above you." It's so true. As leaders, we're only as good as our teams that support and believe in us. I tried my best to let them grow and to experience just how capable they truly are. Of course, loyalty, respect and trust must be mutually earned and I'm forever grateful to my teams who believed in my vision and passion. Those that had their own agendas, I also thank because I learned from them too. I wish each and every one of my teams great success for the future. And I look forward to working with my future teams and teammates!

Thank you to all my bosses and colleagues. Whether in the businesses, support functions, legal, human resources, finance, risk, or audit, you were incredible partners in weaving the cultural fabric of the institutions where we worked together. Some of you—and you know who you are—are an inspiration to me because of your ethical compass, diligent organization, and passion to get to the right outcome. I'll forever be appreciative. Though there are others with whom our relationships may have been challenging, *c'est la vie*; that's corporate politics.

I couldn't have written this book without my wise and objective editor, Armin Brott as well as Elena Reznikova (designer); and Dina Mangarella (proofreader) who helped produce the book. Armin, you'll forever have my endless gratitude for your objective insights and deep patience with my zigs and zags to formulate, write, re-think, condense, and ultimately produce my book. You kept me focused and creative for the past 15 months. You were and always will be a US Marine, a famed author and radio host as "Mr. Dad" before you met me, and now you're an honorary compliance & ethics officer! And I'm proud to call you my friend.

As an adjunct professor, I am very thankful to the Fordham University School of Law, especially to Program on Corporate Ethics & Compliance senior director Robert Mascola, for your calm leadership, design, and execution of our Master of Studies in Law program. Bob, you and your

Fordham colleagues, and our fellow adjuncts make the program a huge success! And thank you, Bob, for allowing me to refresh my academic knowledge and enabling me to give back to our future generation of compliance & ethics leaders. I enjoy teaching all of my students, especially because they keep me on my toes with challenging questions. Witnessing my students' growth over legal, compliance & ethics knowledge over the course of the program is very fulfilling for me. I am learning from each of you!

Sometimes, we all need executive coaching and an objective lens to re-calibrate how we lead and manage. Athletes continuously need professional coaches to excel and so do executives, including chief compliance officers. I celebrate and applaud each, especially my good friend Charlotte, and to Marc, Lisa, Jean, Karen, and Caryn, each of whom have over my career helped me re-learn how to "hit the tennis ball" with focus and follow through with success. Thank you for showing me the way. Those of you who recruited me are also my coaches. Thank you!

Of course, I cannot close without thanking the dozens and dozens of the incredibly talented friends and colleagues I've already known over the years and also newly met over the past 15 months to help shape and influence my thinking for this book. I couldn't have formulated some of my recommendations without you! These include the following, in no particular order:

Retired Delaware Chief Justice Leo E. Strine, Jr (my hero, for your tectonic-shifting Marchand v. Barnhill and other important judicial rulings which have set an important, new course for corporate directors, executives, and compliance & ethics officers to follow). As co-panelist with you, Chief Strine and Klaros Group partner Jonah Crane, I also witnessed how great judges and a sharp sense of humor can go so well together; Richard Bistrong; Harvard Professor Eugene Soltes for your inspirational book, *Why They Do It*; David Koenig for your governance leadership and book-writing advice; Chris Hetner for your cyber security and national

security leadership; Orrie Dinstein for guiding me at GE and beyond, over all things data and privacy-related; Douglas Chia; David Wright; Margaret Preston; Brian O'Malley; Jonathan T. Marks for your "fraud pentagon" and our common "three lines" views; Mike Koehler for your refreshing candor; Torben Ostergaard; Jeffrey Martino for your impressive, intellectual and thoughtful anti-trust views; Oonagh van den Berg; Nicole Rose; Erica Salmon Byrne of Ethisphere; Frank Raimond; Charlie Middleton; George Bradt; Ross Delston; Mary Gentile; Alison Taylor; Bruce Karpati; Bob Kolasky of US Homeland Security; Herve Duteil; Nagaraja Deevi; Ellen Hunt; Karen Moore; Irina Samoylova Kunces; Lisa Beth Lentini Walker; Friso Van der Oord of the NACD; John Cusack for your continued financial crimes & corruption compliance leadership; Wayne Fox; Mike Shapiro; Michael Blackshear; Andrea Bonime-Blanc; Lucy Fato for our collective and aligned success; Adele Hogan; Paul Tufaro; Allen Love; Erin Schrantz; Carolyn Renzin; Jim Nortz; Elizabeth Simon; Mirea Raaijmakers; Anna Romberg; Thierry Dupiot; Natasha Vernier; Wies Waagenar; Ellen Zimiles; Maryanne Bullion; Anna Bond; Greg Montana; Lawrence Zelvin; and Simon Brady. I'm sure I've forgotten many others, for which I apologize.

I'm very appreciative for being interviewed/invited as speaker/panelist including (in no particular order): Tom Fox; Nick Gallo; Julie Myers-Wood; Vince Catanzaro and Jeff Niebuhr; Heidi Weber; Matt Kelly; Reuters; The Wall Street Journal; and Forbes; Jack Kelly; NICE Actimize especially Lee Garf, Chris DeNigris and David Ackerman; the New York City Bar Association; Minnesota Continuing Legal Education (CLE); the Society of Corporate Compliance and Ethics/Healthcare Compliance Association CEO Gerry Zack and Adam Turteltaub for believing in my vision; Association of Certified Financial Crime Specialists (ACFCS) President Joseph Yerant; Brian Kindle and Brian Monroe; National Society of Compliance Professionals (NSCP); Ethics & Compliance Initiative CEO Pat Harned;

Clifford Kirsch and the Julia Kirsch Foundation for their humanity; and especially, Rebellion Research CEO Alexander Fleiss.

A shout-out to my Columbia University classmates including my good friend, Bruce G. Paulsen (yes, another attorney!) who together with me took Ethics, and many other philosophy, literature, art, and music classes. Indeed, it was John Rawls' Theory of Justice which inspired me to consider pareto optimality in every moral dilemma as a compliance & ethics officer.

Thank you to my followers and those I follow on LinkedIn. Your thoughts and leadership fuel and inspire me.

I applaud and embrace our legislators, prosecutors, and regulators. You enact the laws, enforce, and supervise us to protect our markets, customers, employees, communities, and our society for our future generations. Lastly, we should never forget our employees—particularly those who raise integrity issues in good faith—because companies cannot operate in an ethical and compliant manner without our employees. Independence is declared for you. And finally, thank you to all my fellow compliance & ethics officers, with whom I declare independence!

About the Author:
Eric T. Young

Eric re-engineers governance, risk, compliance & ethics programs to enable strategic, responsible growth. His voice is unique, thoughtful, and provocative, leveraging his chess, tennis, baseball, and 40+ years' experience as a regulator, chief compliance officer (CCO) and financial crime specialist with the Federal Reserve, JP Morgan Chase, General Electric, S&P Global (the largest credit rating agency in the world) and four international banks including UBS and BNP Paribas (one of the largest in the world). Very few have the depth and breadth of practical enterprise compliance & ethics risk management experience across multiple industries as Eric. He loves to teach and give back to our future leaders, as an adjunct professor with the Fordham University School of Law's Program on Corporate Ethics and Compliance, in New York.

Eric also provides strategic compliance & ethics advisory services to multiple clients, strategically repositioning firms for an ESG, new cultural paradigm, and compliance technology future, across a cross-section of

industries. For example, he co-developed the "Compliance Solutions Across Industries" conference with the Society of Corporate Compliance and Ethics (SCCE), exploring technology-driven risks blurring banking and commercial siloes.

Eric serves on advisory boards with a number of artificial intelligence, data integrity, and technology firms, including Rebellion Research, WebDoctors.com, HyperVerge, Inc. and AI Data Innovations. Eric is a frequent speaker and author, quoted in *The Wall Street Journal*, *Reuters*, *Forbes*, and the *American Banker*. He is a graduate of Columbia University (Economics), and the GE Management Development Program.

For more information, visit Eric's blog, ethicalpebble.com.